Digital Video Recorders

Digital Video Recorders
DVRs Changing TV and Advertising Forever

Jimmy Schaeffler

AMSTERDAM • BOSTON • HEIDELBERG • LONDON
NEW YORK • OXFORD • PARIS • SAN DIEGO
SAN FRANCISCO • SINGAPORE • SYDNEY • TOKYO
Focal Press is an imprint of Elsevier

Focal Press is an imprint of Elsevier
30 Corporate Drive, Suite 400, Burlington, MA 01803, USA
Linacre House, Jordan Hill, Oxford OX2 8DP, UK

Library of Congress Cataloging-in-Publication Data
Application submitted

British Library Cataloguing-in-Publication Data
A catalogue record for this book is available from the British Library.

ISBN: 978-0-240-81116-1

For information on all Focal Press publications
visit our website at www.elsevierdirect.com

09 10 11 12 5 4 3 2 1

Printed in the United States of America

Working together to grow
libraries in developing countries

www.elsevier.com | www.bookaid.org | www.sabre.org

ELSEVIER   BOOK AID International   Sabre Foundation

Dedication

As was the case in 2008 with my first NAB/Focal Press book, *Digital Signage—Software, Networks, Advertising, and Displays: A Primer for Understanding the Business*, I inevitably pay a remarkable tribute to my immediate family: my most loving wife, Diane, and my three outstanding children, Willy, Jessica, and Cory.

Yet, for this second NAB/Focal Press book, *DVRs: Changing TV Forever*, I am compelled to add a few more remarkable individuals. My late parents, Willy and Betty Schaeffler, sacrificed in ways that are most recently becoming so much more apparent, for me to have the advantages they provided, especially a remarkable education. I also thank those remarkable educators from the earliest days, namely, Mary Jo Osborne, Tom Hamill, Barbara Miller, Norman Ellis, Frank Keith, Ed Brown, Tom Trutner, Bob Leichtner, Joseph Tussman, Kojo Yelpaala, and Judge Anthony Kennedy.

To all of you, I offer sincere thanks, and I dedicate this book about DVRs.

Contents

Acknowledgments

Once again, those that got me started on this road to finishing another book were my interns from the Monterey Institute of International Studies (MIIS), in Monterey, CA. This especially included Chris Dempsey, as well as in the late stages, Scott Hernandez, and Niresh Kumar Gunasekaran. Also, because they are so many, I need to thank those at each of the companies and trade groups I consulted but suffice it to say, "They know who they are." I would be remiss if I were to leave out Marc Beckwitt at Digeo and Krista Wierzbicki at TiVo, as among the best. In addition, in its final stages, the book got done at all because my three children, Jessica, Willy, and Cory, and my dear wife, Diane, made it happen.

Thanks guys.
Jimmy Schaeffler
Carmel-by-the-Sea, CA

About the Author

Jimmy Schaeffler is the chairman and CSO of The Carmel Group, a telecommunications, computer, and media industries consultant, conference organizer and publisher, located in Carmel-by-the-Sea, CA. Since 1995, The Carmel Group has provided these services to a broad range of clientele in the private, public, government, and nonprofit sectors. The Carmel Group's website can be accessed online at www.carmelgroup.com.

While being widely sought for his expertise on satellite TV, cable, wireless, and telephony, Schaeffler has already earned a position as a leading authority on such new, advanced cable, telco, DBS, broadband, and broadcast services as video-on-demand, digital video recorders, high-definition TV, satellite radio, and digital signage, to name just a few.

Today, scores of the world's largest telecommunications, computer, and media companies seek Mr. Schaeffler's insights for studies and conferences, etc., and his views are reported regularly in such publications as *The Wall Street Journal*, *Investor's Business Daily*, *Business Week*, and *Time* magazine. He is the author of the best-selling 2008 NAB/Focal Press book *Digital Signage—Software, Networks, Advertising, and Displays: A Primer for Understanding the Business*. Mr. Schaeffler is the author of numerous other telecom books and has been a frequent participant in domestic United States and global industry conferences and activities, going back to the mid 1990s. These include *CES, NAB, NCTA, CeBIT, Bileshim Eurasia*, and *IBC*. A "google" of his name delivers literally thousands of entries.

Mr. Schaeffler holds a bachelor's degree, with honors, from the University of California, Berkeley, and a Doctor of Jurisprudence degree from the University of Pacific, McGeorge School of Law in Sacramento, CA, where he served as a staff member on the law school's *Pacific Law Journal*. He is licensed to practice law in California, Minnesota, Colorado, Washington, D.C., and before the U.S. Supreme Court.

Executive Summary

Digital video recorders (DVRs) are—fairly rapidly—taking over most of North American television.

In a handful of words, DVRs are taking over TV in the United States and Canada, because they present such a vast improvement over the viewing of so-called linear, or real time, scheduled TV.

DVRs are also taking over because a number of important drivers are in place, both on the business (or enterprise) side and on the consumer side.

On the business side, DVRs mean money. Often that route is not as direct, and the margins are not as clear and instantaneous, as impatient business people might wish, but they are evident. DVRs cost money to develop as hardware and software systems, indeed, they cost significant money; however, once in place, some of that investment can be quickly made back by charging consumers upfront for the hardware, or later down the line for the leasing of the set-top box or the monthly leasing of the electronic program guide/interactive programming guide.

Yet, the real value of DVRs for TV business people is actually defined more subtly. First, DVRs stem competitive losses of subscribers to rivals that have DVRs and would take those customers away whenever possible. Second, DVRs are a solid investment for business people, especially multichannel TV operators, because they take existing subscribers and make them happier. Once happier, and satisfied by the value of digital services in the form of DVRs, consumers are that much likelier to want to add on additional digital services, such as video on demand, HDTV, and interactive TV. Further, the addition of each of these usually means those customers pay extra for each new service, often having a marked increase on average revenue per unit or ARPU. In short, again, DVRs make money.

Also, on the business side, DVRs tap into a new trend toward personalized video, which, like DVR functionality, appears inevitable. It is because of this new trend that advertisers and their agencies (those once so threatened by DVRs) are now in a position to capture that trend (working with DVR operators to mine consumer use data), and create an entire new paradigm of two-way, interactive commercial relationships with hundreds of millions—or one day, billions—of DVR users.

On the consumer side, a positive link exists in the form of DVRs making video customers happy. By permitting users huge flexibility as to what and when they watch all TV, DVRs massively expand the usability of just about all TV. Typical customer survey materials, such as those included in several places within this book, indicate the level of passion customers feel toward these devices, which is remarkable. It is also worth predicting that consumers will adapt to and seek out well-developed and well-presented content, including advertisements, in the future. This will be the case especially for personalized content, again including advertisements.

It is easy to focus a time in the future when all TV homes in the United States have DVRs, indeed when video using a DVR or DVR-like function becomes the standard. Further, as it relates to the future, it is difficult to see a time when DVR functionality will not be important to consumers or when it will not be growing in popularity.

This leads us to the two final chapters of this book, *Digital Video Recorders: DVRs Changing TV and Advertising Forever*. Chapter 7 is a look at some key international markets, where the real long term of growth of the DVR industry will occur. Chapter 8 provides a solid look at the future of the service and product side of DVRs and DVR-like functions, which will find their way into just about every device, wherever people find themselves, recording every type of content, for posterity. The only foreseeable glitch to the existing business model is the idea of most or all the content storage moving from in-home individual DVRs to a central storage facility, away from the home and the living room of the consumer. This storage facility thrives in the future because it is cheaper for the operator and the consumer. It also thrives in the future because, unless operators build it out and do it properly, consumers will not continue to accept and pay for it. And, if that happens, operators will lose a great deal of future profit.

In short, DVRS are emerging at a rapid rate because, in general, they work. Yet DVRs will keep working and keep getting better, because those in and those about to be in the DVR industry, will do their homework, understand their audience, understand their medium, and do it right. This book is written with the express vision of helping to make that happen.

Introduction

The advent of the DVR has transformed a world of ever-increasing TV choice into a manageable environment, with increasing personal control. Television can now be personalized by the viewer—enabling each person to watch what he wants, when he wants to watch it. TiVo guarantees that there will always be something good on when the viewer turns on the TV. We have entered a new reality, whereby viewers are in control and can effortlessly pause, fast forward, and rewind the content of their choice with the push of a button. It has long been said that "time waits for no man"... all evidence to the contrary.

—Tom Rogers, CEO, TiVo

All too occasionally, a technical and marketing marvel enters the telecommunications arena and really changes forever the way human beings do something. Without question, the development and marketing of the digital video recorder (DVR)—like the emergence of radio, basic television, and color TV before it—is an example of that remarkable progress within the realm of video and audio, as well as within the areas of content storage, distribution, and presentation. This is the reasoning behind the title of this book, *DVRs: Changing TV and Advertising Forever.*[1]

For people who own or have used a DVR, it is rare to find a person who is not totally enamored of the DVRs capability and functionality. Some users even call it "magical." This infatuation with, and excitement over, DVRs and what they do typically holds true, no matter which DVR device is in operation. Thus, from the ultimate, top-of-the-line models (like that of TiVo's series 3 model no. TCD648250B high definition (HD) DVR; or that of Digeo's model no. MR-1500T3 HD DVR; or EchoStar's ViP 922 model combination HD/DVR with Sling Media capability); to the most basic consumer model offered by a multichannel TV operator, such as DirecTV or Comcast, customers appreciate the "three C's" of the modern-day DVR deployment: the *convenience* of usage, the *control* over the video, and the *choice* over which content to view. The fact that DVRs eliminate the need to buy and manage cumbersome tapes and disks—which the predecessor video cassette recorder (VCR) required—is yet another reason behind the success of the DVR today.

Telecom industry players, especially multichannel television operators, are also favorably inclined toward the revenues produced by DVRs, from both the service subscription fee and the hardware revenue points of view. DVRs

---

[1] In a vein similar to that of this "time waits for no man" quote offered by TiVo CEO, Tom Rogers, the author's company, the industry consultant and analyst of The Carmel Group, has authored several annual studies about DVRs, going back to 2006, each entitled *Digital Video Recorders: Time in a Magic Box.* These studies have been and are intended to bring out the real wonder of DVR technology and what remarkable things the DVR does for consumers. Descriptions of these detailed DVR studies, based upon detailed consumer surveys of thousands of consumers, can be found at The Carmel Group's Web site at http://www.carmelgroup.com.

bring system operators new subscribers, while also helping to satisfy existing subscribers (thus keeping those customers from churning or leaving the existing service). Indeed, the two key remaining members of the current DVR multichannel revenue chain that appear to be most challenged as they feel their way through the new labyrinth that DVRs represent are the advertisers and their agencies, on the one hand, and the large scale consumer electronics (CE) dealers, on the other hand. But interestingly, both probably have reasons to be sanguine. This is because the measurement capabilities offered by DVRs offer much in the way of personalization and customization of advertisements, thus presumably enhancing a specific ad's attractiveness as it relates to the specific consumer interested in that product or service.

Properly managing this challenge will be the truest long-term measure of the DVR industry's long-term impact and profitability. Advertisers who "get it," will survive; those that do not, likely will not survive. As for the large CE dealers, their opportunities will come as more and more device and service manufacturers, such as satellite radio suppliers, turn to CE industry suppliers for new DVR and DVR-type devices. Those in the CE chain will also likely benefit from a loosening of the monopolies or duopolies that now dominate the cable and satellite and telco set-top DVR supply chain.

This book is intended to capture a good deal of that industry and consumer excitement—and angst—as well as to explain the DVR industry's basic ingredients. These ingredients range from just what a DVR is and how it operates, to how many DVRs are estimated to be sold during the next 5–7 years, to what it is that consumers like—and dislike—about DVRs.

Addressing the future, significant time is spent looking at issues like what products and services threaten to replace or invalidate the DVR business. For advertisers and agencies, this book is also meant to try to dissemble and reassemble the disruptiveness, the paradox, the real challenges, and the apparent opportunities that face them in the Brave New World of DVRs (and the progeny of today's DVRs). Other questions asked and answered will include the impact of DVRs on, and their expectation to permanently change, the global advertising world, as well as the advertising community's ability to change and adapt relative to ad-skipping and other DVR-type threats.

About this Book

Almost 20 case studies support the main text in the eight chapters of this book. Dozens more charts and photos help clarify the DVR message of that general text and case study material.

The case studies are sought out and completed with the goal of providing additional information and real-life applications and approaches to problems that a normal DVR chapter analysis might miss. The case studies are also intended to give the reader a chance to zero in on specifics, in a larger context and in greater detail. One example is the Sony case study in Chapter 1, showing where a true CE pioneer took the business (and art) of DVR, how that vision became frustrated, but how that view might improve in the not-too-distant future. Another example of case studies, on the other side of the book, is in Chapter 8, where the lessons of both a multichannel operator, DirecTV, and of an important advertiser, Hill Holliday, are presented. Worth noting in between are also case studies involving survey data from companies such as Nielsen, Arbitron, and the Consumer Electronic Association.

Chapter 1 presents a broad overview of DVRs, tracing back its history, the types of DVRs, comparisons of DVRs to other products (such as VODs and digital signage), detailed discussions of key industry players, a look at past and future growth prospects, and a look at DVR hardware and software, technology, trends, challenges, and opportunities. Also, a brief look at the future is presented to keep the DVR overview in context; however, the reader is strongly encouraged to read all of Chapter 8 to get the best picture of the future of DVRs.

Chapter 2 moves more specifically into the question of, What is a DVR? Additional questions asked and answered include where (DVRs work), why (a DVR works), and when (a DVR works). This chapter is important to help the reader specifically answer core questions about the fundamentals underlying DVRs.

Chapter 3 takes a hard look at the business of DVRs. Legal and regulatory matters have been an important part of the DVR industry thus far, so a fair sum of material is dedicated to that discussion. Financial, marketing, distribution, and technological matters are also given additional attention in the business context. Further, before an excellent case study involving multichannel operator and DVR pioneer EchoStar closes the chapter, a full set of two types of frequently asked questions is presented from both an advertiser/agency, and a DVR provider, point of view.

Moving to Chapter 4, DVR uses and applications are detailed. This chapter chronicles not only the current consumer DVR uses and applications, but also those of the future and those of related devices and software. Thus, not only are single- and multiroom applications discussed, but also those in the cable, satellite, and telco realms, as well as the up-and-coming mobile arena. A brief review of DVRs in the security context precedes review of DVR control devices, transferring content, and current on-screen DVR information.

DVR business models make up Chapter 5. In this chapter, specific review of the moneymaking aspects of DVRs, from the various operator, manufacturer, and standalone DVR maker perspectives, is presented. A look at the business models of software and other miscellaneous DVR industry players rounds out Chapter 5, along with a look at advertisers (and their agencies), networks, and broadcasters.

Chapter 6 is a chapter that focuses on the consumer. It contains a good number of the projections of future growth and of the survey material drawn together by a prominent industry researcher in an effort to better understand consumers and their love of DVRs. It also gives consumers ideas about whether to rent or buy their DVR upfront, including dozens of questions prepared specifically for consumers, as they wend their way through the maze that can be a DVR purchase (or rental).

Chapter 7 is a snap shot of the DVR World, literally speaking, with a focus on Asia and Europe, as well as U.S. North American partner, Canada. Note that this chapter is not intended as an all-inclusive look at all global DVR deployments but rather as a set of examples that tell the global DVR story relatively well. Because other countries present such different cultures and paths to the development of DVRs, their stories tend to be particularly refreshing and instructive as it relates to other DVR options and alternatives that are possible.

Chapter 8, finally, talks about the future of DVRs. This chapter tells the reader what to look for in the where, and the how, and the when of next generation DVRs and the later stages of the DVR growth cycle. Key to this is a discussion of the remote storage DVR and why it makes such good sense among cable and telco multichannel TV operators. Perhaps as importantly, Chapter 8 talks a good deal about where other important players, such as broadcasters, advertisers, and networks again, are expected to go with—and take—the DVR world into the future. A look at the DVR of the future concludes the chapter.

Beyond the formal chapters, a glossary of terms is presented at Appendix A, and Appendix B lists the key players in the DVR world today and an brief overview of what they do.

In summary, a lot of good business is ahead for the DVR industry, and a lot of good TV pleasure is ahead for the world's DVR users.

It is the author's sincere hope that many of those businesses and consumers will look back at the process of getting there and determine that this book helped.

Jimmy Schaeffler
Carmel-by-the-Sea, CA, USA

1 An Overview of Digital Video Recorders

The DVR is rapidly evolving far beyond its original, and quite limited, role as a time-shifting device. The DVR will become a more multifaceted product, one that can conveniently access and store both broadcast and Internet Web media. Very soon, endusers will gather, sort, and access videos, photos, music, podcasts, and RSS feeds.[1] And, with the intelligence available in the next generation of DVRs, connections between various content choices will be recognizable, such that meaningful recommendations as to related content and choices amongst all enduser media will become the enduser's favorite feature—a trusted friend, of sorts. Best of all, it will all be readily accessible anywhere within the home and, when the enduser is out and about, via the Net.

—Greg Gudorf, CEO, Digeo, Inc.

Users with DVRs in their homes quickly change their viewing behavior and appreciate newly gained editorial and scheduling control.
—Loebbecke and Radtke, "Business Models and Programming Choice: Digital Video Recorders Shaping the TV Industry"[2]

Once also called a personal video recorder (PVR), but now known almost exclusively among aficionados and most laypeople as simply a digital video recorder (DVR), the DVR device is essentially an in-home computer. In its typical forms, the DVR is either its own standalone set-top box (that only functions as a DVR) or is part of a cable, satellite, or telephone[3] company's set-top box. This would be the set-top box that sits beside, below, or on top of a TV and also permits access to that company's multichannel content. The DVR contains a mechanism—called a hard drive—onto which the live, real-time audio and video digital content is recorded. This content is then delivered to the TV (or similar) screen upon command by the user.[4] In other words, instead of saving documents or files like a personal computer (PC) does, the DVR saves the

---

[1] RSS feeds are known to most consumers as the type of scrolling stock or news information that moves across the bottom of a CNN screen, below the on-screen video, for example. The term, RSS, stands for "Really Simple Syndication."

[2] See *Proceedings of the Eleventh Americas Conference on Information Systems*, Omaha, NE, August 11–14, 2005, which is a good review of various business models in the new world of DVRs.

[3] A telephone company will henceforth be referred to in this book using its industry term, "telco."

[4] Although currently the predominant form of content storage in a DVR is onto a hard drive, it is expected that future forms of storage, such as flash, will also be incorporated into DVRs.

actual digital video and audio signal that arrives at the DVR and the monitor(s) it serves. This digital content is recorded, of course, back onto the hard drive for later manipulation by the DVR user.

Other newer or less popular versions of DVRs are found in the software for PCs, which enable video capture and playback to and from a disk. As detailed below, some consumer electronics (CE) manufacturers have begun to offer televisions with DVR hardware and software built into the television itself. Further, use of a DVR has also become the main way for security-based closed circuit TV (CCTV)[5] companies to record their surveillance, because the DVR provides far longer recording times than the previously used video cassette recorders (VCRs).

Once the digital content is recorded onto the hard drive, that content on the DVR hard drive is then managed via a remote control in the hands of the DVR user. This control typically comes in the form of a viewer pushing the "pause," "forward," and "reverse" buttons: he or she can pause (or freeze the frame of) the content on the TV monitor for long periods of time; he or she can rewind and replay the content, often returning to the very beginning of a show of almost any length; and he or she can fast forward the recorded content material right up to the point where the on-screen content is actually live or real time. The industry term that captures these concepts of viewing in the future, viewing at will, and viewing only what is desired is called "time-shifting."

Moreover, because content is typically stored inside the consumer's set-top box, there is no need to handle, organize, label, and store tapes and other portable hardware (which is required of a VCR). Most DVRs automatically record up to 30 minutes of any given show that is showing live on the TV set at the time. They begin this automatic recording the minute the TV is turned on. This is the function that allows viewers to manipulate a live program they are watching at the time.

If the phone rings, the baby cries, or the viewer just needs to take a break, the viewer pauses the program, without missing anything. While paused, the DVR continues recording the program and when the viewer returns, he or she simply hits the "play" button, and viewing continues from the point of the pause. Or, at that point, the program can be rewound or fast-forwarded. The DVR also allows a viewer to automatically record a favorite show every time it airs. Thus, there is no more searching for a blank VCR tape, or worrying about recording over a previously-recorded piece of content. DVRs thus save the cost of tapes, while offering usually adequate storage, and providing better picture quality than a VCR, as well as networking capabilities. Note, though, to be clear, unlike VCRs, DVRs typically cannot playback content stored on other forms, such as tapes or DVDs. Typically, the DVR only plays back content that has been transmitted to it, and that is the only content it records.

---

[5] A CCTV system is one where video cameras are used to transmit a signal to a specific and mostly limited set of TV monitors.

Viewer control also comes in the form of DVR users turning to a screen that presents a grid of shows being aired currently (or yet to air) and clicking to highlight a particular show to then have the DVR record or store it onto the hard drive. In industry parlance, this screen is called an electronic program guide (EPG) or an interactive programming guide (IPG).[6] Once that choice has been made by the viewer and registered by the DVR, at a time in the future, the recording will be made by the DVR unit. Then, when the viewer chooses to view that stored program, or the entire series of those programs, the viewer simply retrieves the recorded list, clicks on or highlights the recorded event, and the viewing begins. What is particularly attractive to most DVR users viewing this form of previously recorded content is that advertisements or other unattractive content can be avoided or minimized by running the DVR in one of several fast-forward speeds. Thus, for example, a 30-minute long evening news program can be boiled down to about 22 minutes of programming content that is not dedicated to ads, making one's news viewing time that more efficient (assuming one wants to fast forward through the 8 minutes, worth of ads).

Another part of a DVR EPG/IPG that is important is the ability of a viewer to select an author, actor, genre, or other delineation of show type, and the DVR will act to seek out that type of program with that or those characteristic(s) and display it for future selection by the viewer. Further, with recommendation software built into a TiVo DVR, for instance, the DVR will determine programs that match the criteria for the kinds of shows you watch, and later display titles for those programs as they are available.

Additionally, a DVR permits a viewer who is watching a show live or in "real time", as the industry knows the expression, to push a button on the remote control that will instantly begin recording the live show from that point onward. This also permits the DVR user to view the live show at a later date. Additionally, in some instances, and on some devices, if the show being recorded on a DVR device goes long, the device can be programmed to continue recording so that it can catch the entire program. In addition, DVRs typically include a function that allows the viewer to run a program in slow motion. In short, the viewer simply chooses the program he or she wishes to record, and the DVR does the rest.

1.1   Main Types of DVRs

There are currently three main types of DVRs: one is a standalone DVR, one is an integrated set-top box DVR, and one is known as a remote storage DVR. Note that the remote storage DVR concept and its attempted deployment are presently embroiled in significant controversy and litigation, as noted below, and

---

[6] For the sake of clarity, future uses of both or either acronym EPG or IPG will be written in the form of simply EPG/IPG, indicating that within the TV business, the two terms are synonymous. Nonetheless, to maintain the integrity of the quotation, wherever someone uses only one or the other form in a quote, that form alone will be noted.

thus, there are few remote storage DVR users. Nonetheless, the author and many other observers and analysts see great possibilities for the remote storage DVR business models, once licensing and copyright challenges have been resolved with Hollywood, network TV, and other content owners.

1.1.1 Standalone

A standalone DVR is one that typically serves only as a DVR. In other words, a standalone DVR set-top box does not also allow multichannel TV—such as that offered by the cable, satellite, or telco operator—to be accessed by the TV viewer using the same set-top box. Since digital cable, satellite, and telco-delivered services are scrambled (or encrypted), and can only be descrambled (or decrypted) by cable-, satellite-, or telco-provided set-top boxes, tuning digital cable, satellite, and/or telco channels—and recording them—is a capability that standalone set-top boxes lack. DVR developers, such as TiVo (and earlier forms of the TiVo rival, ReplayTV), typically offer(ed) only standalone DVRs as part of their first generation of DVR lineups. Photographic examples of a standalone set-top DVRs typically look nearly the same as integrated DVRs, such as the integrated set-top depicted in Figure 1.1.

1.1.2 Integrated

Another type of DVR is the integrated set-top DVR (Figure 1.1), which typically is part of a set-top box that has a broader function, as well, that is, that of delivering and decoding cable-, satellite-, or telco-delivered signals for presentation onto

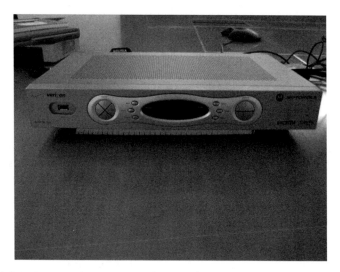

Figure 1.1   An integrated set-top DVR box, in this case supplied by Verizon to its video/DVR subscribers. (Copyright 2009. Property of Verizon. Used with permission. All rights reserved.)

the viewing monitor. Cable, telco, and satellite operators typically deliver set-top decoder boxes to consumers these days, with DVRs already built into them at the factory. In more recent years, cable set-top boxes with a cable card and DVR built into them are also available at retail, permitting cable subscribers to own their integrated DVR set-top following purchase (rather than only being permitted to lease their set-top from the cable operator, via the traditional cable distribution model).

1.1.3 Remote Storage

A third type of DVR is also provided by a cable operator, yet the storage function is built into a remote server, that is, one that is housed elsewhere than in the consumer's home, and thus also is controlled, in part, by the operator. Typically, the storage center location is miles distant from the user's home and contains large sets of storage boxes or servers that are connected by miles of cable lines to a viewer's in-home set-top box. When the viewer selects his or her content, the remote recording device in the distant storage center location then records the content for that individual user.

New York City-based Time Warner Cable, in the 2002–2003 time frame, is generally believed to be the first to attempt to implement this type of alternative to the in-house set-top box DVR implementation, albeit unsuccessfully.

Cablevision Systems of Long Island, NY, is a more recent example of a cable company that has tried this type of storage infrastructure. Cablevision stated that two of its goals were to (1) lower the price of the DVR-type experience (because neither the cable company nor the consumer would be required to purchase a DVR set-top for the home) and (2) bring larger numbers of consumers into the development of DVR-like features (because the remote server could then be more simply and economically deployed, by both the system operator and the consumer). This remote storage device called the remote storage (RS-DVR) would, for a rental fee of less than $9.99 per month, offer users 80 gigabytes (GB)[7] of storage space on the Cablevision server (or recorder), on which the consumer could then remotely record shows to be watched at his or her convenience, in true DVR-like fashion. Key members of the content community, however, have challenged Cablevision in court proceedings—arguing concerns about copyright infringement—which has slowed the deployment of this form of DVR. Presently, the concept and development of the RS-DVR remains embroiled in litigation, Cablevision having lost and subsequently appealed and won a U.S. district court opinion supporting the content-owning plaintiffs.[8] This case is now before the U.S. Supreme Court on a final appeal, which will result in a final court judgment.

---

[7] 80 GB of hard drive storage is the equivalent of approximately 8 hours of HDTV programming stored on a DVR, or approximately 55–60 hours of standard definition (SD) TV programming stored on the same DVR. See also Table 1.2, showing these conversions.

[8] See http://arstechnica.com/news.ars/post/20070323-broadcasters-win-legal-fight-against-cablevi-sions-networked-dvr-or-cablevision-loses-networked-dvr-case.html, for an *Arts Tecnica* article by Eric Bangeman, dated March 23, 2007, about this dispute.

1.1.4 Miscellaneous and Future Devices

More hardware devices that deliver content to consumers are likely to include hard drives or other forms of instant storage, in various media, allowing content manipulation, as the DVR trend expands. Already, satellite radio manufacturers have created portable satellite radios that serve a DVR-like function. As mentioned later in this chapter, some Asian-based TV monitor manufacturers have begun to implement TVs with DVRs automatically built into the same unit (see the "Forms" section). In part, because it is such a logical, efficient, and elegant combination, it is merely a matter of time before DVRs built into TVs become more common in the United States.

Indeed, in the future, the list of types of DVRs will grow significantly, as DVR functionality gets built into satellite radios, mobile DVRs, gaming devices, cell phones, and personal digital assistants, as well as many other devices and form factors that have not yet been developed or defined. A good example of this future growth that is already well on its way is the recording function that is now provided in newer forms of gaming systems, such as the *Xbox 360* from Microsoft. The DVR function inside this box contains a 120-GB hard drive, which is quite large by today's standards. Common sense suggests that future generations of video- and audiophiles will expect that whenever they are listening to music and/or viewing video, a DVR or a DVR-like device will be recording it and storing it for later personal playback [but not for anything more than limited distribution, as that would create copyright and digital rights

Table 1.1 The Different Types of DVR Makers.

DVR Provider and Model	Type of DVR	Up-Front DVR Cost	Service Cost	Type of Set-Top Box
Digeo MR-1500T3	SD/HD standalone	$799.00	Included in up-front cost	Standalone
TiVo® Series2 DT	SD standalone	$149.99	$12.95/month	Standalone
TiVo® HD DVR	HD standalone	$299.99	$12.95/month	Standalone
TiVo® HD DVR Lifetime Service	HD standalone	$299.99	$299 for the lifetime of the DVR box (transferable)	Standalone
DirecTV® Plus HD DVR HR20	HD standalone	$99.97 (with rebate) or $198.97	$54.99/month (including DirecTV and DVR service)	DBS
DirecTV® Plus DVR	SD standalone	Free with service	$44.99/month (including DirecTV and DVR service)	DBS

(Continued)

DVR Provider and Model	Type of DVR	Up-Front DVR Cost	Service Cost	Type of Set-Top Box
DISH® ViP722 DVR HD	HD standalone	Free with service (OAC)	$5.98/month	DBS
DISH® Player DVR 625	SD standalone	Free with service (OAC)	$5.98/month	DBS
Comcast/ Motorola—DCH 3200	HD integrated	Included in service fee	$13.95/month	Cable
Comcast/ Motorola—DCH 70	SD integrated	Included in service fee	$8.99/month	Cable
Charter/Digeo	SD/HD integrated	Included in service fee	$15.00/month	Cable
Time Warner cable—SA various	HD integrated	Included in service fee	$14.15/month ($6.95 svc + $7.20 STB)	Cable
Charter communications SA or Motorola	HD integrated	Included in service fee	$15.00/month (HD included)	Cable
Cox communications— SA various	HD integrated	Included in service fee	$17.20/month ($11.95 svc + $5.25 STB)	Cable
Cablevision systems—SA various	HD integrated	Included in service fee	$16.45/month ($9.95 svc + $6.50 STB)	Cable
Verizon FiOS TV	HD integrated	Included in service fee	$47.99/month (including Verizon Cable and DVR service)	Telco
AT&T—U-Verse TV	HD integrated	Included in service fee	$44/month (including AT&T Cable and DVR service)	Telco

Table 1.2 Different Conversions and Other Data for SD vs. HD Comparison.

Comparison Point	SD	HD	Description
Typical Storage Size	60 to 320 GigaBytes (GB)	160 to 500 GB (up to 1 TerraByte in 2009)	Storage capacity is the Holy Grail of DVRs. Within a reasonable price, the more the better. Consumers tend to be greedy when it comes to value.
Record time (hours\)	25 to 200 hours	20 to 55 hours	See above.
1080p	No	Exists on some HD models	This is the future of HD standards.
Analog over-the-air tuner or analog support	Exists on some SD models	Exists on some HD models	Analog is disappearing, so its importance in the U.S. dimishes quickly, especially after February 17, 2009.
MPEG4	No on cable, yes on some satellite models	Exists on most HD models	MPEG4 as a compression standard is a vast improvement over its predeccors, MPEG2, and simply allows TV operators to do more with a given signal, again, to deliver either greater margins or better value, or both.
Caller ID	Primarily on satellite	On satellite and some cable boxes	Is a "bell and whitle" now that will increasingly become standard.

management (DRM) conflicts with the content copyright holders]. Moreover, like the earliest development of the DVR (which we will see in the "History" section of this chapter, includes crude implementations of a home media center), the home media center of the future will, one day, likely be a core system supporting en masse the deployment of DVRs (or a DVR-like device).

1.2 DVRs vs. VCRs

It is no surprise then that many refer to a DVR as a "VCR on steroids." This occurs because the DVR not only can record content as it is being telecast, but, unlike the VCR, it also allows the viewer to manipulate that content while it is being telecast *live*. The DVR also eliminates the need to handle or later deal with tapes or disks that are the physical media that records and stores the content. A DVR uses an internal hard drive to store the audio and video. Also, DVRs typically offer two or more tuners, which are devices which enable two or more channels or streams of content to be recorded or viewed at the same time. Figure 1.2 shows a photo comparison of a VCR set-top to that of a DVR set-top, while Table 1.3 compares the features of a DVR vs. those of a VCR. This chart is intended to emphasize the advances that are offered by the DVR over the VCR [and why the DVR has already, along with the digital versatile disk (DVD) device, almost entirely replaced the antiquated VCR fairly well].[9]

Note that a DVR, as its name implies, is only capable of recording digital content. Audio and video content that is delivered in an analog format cannot be recorded on a DVR, unless a special adaptive device is placed inside the DVR set-top box to transfer the signal from analog to digital form. Analog content includes video, such as standard over-the-air broadcast TV signals from local network TV affiliates, which currently the government will only allow those

Figure 1.2   A DVR set-top box (top) and a VCR set-top (bottom). (Copyright 2008. Property of Willy Schaeffler. All rights reserved. Photo used with permission.)

---

[9] It is also interesting to note that although DVRs and DVDs have replaced VCRs (see Chapter 8, "The Future of DVRs"), the two do have a "working relationship" of sorts: the DVR pioneer, TiVo, includes a functionality in its DVRs, which enables VCRs to be used to archive stored DVR content (for later playback and to free-up additional space on the DVR hard drive). Similar back-up recording functions are being designed for use with DVR-DVD set-top combinations. In this way, the DVR user can get what the VCR has always offered: a separate piece of hardware on which to store and perhaps later share the content with someone else, or play the content on another machine in another locale.

Table 1.3 A Comparison of a Standard DVR to that of a Standard VCR.

VCRs vs. DVRs: The Old vs. The New

Comparison Point	VCR	DVR
When developed	1965	1998–1999
Core developers	Ampex, Sony, Philips	OpenTV, TiVo, ReplayTV, EchoStar
Standard form of storage	Video tape	Computer hard drive
Storage function	Subsequent viewing of recorded programs	Manipulation of live content, as well as subsequent viewing of programs recorded
Standard storage length	2-hour video cassette tape	Various hard drives (some offering 10 hours of storage time, to those offering scores, or hundreds, of hours)
Source of content	Live TV content and cassettes with pre-recorded content	Only live TV
Key features	Pause, rewind, and fast forward previously recorded TV content	Pause, rewind, and fast forward live and previously recorded TV
Number sold as of year-end 2007	88,000,000[1]	19,327,000[1]
Average unit pricing when introduced	$600	$600
Average unit pricing at 10-year growth stage	$100	$50
Average monthly fee	None	$0–12.99
Where sold or distributed	CE dealers	CE dealers and multichannel TV operators
Major distributors	CE dealers	DISH Network, DirecTV, major cable operators, major telco video providers, retail CE dealers
Major manufacturers		TiVo, ReplayTV, Scientific-Atlanta, Motorola, DISH Network, NDS, Digeo
Related functionality	None early on; DVRs more recently	Ties in with home networking devices and functionality
Replaced by	DVDs, DVRs	Home network unit; VOD someday?

[1]Source: Nielsen.
Source: Consumer Electronics Association. Used with permission. Copyright 2008. Property of Jimmy Schaeffler. All rights reserved. From Admiral, Aiwa, Ampex, Canon, Daewoo, Emerson, JVC, Kenwood, Magnavox, Panasonic, RCA, Samsung, Sony, Toshiba, and Zenith.

stations to carry until June 12, 2009.[10] After that date, all over-the-air signals will have to be carried in a digital—and a digital only—format. Inevitably, this "digital deadline" event, in mid-June 2009, should have a very positive effect on the growth of DVRs. This is because the question of whether an over-the-air program is carried in digital format or not will quickly become irrelevant. Almost all content, delivered via over-the-air terrestrial broadcast, cable, telco, Internet, or satellite, will be digital as of Qz 2009, and thus capable of storage on a DVR and manipulation by a DVR user.

In addition, to utilize the full DVR functionality, a user must also have a subscription to a programming service, such as a cable, satellite, telco, or a similar multichannel distributor. This is necessary to have access to the operator-supplied EPG/IPG. The EPG/IPG allows users to see currently playing and future scheduled programming. This programming guide (or menu or grid) then permits the viewer/user to interact with the scheduled programming, by selecting, playing, and/or recording those programs for later use. Other typically more advanced EPGs/IPGs are also available from consumer companies, such as TiVo or Digeo, to substitute for cable-, telco-, and satellite-created EPGs/IPGs.

Importantly, since the midpoint of the new millennium's first decade, newer versions of DVR set-top boxes have allowed the recording and manipulation of digital content that is delivered in high definition (HD) quality, as well as content that is delivered in lower quality standard definition (SD) digital versions. Additionally, DVRs with added recording devices, known as tuners, are capable of recording and storing more than one program that is being telecast simultaneously on different channels. Thus, for example, a DVR with two tuners could play one show for viewing live, while concurrently recording and storing two other shows for later playback.

1.3   DVRs vs. VOD

In the context of DVRs, video on demand (VOD) is important for several reasons. VOD can be seen as a technological competitor to DVRs, because some multichannel operators and some consumers will not choose both, and thus, in many instances, will choose VOD over DVRs. VOD has advantages in this way because it does not require up-front consumer, company subsidy, or investment in consumer hardware. The only VOD investment is typically made by the operator in the cable center servers and in the content that reaches those VOD consumers. Moreover, one after another, consumer purchases of that content have the potential to add significant sums to the coffers of savvy multichannel operators.

---

[10] The U.S. government, in the form of Congress and the Federal Communications Commission (FCC), has mandated that all over-the-air terrestrial broadcast TV signals shall be delivered in a digital form *only*, as of June 12, 2009. The FCC states that this is being done now as an effort to enhance the quality of TV signals and actual on-screen programming, and to make more efficient use of the limited spectrum used to carry TV and other telecommunications signals.

Conversely, VOD is also important to multichannel operators and to consumers because the savviest of those operators and consumers realize how well VOD and DVRs go together. Indeed, the combination of VOD and DVRs is ideal for most consumers and goes a long way not only to bring in additional operator revenues, but also to reduce churn (or consumer turnover) and to bring in new subscribers for operators who are wise enough to install both services. VOD permits choice and control of content stored on servers by the cable

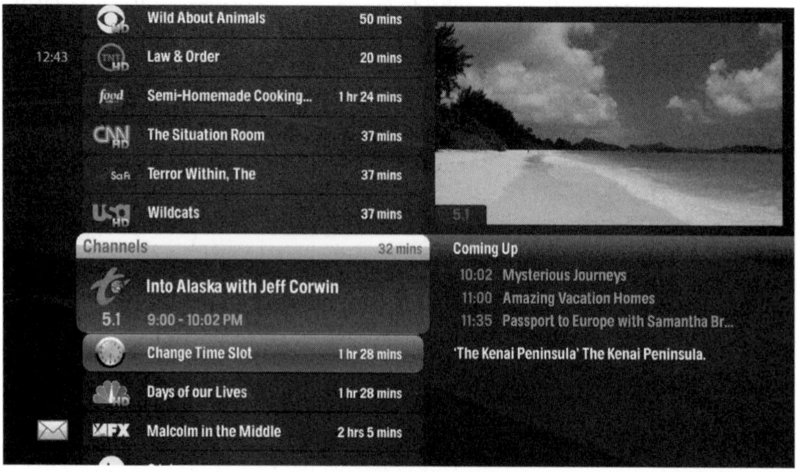

Figure 1.3 A top-rated DVR on-screen guide from Digeo. (Copyright 2008. Property of Digeo. All rights reserved. Photo used with permission.)

Figure 1.4 A VOD on-screen guide. (Copyright 2008. Property of Comcast. All rights reserved. Photo used with permission.)

Table 1.4 A Comparison of a DVR Service to that of a True VOD Service.

DVR vs. VOD			
Comparison Point	DVR	VOD	Description/Explanation
Initial investment	Requires up-front company subsidy and consumer investment in consumer hardware, or consumer investment in monthly hardware lease.	Does not require up-front consumer/company subsidy investment in consumer hardware; does require significant investment in servers by company.	VOD can simply be integrated into the current programming of most consumers. Because DVR requires a hard drive, new set-top box must be purchased.
Later investment	Typically requires monthly fee to use EPG/IPG and similar software (although some companies allow payment of this fee by a consumer for lifetime, up front).	VOD titles, especially in the movie category, cost additional sums per order.	Typically DVR accounts for two revenue streams, up-front and monthly; VOD revenue stream is typically via individual orders of content titles.
Choice and control of content	Live telecast delivers signals to set-top box with DVR typically, for later storage.	Content stored on servers or company/operator.	VOD permits choice and control of content stored on servers by the cable operator. On the other hand, DVRs permit choice and control of content telecast live, which can then be stored by the customer on his or her DVR.
System/device promotes content for sale	No	Yes	Cable operators load for purchase content onto the VOD programming interface. This has the potential to add significant sums to the coffers of savvy multichannel operators.
On demand capabilities	No	Yes	VOD is the only system that can deliver content immediately, on demand. DVRs require that program first be telecast as part of linear programming.

operator; DVRs permit choice and control of content telecast live, which then can be stored by the consumer on his or her DVR. Figures 1.3 and 1.4 compare the on-screen guides for a DVR service (in this case, that of a Comcast DVR) and that of a VOD service (in this case, that of Time-Warner Cable).

From the perspective of the future of DVRs, many say that either VOD will eventually eliminate the need for DVRs or that operators will eventually begin delivering DVR services via the remote server—just as all true VOD systems do today—and that this development of a remote storage system for DVR and VOD will subsume DVRs within the infrastructure that today is only made for the VOD side of the content service industry.

The chart in Table 1.4 shows a side-by-side comparison of the features of a DVR service with those of a true VOD service, the latter capable of being offered only by cable and telco operators with true two-way interactivity and the capability to immediately deliver a program to a consumer upon demand. Satellite TV operators, on the other hand, are only capable of delivering content well after the time of consumer demand, via typical nighttime downloads of movies to set-top box DVR hard drives, for later viewing (typically by consumers the next evening). As such, satellite operators are not yet capable of delivering true VOD (although, for example, DirecTV claims that in Q3 2008, its new Internet-delivered VOD service began working in sync with its satellite-delivered DirecTV service).

1.4 DVRs vs. Digital Signage, DVRs and Digital Signage

Another new technology that some might find in conflict with DVRs is the digital signage. This is because from a display point of view, both products and services are driven by the concept of stored content being replayed for viewers. Thus, when looking at digital signage usage in a home environment, a digital photo frame has a chip that stores photos and then replays them on the screen for the viewer. In the same vein, a DVR records video and replays it later for the viewer. However, simply put, presently, most home digital signage is still images, whereas almost all DVR content is made up of active video together with audio. However, soon in-home digital frames will also include video and audio, and thus, the digital sign and the DVR in the home will be in conflict.

More importantly, today, however, DVRs and digital signage have one key element in common: both DVRs and digital signage thrive when the content they deliver is personal and relevant to the viewing audience. This is a critical concept. As viewers achieve more choice and control using their DVRs, they will expect more and more that other forms of media deliver the same options of choice and control. As repeatedly emphasized in this author's NAB/Focal Press book titled *Digital Signage—Software, Networks, Advertising, and Displays: A Primer for Understanding the Business*, the future of almost every screen showing content from here forward will turn on its ability to deliver viewers content that they want to see, content that helps them, content that is relevant. A great deal of what will allow DVRs to do that more efficiently in the future will be the ability of the DVR technology to appropriately collect, measure, and decipher a DVR viewer's viewing preferences, and then appropriately deliver those choices to the consumer for action. The more that both DVR operators and digital signage operators do just that, the more successful their mediums will become.

TiVo cofounder Jim Barton, in an April 2006 article, titled "TiVo-lution: The Challenges of Delivering a Reliable, Easy-to-Use DVR Service to the Masses," notes, "Privacy must be fundamental to the design. People are understandably concerned about their viewing habits being exposed to others or used in unexpected ways. On the other hand, anonymous viewing information can be used to measure general behavior and to improve programming. Therefore, the system must be designed to protect the viewer's privacy while allowing for collection of relevant information."

Further, in the future, just as DVRs have become an important part of the security monitoring sector (discussed in more detail in the next section), DVRs are likely to become a greater part of the digital signage business, especially for those digital signage implementations that will wish to measure and monitor the audience receiving the messages on any given digital sign. Thus, a digital sign with a small camera placed nearby will record a user's impressions and reactions, in sync with certain types of video, which will then be recorded for playback on a DVR, and used to assess the effectiveness of and relevance of certain content with certain audiences at certain times.

1.5 History

The history of DVRs is a metaphor for the history of the core industry segments within which DVRs reside, that is, TV and computers. This is because the development and growth of DVRs did exactly what the development and growth of TVs and computers did: it vastly improved most people's quality of life, allowing them enhanced access to information and entertainment. Although today, more and more, the two realms are emerging and overlapping, in their earliest days, computers primarily meant access to information in the business environment, while, correspondingly, TVs meant access to entertainment in the personal environment. DVRs, realistically, will skew more toward personal use, as has been the case with TVs; however, more and more DVRs will also be important in the enterprise context, such as DVRs being used in security and corporate training applications. This historical section of this chapter tracks the growth and development of DVRs, focused, necessarily, on the key early players and the key parts of the TV and multichannel pay TV worlds. For the sake of convenience, the timeline following allows readers to quickly scan and understand a more than 15-year time frame within the course of a few minutes.

1.5.1 Computer Beginnings

The earliest roots of DVRs are in computers, plain and simple.

Indeed, for several years now, many knowledgeable technologists have thought of DVRs as just another form of a PC. In more recent times, especially as the technical sophistication of DVRs and DVR-like devices increases, it is hard to think of a DVR as anything but a highly sophisticated computer (no matter who is doing the judging). One of Sony's PlayStation 3s, with a built-in DVR, is another perfect example of a device that is not that dissimilar from the basic PC.

The listing for DVR on *Wikipedia* begins with a history section and a brief discussion of DVR-related development in the early 1960s. This includes discussion of television network inventions tied to commercial recording of video and audio programming for rewinding and freeze frames of sports programming in the mid-1960s. It was not until 20 years later, in 1985, that home-based designs were developed and patented by Honeywell employee David Rafner. This device included a hard drive that made ad-skipping and so-called time-shifting possible and was described in patent materials as permitting applications such as "... streaming compression, editing, captioning, multichannel security monitoring, military sensor platforms, and remotely piloted vehicles."

The first DVR-related patent, known in the DVR industry as the Goldwasser Patent [after inventors Eric Goldwasser (father) and Romi Goldwasser (daughter), of Yorktown Heights, NY], was applied for in 1991 and was issued by the U.S. Patent and Trademark Office in late August 1993. In Q1 2005, TiVo's top-level executives, lawyers, and engineers, in the company's 8-K document filed with the U.S. government's Securities and Exchange Commission, described the Goldwasser patent as covering "... devices which permit the simultaneous recording and playback of video material with a variable time delay between recording and playback of a given program segment." This definition would later be shortened to the industry terms "time-shifting" or "time warp." With this patent in place, a great variety of intellectual property began to grow up and around the soon-to-be-developed DVR industry, spread around many different companies, which was to make for some very interesting and very complex business, technical, and legal arrangements during the ensuing years.

1.5.2 TiVo and ReplayTV

Following these early foundational inventions, and dependent on who is asked, the earliest ideas for the development of a business built around sales of DVR devices and services were either (or both) that of Anthony Woods, who built his DVR company, ReplayTV, during the 1997–2001 time frame and/or of Michael Ramsay and Jim Barton, who built their TiVo business, in the 1997-to-present time frame. Both sets of players would combine their visions and these early inventions with ever-cheaper hard drives and new chip designs that permitted real-time encoding of analog signals into digital signals. In the late 1990s, these were the core developments that jump-started the DVR revolution.

Other DVR roots are found in the process of the telecom industry planning for the development of a telecom infrastructure within the American home of the future. For example, TiVo's earliest ramblings were based on the idea of a large, server-like device in the garage or attic of a typical home. This "super box" device would then collect signals from many different sources (including fax, TV, telephone, radio, and others) and display those signals in many rooms and via various devices around the home. The idea of a specific set-top box that would be a part of the grander in-home system was the genesis for TiVo's focus on what it claims was the first commercial deployment of a DVR in late March 1999. TiVo's deployment of the DVR was preceded by WebTV's January 1999 Consumer Electronics Show (CES) announcement with partner EchoStar of its new set-top box, which combined DISH Network programming with DVR capability and Internet access from the home TV set. Following TiVo's March 31, 1999, unveiling of its first set-top standalone box, within a few days or at most weeks (depending on who is speaking and what definitions are used), ReplayTV launched its first set-top DVR in April 1999. Indeed then, the DVR race was on.

Still other DVR roots include the transition from analog to a much more efficient digital carriage of video and audio signals. This evolution was brought to fruition by DirecTV during the launch of its satellite TV system in the early 1990s. The "Technology" section in this chapter further details this analog-to-digital

Figure 1.5 The first-generation logos for the DVR industry pioneers, TiVo (left) and ReplayTV (right). (Copyright 2008. Property of TiVo and ReplayTV, respectively. All rights reserved. Used with permission.)

transitional development. This transition was pivotal for all DVR makers, because the best of DVR technology works best in an all-digital environment.

TiVo

For TiVo itself, it did many things quite well as it battled rival ReplayTV for first—or at least early—dominance of this unique new sector, called DVRs. A list of those well-managed items is actually quite long, as TiVo's continued presence in the DVR world today signifies. They include the following:

1. Early and ample financing
2. In-the-home upgradeable set-top boxes and software
3. Attractive form factors for both set-top boxes and remote controls
4. Attractive and innovative user interfaces
5. Design of the system to allow subsequent software downloads whenever upgrades were necessary
6. Simple-to-use products and services, without surprises, and
7. Establishing a subscription service fee to go along with the up-front hardware fee.

Indeed, three dominant themes guided the start-up team in the late 1990s, as it rushed to be the first real DVR manufacturer to unveil a consumer-ready DVR. These themes were that the TiVo product and service be reliable, simple, and generally attractive (all as they relate to the consumer). Early agreements were entered into with the large CE manufacturers, Philips and Sony, to build the new TiVo DVR set-top boxes and remote control devices. Bob Poniatowski, the # 4 TiVo employee (just after founders Jim Barton and Michael Ramsay), currently TiVo's director of DVR services, notes, "Like every new start-up, you have to reach out and collect advice and information, and you have to listen to others. We did that."

Yet, not unlike nearly every other company facing such challenges, there were a handful of things that TiVo did not do well (or at least such an argument can be made). In fact, *The Wall Street Journal's*[11] Walter Moss, in a 1999 article comparing the first-generation set-top DVRs offered by the Silicon Valley rivals, TiVo and ReplayTV, gave a superior review to ReplayTV, due, in part, to what he described as "glitches" in the TiVo device. Table 1.5 compares TiVo's first generation of set-top DVRs to those of rival ReplayTV.

Other early TiVo challenges included struggles with trying to inform and educate consumers about both the concept of DVRs and the ease with which a DVR could be used. Additionally, TiVo (and its allies) chose to subsidize the cost of the TiVo hardware, such that consumers could purchase the set-top boxes and remote control devices for less than it took to manufacture and distribute them. Many critics today believe subsidies like this are unnatural ways to encourage markets to deploy new creations. Also, at some points, TiVo

---

[11] See *The Wall Street Journal*, April 8, 1999, page B-1, written by Walter Mossberg, available at http://www.wsj.com.

was roundly criticized for developing its hardware based upon a new "open" platform from a Silicon Valley company called Linux, rather than to go with the more accepted but proprietary computer program offered by Linux rival Microsoft. Interestingly, many today believe that this early decision to favor Linux turned out to be one of TiVo's better early choices in the design of its system. Furthermore, although TiVo did create a very lucrative association in the late 1990s with the then-dominant satellite TV provider, DirecTV, TiVo

Table 1.5 A Comparison of DVR Maker TiVo to DVR Maker ReplayTV, Focused on the First Generation of Set-Top Boxes and Services they Both Unveiled, Late in the First Half of 1999

TiVo vs. ReplayTV: Comparing the Businesses			
Comparative Point	TiVo	ReplayTV	Description/Why it Mattered
1st model launched	Mar-99	Apr-99	First to market is important for internal and later sales goals.
1st model available from multichannel operator	2000	Never	Base of large multichannel operators is important for long term survival.
Later models available from multichannel operator	Yes	No	Base of large multichannel operators is important for long term survival.
Special features	User interface (UI)	Quickskip and instant replay	Attracts subscribers, creates word of mouth.
Financing	Went public earlier, was more aggressive, for example, got AOL money, which was very important at the time.	More conservative about seeking financing	Up-front financing may have made the difference between surviving and not surviving.
Business model	Monthly fees	CE, no monthly fees	Price and perceived price can be make or break important.
Demographic sought	More of a mass market.	Higher end, early adopter stage, more connectors on back of the box	TiVo sought the common man, ReplayTV sought the technophile and early adopter.

(Continued)

Table 1.5 *(Continued)*

	TiVo vs. ReplayTV: Comparing the Businesses		
Comparative Point	TiVo	ReplayTV	Description/Why it Mattered
Features	Background behind navigation screen moved subtly.	Home theatre focus; Ethernet on back of box; included firewire in early versions.	Often the icing on the cake and, again, the key to good word of mouth and sales at retail.
Remote	Had fewer buttons, very simple and basic as not to confuse the new consumer.	More buttons = early adopter enticement; universal application (could use the remote to change the volume on the TV).	Remote is the first and last thing customers' touch, almost daily.
UI	Did a lot to help the consumer. Had more screens; was very user friendly; made it very clear for consumer what next steps should be taken when navigating.	Required fewer clicks to achieve a task, but was less intuitive.	Making it fun, easy, and attractive, for little more money, can always evoke passion and interest, if done correctly.
Form factor	Invested more in the remote; made it more ergonomic.	Used a remote that was off the shelf from a vendor; its industrial design was not as good.	Always try not to make it ugly.
Employees	Had 50% more staff on a regular basis.	Ran a very lean organization, staffwise.	This cuts both ways and, in a perfect world, it is always nice to have the funds to maintain more of the right kind of employees.
Marketing	Spent more on brand marketing.	Was more direct and targeted in its spending (to get to the early adopter).	Without good marketing, even the best product very often goes nowhere when it should.

failed early on to aggressively and effectively develop a strong relationship with the top cable operators, creating a delay of several years, which badly injured TiVo's future growth prospects, especially during the 1999–2005 time frame.

ReplayTV

Perhaps no other example of the TiVo vs. ReplayTV battle is as emblematic of their differences as a look at their respective remote controls. While TiVo's remote control was simple and designed to fit specially within the hand, it offered a very minimal number of buttons, apparently designed for a mass audience user; ReplayTV's remote was much more complicated, with more buttons, apparently designed for a more sophisticated and technically comfortable user.

For ReplayTV, the other key player in the early DVR historical mix, it too, did things quite well as it battled rival TiVo for dominance. A list of those well-managed items for ReplayTV included the following:

1. A good longer term business model
2. Portraying itself as being particularly sophisticated, with an eye toward the technophile or so-called early adopter
3. Being very aggressive when it came to development and implementation of devices that skipped both ads and shared content

Interestingly, as time developed, this early and positive drive toward enhanced ad-skipping and program sharing capabilities later became a significant dilemma, because these actions prompted a troublesome and costly lawsuit, filed in October 2001. This lawsuit pitted defendant ReplayTV and its new owner, SonicBlue, against several prominent plaintiffs, that is, most of the big Hollywood studios; all the TV networks; and several large cable networks.[12]

Yet, not unlike nearly every other company facing such challenges, there were a handful of things ReplayTV did not do well, several of which eventually led to its demise, in the form of its sale to SonicBlue in 2001 and the bankruptcy of SonicBlue in 2003. Those apparent stumbles included an early focus on marketing to technophiles and early adopters, gambling that, at least early on, those "techies" would be the ones to successfully propel the new ReplayTV business. Nonetheless, others like former ReplayTV vice president, Michael Kornet, argue that all along, features like the 30-second ad-skip and the set-up of the ReplayTV on-screen EPG/IPG and user interface (UI) showed just the opposite, i.e., that ReplayTV was the more consumer friendly company.

In whichever way that argument is concluded, in the end, the aggressiveness with which ReplayTV pursued ad-skipping and program-sharing features

---

[12] This case was titled *Paramount, et al vs. ReplayTV*, and it was ultimately settled in mid-2002, causing ReplayTV (and its subsequent owners, SonicBlue, Denon & Marantz, and DirecTV) to significantly modify and reduce the company's ad-skipping and file-sharing functions. See http://www.eff.org/cases/paramount-v-replaytv, for a more thorough description of the case, its developments, and resolution.

proved to be quite problematic as it related to relationships with the very content owners who backed ReplayTV and whose programs made DVRs possible in the first place. Even Kornet agrees with the premise that ReplayTV was disadvantaged when it came to trying to keep up with TiVo's superior financing results.

1.5.3   DirecTV, WebTV, UltimateTV, EchoStar, NDS, Digeo, and Macrovision

For a half dozen or so other key players in the early days of DVRs, this new business of "program manipulation" offered many varied opportunities and challenges. To observe, this set of players is also to observe DVRs going from their earliest days, where a DVR was a premium, upscale item of some relative luxury; to their most current iteration, where, in most multichannel TV homes, a DVR is a standard commodity-like product offered to just about any qualifying subscriber.

DirecTV

El Segundo, CA-headquartered DirecTV first ventured into the waters of the DVR pool in the late 1990s, eventually offering coveted relationships to both TiVo and TiVo's rival, Microsoft's *UltimateTV* product and service. Within a handful of years, especially following the success of the DirecTV-TiVo integrated set-top box, DirecTV had become the leader in the U.S. deployment of DVRs. Currently, new DirecTV subscriber promotions sent frequently via newspaper fliers, by newspapers across the United States, typically offer several rooms' worth of DVR installation for $5.99/month/DVR.

Both EchoStar's founder, CEO and chairman, Charlie Ergen, and DirecTV's then-executive vice president, Larry Chapman, talked repeatedly during the 2000–2003 time frame of DVRs as a vehicle to more and happier subscribers, which led to greater revenues and typically greater profits.

WebTV and UltimateTV

Englewood, CO-based EchoStar was among the very first to show interest in DVRs, beginning with its early investment in and deployment of Microsoft's combination of DVR, Internet-connected, and DISH Network-connected *WebTV* set-top box device in early 1999. Microsoft had purchased the *WebTV* technology in August 1997 from early set-top inventor, Steve Perlman, who later built a related company, calling it Reardon Steel, which he also later sold, this time to Microsoft co-creator, Paul Allen. *WebTV* also later became the underpinnings for the *UltimateTV* service, which Microsoft and DirecTV introduced—as competition to TiVo—in late October of 2000 to subscribers of the DirecTV system. Features of the *UltimateTV* set-top product and service included a hard drive with 35 hours of storage capacity and on-screen software that included so-called picture-in-picture.[13] Thousands of *UltimateTV* devices are still supported by DirecTV today; however, the service was not successful during 2000–2003 and, as such, Microsoft and DirecTV abandoned the further marketing of *UltimateTV* set-top boxes in 2003. Many believe today that while much of TiVo's success is found in its simple focus on DVR functionality (and *only* DVR functionality, at least early on), conversely, *UltimateTV's* failure resulted in its varied and broad focus on doing (and being) too many things—including a TV, a DVR, and an Internet service, running side-by-side, concurrently, all as part of the same set-top box. Indeed, it is probably not unfair to say that the first generation of *UltimateTV* was just a little bit too much ahead of its time.

Echostar

EchoStar had a falling out with Microsoft following the launch of WebTV, which actually helped move EchoStar and its technology division to build their own version of a basic model integrated set-top box and DVR, labeled the DISHPlayer 500, in 2000. Thus began a long history of DVR deployments for EchoStar's DISH Network subscribers, to the point today where an estimated 50+% of EchoStar's 14 million DISH Network subscribers have DVRs. Indeed, these days, just about any new subscriber to DISH Network, DirecTV, or any major cable company, will be supplied with a new integrated DVR set-top box for free (if they either agree to a certain programming package for a given number of months, and/or pay a monthly fee for the DVR product/service). In addition, currently, new EchoStar DISH Network subscriber promotions sent frequently via newspaper fliers, by newspapers across the United States, typically offer several rooms' worth of DVR installation for anywhere from $0 to $5.99/month/DVR, dependent on the programming package a consumer accepts. For subscribers buying into the highest end DISH Network packages, for example, $94.98/month for a total channel package of over 280, the DVR fee is typically waived. Plus, like DirecTV, DISH Network will also install DVRs in up to four rooms in any household, for no additional fee, assuming certain other programming package guarantees are in place.

Nevertheless, along the way toward EchoStar's development of DVRs, rival standalone DVR manufacturer (and rival DirecTV ally), TiVo, filed suit against EchoStar for patent infringement; in yet another piece of early DVR intellectual property litigation, *TiVo vs. EchoStar* was filed in the eastern district of Texas federal court in January 2004. A May 2006 jury verdict and subsequent appeals all the way to the U.S. Supreme Court have gone against EchoStar, which resulted in a large monetary verdict for over $100 million in October of 2008. Meanwhile, EchoStar in May 2008 filed a petition for declaratory judgment in

---

[13] As noted in the "Vocabulary" section following the chapters in this book, "picture-in-picture" delineates a software feature of a DVR or other device that permits a viewer to observe a condensed version of a video (and audio) signal displayed as a smaller part of a larger video (and audio) on-screen display.

a Delaware State court, asking for a ruling that EchoStar's new DVR software product (or "workaround," as it is called in legal and technical circles) does not infringe on TiVo's patent. Rolling into 2009, EchoStar is scheduled for a bench trial on that "workaround" motion, having avoided a court-ordered injunction in November 2008.

NDS

Once Rupert Murdoch finally gained control over DirecTV in January 2004, he immediately began to substitute his own conditional access and set-top box technology company, NDS, wherever he could. Thus, in the area of DVRs, DirecTV sought to quickly limit long-time partner, TiVo's, participation, instead bringing in NDS' xTV-model DVRs. Unfortunately for NDS, it underestimated the complexity of the DVR tasks and early consumer and expert reviews of the first-generation NDS boxes were not glowing. Nonetheless, NDS set-top boxes are the standard issue deployment today for any current DirecTV customer. They are also standard issue for just about any News Corp.-controlled multichannel TV operator.

Digeo

Kirkland, WA-based and Paul Allen-owned Digeo had its earliest roots in a super set-top box crystallize when it merged its expertise in UI and middleware development into the hardware designs of Silicon Valley inventor Steve Perlman's Reardon Steele, which Allen purchased in mid-2002. Digeo today, mostly in the form of its *Moxi Media Center*, has shipped more than 450,000 DVRs to clients comprising nine cable multichannel providers. The *Moxi Media Center* also often serves as an alternative to the traditional set-top boxes large cable operators deploy, due to deals established with major cable set-top providers, such as Motorola and Scientific-Atlanta (now called Cisco). Digeo's software is currently being evaluated for deployment within other manufacturers' set-top boxes and for use in various CE retail applications, mainly because Digeo's attractive networking and UI features. In addition, Digeo has recently rolled out its own version of a standalone DVR sold at retail, which will compete directly with TiVo standalone DVRs.

Macrovision

Santa Clara, CA-headquartered Macrovision is best known for its software expertise. In the DVR space, Macrovision distributes its multiroom DVR (MR-DVR) software, which Macrovision states, "… allows cable subscribers to view their stored programming anywhere within their home cable network." Typical clients include smaller-to-medium-sized cable operators in the United States, such as Lawrence, KS-based Sunflower Broadband. Through the MR-DVR application (which the operator would then load onto its own integrated set-top DVR), viewers can watch a show on a set-top DVR in one room, stop the show, and resume watching via a set-top DVR in a different room. A case study in Chapter 2, "What Is a DVR?" further defines Sunflower Broadband and its deployment of DVRs.

1.5.4 Cable and Telco Plays

2002 is generally considered the year in which the cable industry began to solidly establish itself in the business of DVRs. Thereafter, just about every major cable multiple system operator (MSO) in the industry acted quickly to create the cable industry's answer to the more than two-year lead and success already experienced by the U.S. satellite industry. Indeed, the satellite operators, DirecTV and EchoStar, surged ahead during the 1999–2003 time frame, proving that DVRs brought not only new subscribers by the hundreds of thousands, but also greatly reduced churn (or subscriber loss), while concurrently raising average revenues per unit (ARPU). Figure 1.6 shows the growth of DVR installations over the last decade.

Prior to 2002–2003, cable operators like Comcast and Time Warner had reviewed the business of DVRs and determined their better response was to rollout a differentiated and arguably competing technology, called VOD, which they believed would bring them more and better subscribers and better ARPU. Indeed, at a National Cable Telecommunications Association (NCTA) show held during the 1999–2002 time frame, Comcast chairman Brian Roberts delivered the cable industry's then VOD-centric message opposing DVRs, in a large measure because of the perceived superiority of VODs and the perception of copyright and DRM infringement problems that emanated from consumer use of DVRs.

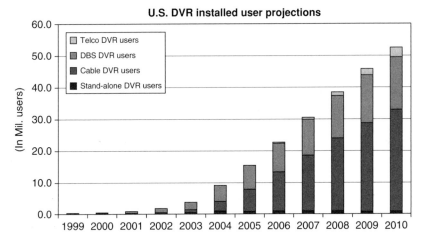

Figure 1.6 The Carmel Group predictions indicating the growth of DVRs in the United States from the end of 1999 to 2010. (Copyright 2008. Property of The Carmel Group. All rights reserved. Used with permission.)

Then, in June 2002, led by Time Warner, the United States' second largest cable MSO, the cable industry went head-strong into the DVR business, starting with Time Warner's installation of the Scientific-Atlanta DVR-enabled set-top model Explorer 8300 into thousands of consumers' homes. As a measure of the power and capability of the U.S. cable industry, some 5 years later, in 2007, the combination of U.S. cable operators had more DVRs deployed and operational than did the pioneer satellite operators. This lead was developed despite the fact that the satellite operators—DirecTV and EchoStar—led the cable industry in the deployment of DVRs by almost 3 full years. Another important milestone in the cable development of DVRs was the agreement finally entered into in March 2005, by TiVo with the Number One U.S. cable operator, 25 million strong Comcast, to deploy TiVo DVRs within integrated Comcast set-top boxes.

Most recently, Internet protocol-based television (IPTV) services offered by various cable and telco operators have also begun to offer DVR capabilities. An example includes cable overbuilder, SureWest Communications, and its system in Roseville, CA, a nearby suburb of Sacramento, CA. In April 2008, *CED* magazine article by Traci Patterson notes the SureWest-supplied DVRs offer access to HD and SD channels and standard DVR industry features, such as rewind and playback of live TV, together with three tuners per set-top DVR box, and, she notes, "The DVRs can also act as a 'home server' for a home entertainment network." Companies servicing IPTV DVR capabilities include such industry leaders as Microsoft. Microsoft's *Xbox 360* gaming device offers such DVR capabilities and is concurrently able to access operators offering IPTV infrastructures.

HughesNet, on the other hand, via its recently acquired subsidiary, Helius, also offers corporate users DVR functionality using an IPTV infrastructure designed for a business environment. Employee training and other corporate uses are the focus for Helius DVR customers, including General Motors, JC Penney, Edward Jones, and Safeway.

Putting the DVR evolution into further perspective, as of mid-2008, DVR industry researcher and analyst The Carmel Group estimates there are more than 30 million DVRs installed in the U.S [among an estimated 110 million U.S. TV households (TVHHs)]; among that 30 million DVR numbers, nearly two thirds are DVRs deployed by a combination of Motorola, Digeo, and Scientific-Atlanta into the cable market; EchoStar and DirecTV, between them, have deployed approximately 8 million DVRs as of mid-2008. By the end of year 2010, The Carmel Group estimates the same numbers will reach approximately 52 million DVRs installed in the United States (among an estimated 113 million 2010 U.S. TVHHs); among that 52 million DVR numbers, nearly 32 million will be DVRs deployed by a combination of Motorola, Digeo, and Scientific-Atlanta; and EchoStar and DirecTV, between them, will have deployed almost 14 million DVRs.

The other major multichannel provider that delivers its signals largely via terrestrial cables, that is, the telcos, has also entered the DVR-provider pool, realizing that, as new competitors in the audio/video and TV realms, they needed advanced services like DVRs, mostly to attract new subscribers to their

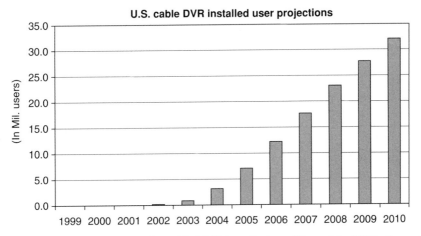

Figure 1.7   Future projections for cable DVR installations. (Copyright 2009. Property of The Carmel Group. Used with permission. All rights reserved.)

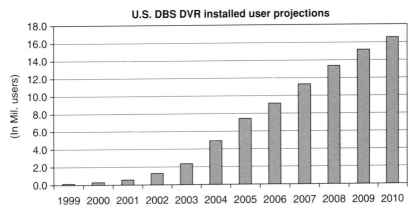

Figure 1.8   Future projections for satellite (DBS) DVR installations. (Copyright 2009. Property of The Carmel Group. Used with permission. All rights reserved.)

fledgling offerings. Indeed, Verizon, AT&T, and Qwest all offer DVR products and services these days.

Figures 1.7–1.9 show further industry estimates for actual and future projections for cable, satellite (DBS), and telco sectors of the U.S. DVR industry.

AT&T

AT&T offers what it calls its *U-Verse* TV DVR, which is HDTV capable, and is included today along with most AT&T audio/video TV programming packages. AT&T customers have the ability to record up to four programs at once—something AT&T claims no other provider offers today. Customers who

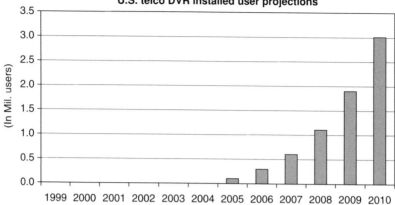

Figure 1.9 Future projections for telco DVR installations. (Copyright 2009. Property of The Carmel Group. Used with permission. All rights reserved.)

subscribe to *U-Verse* TV and Internet services can access their DVR remotely from any Web-connected PC in the world, using their AT&T Yahoo! Account, notes AT&T. *U-Verse* TV and Internet customers can also take advantage of remote access to their DVR from an AT&T wireless phone or device.

In the latter half of 2008, AT&T states it also began plans to offer a "whole home" DVR, meaning that—like telco sibling Verizon—one DVR can serve multiple rooms in a single dwelling.

In its package aimed more at rural consumers, called *HomeZone*, AT&T has allied in the past with the satellite provider, EchoStar, so that AT&T's customers to those packages have received their DVRs from DISH Network's list of DVR packages. That AT&T-EchoStar DISH Network alliance, however, was not renewed, as AT&T announced in mid-2008. Instead, AT&T switched to rival DirecTV for delivery of video services to its *HomeZone* video subscribers.

Verizon

Verizon, like AT&T, has two TV audio–video packages for its customers nationwide: one offering video via DirecTV and the other offering fiber to the home (FTTH), called *FiOS TV*. For DirecTV Verizon subscribers, they get their DVRs from DirecTV. The *FiOS* packages include a MR-DVR offering; however, there is a charge for the service monthly, ranging from $12.99 for SD quality to $15.99 for HD quality, and $17.99 and $19.99 for SD and HD MR-DVRs, respectively, termed Home Media. With the Verizon Home Media DVR, Verizon states that viewers can watch separate recorded shows on up to three TVs at the same time. Also, viewers may pause a recorded show in one room and later pick it up in another room. As of this writing, Verizon leads the multichannel TV market among providers of MR-DVR functionality.

veri/on

Verizon[14]

Based in New York City, NY, Verizon Communications' (NYSE: VZ) group product manager Angel Cordero has been with his company since 2004, when Verizon first began creating its *FiOS TV* division (pronounced FYE'-ose). Verizon and Cordero, for this case study, describe *FiOS* as, "The new suite of fiberoptic services delivered over Verizon's advanced fiber-to-the-premises (FTTP) network. FTTP is an advanced fiberoptic technology that connects a home or business directly to Verizon's network. FTTP replaces the copper wires that connect customers to the Verizon network today, and it delivers unprecedented broadband speed and a totally new home entertainment experience. It provides the bandwidth and speed to make available an array of new services called *FiOS*: super-fast, high-speed Internet access, crystal-clear voice, and a full-suite of video services. *FiOS* TV is designed to compete with cable and satellite, and win."[15]

Cordero tracks the early days of the DVR at Verizon, back to Verizon's partnership with Microsoft (NASDAQ: MSFT).[16] Parsing out the remote

---

[14] As was the case with the Digeo case study, Verizon provided extraordinary cooperation for this case study. Thus, as was the case with Digeo, the author chooses to reward that forthright communication and dialogue by including as many relevant parts as possible in this Verizon DVR case study. Therefore, it, too, stands at greater length than most of the other case studies in this book.

[15] Further reference to and information about *FiOS* includes the following: (1) FiOS is the Verizon plan to run fiber optic lines directly to customers' homes; (2) *FiOS* supports TV, data, voice, and possibly other services in the future; (3) *FiOS* offers an "... easy-to-use electronic programming guide (EPG) that integrates HD programming, video-on-demand, and the DVR, along with broadcast television," into what Verizon calls "a seamless user experience"; and (4) *FiOS TV* was first launched by Verizon for general availability in Keller, Texas, on September 22, 2005. Verizon's choice to launch *FiOS* in Keller, TX, is interesting strategically, because it is quite close to telco brethren AT&T's former headquarters in San Antonio, TX.

[16] The first Verizon DVR, a DVR model number 6416, manufactured by Motorola, contained an EPG—or, as Verizon terms it, an Interactive Program Guide (IPG)—developed by Microsoft. This EPG/IPG was part of the Microsoft Foundation Edition version of what Verizon later termed its Interactive Media Guide (IMG, as opposed to the standard

control chapter of Verizon's DVR development, Verizon launched with a remote control protocol, the Motorola IR, in the form of a simple DRC 800 model.[17] Finally, as it relates to the history underlying what might be termed a "traditional telco DVR deployment story," the part of it that describes Verizon DVR set-top boxes, also describes a first-generation SD DVR set-top box, which has since been replaced by a standard SD/HD DVR set-top box, across Verizon's entire system.[18]

Verizon describes the decision to deploy or be involved with DVRs as one based on a strong business plan that relied on projections of extra revenue from DVR set-top boxes, and a strategy that stated DVRs were required for the telco to be "... competitive with the incumbent cable MSOs and satellite video providers," adds Cordero. Moving forward to measure the criteria used by Verizon to assess the effectiveness of its deployment of DVRs, Cordero lists four key criteria: (1) the take rate, (2) the

industry terms, EPG and IPG). Cordero states, "Calling our IPG an IMG really helped us internally to focus on making it media rich and on the concept of accessing different types of media. Externally, this also helped us set our IPG apart from other MSOs." As an example of its capacity and user friendliness, Cordero points to the IMG's grouping of recordings into user folders. "Instead of having 15 *Simpsons* episodes, you have one *Simpsons* folder in your recordings view, and then if you drill in from there, you see your 15 separate, individual *Simpsons* episodes.

[17] This remote control device, the DRC 800, included features such as a shortcut to the DVR, as well as various media control items, including play, pause, stop, rewind, and fast forward. The DRC 800 also offered a "go to live TV" button and an instant replay button. Software provides other functions, like slow motion. For a brief period of time (involving inventory problems with the VZ model 144 remote), Verizon had a Scientific-Atlanta model 8550 RC remote control. The VZ 144 is Verizon's advanced remote control for DVR users. It has skip back, skip forward, play, pause, rewind, fast forward, a "live button" (physical and logical), and a shortcut to DVR recordings list. Verizon's in-box software provides other functions, such as slow motion.

[18] Cordero notes that, "For a brief moment in time (perhaps 1 year) Verizon deployed a set-top model 2708 SD DVR. This model was discontinued in 2008. It was an SD DVR only. It had an 80-GB hard drive. On the other hand, it could be a terminal to the MR-DVR hub, but ultimately, it could only access SD content. To better serve our customers, we decided that from now on everyone requesting a DVR is getting a SD/HD DVR model." In that vein, Verizon relies on the SD/HD model number 6416/7216 SD/HD DVR. The 7216 is an updated version that also satisfies the FCC mandate that all of Verizon's high-end boxes containing separable CableCards. Verizon states further that it does not recompress content to maximize the number of channels and content that the DVR can handle, which, according to Cordero, "... has meant that while some DVR providers may have recordings that look worse than TV, our recordings always look as good as the original." Verizon offers two boxes: high definition, which includes HD channels, for $9.95 per month; and a digital video recorder set-top box, with HD channels, for $12.95 per month. Finally, Cordero notes that Verizon reserves a small amount of disk drive for IMG applications and other features, such as caching. Nonetheless, in general, a 6416/7216 DVR set-top box has a 160 GB hard disk, and of that 160 GB, about 140 GB is used for content.

recommender scores,[19] (3) blogs and online forum comments from users, and (4) support center call volume. In terms of current benefits of the Verizon DVR offering, the list includes "Being seen as an innovative leading entertainment company, continued positive revenues, and satisfaction of the requirement that Verizon, as a competitive multichannel pay TV operator, offer everything and more than what its competitors offer."

Today, Verizon DVR penetration rates are on track with its business plan.

Referencing the question of the "Biggest motivator for Verizon to deploy or otherwise be involved in DVRs?" Cordero lists, in order: (1) customer demand, (2) additional revenue, and (3) competitive position. Moreover, although Verizon currently has no plans to discontinue its DVR deployment plans, Cordero and his Verizon colleagues are certainly receptive to technologies that may provide equal DVR capabilities at lower cost. Verizon also is offering MR-DVRs, where users can lawfully access DVR content from other rooms in the same home. MR-DVRs allow users to pause a show and continue watching the same show in another room. Remote DVR programming is available to customers who subscribe to *FiOS TV's* Media Manager service. They are able to remotely program their *FiOS TV* DVRs and set their Parental Controls through select Verizon Wireless handsets and through Verizon's *FiOS TV* Central Web site (http://www.verizon.com/fiostvcentral). And, dual tuners—allowing concurrent viewing and recording of two shows shown at the same time—are part of every Verizon set-top box.

On the distribution side of Verizon's DVR world, sales of the DVR product are implemented via door-to-door, phone, kiosks, and Internet contacts. Installation is, like its cable and satellite TV brethren, handled primarily by way of Verizon-certified installers; a small percentage of users order by mail and self-install their own DVRs. Control of DVR programming on the Verizon system is managed in five ways: (1) remote control by the user; (2) remote access from the MR-DVR (e.g., to play a movie accessed from a hub in another room); (3) from the set-top box itself, via the buttons on the front of the device; (4) from the http://www.MyVerizon.com Web site, allowing one to schedule remote recordings for later viewing; and (5) via select Verizon Wireless handsets.

On the opportunities side of the DVR future, like many in and around the industry (including the author), Verizon believes that the biggest chance for DVRs lies in getting more folks to use DVRs. "This includes older folks, the mass market, and many more multicultural folks. There is still a challenge getting nontechnical folks to understand what a DVR is and what it can do. There are just too many acronyms out there, and these days, most folks are still getting up to speed on VOD, HD, and digital," Cordero says.

---

[19] A "recommender score" is described as a consumer's rating of *FiOS TV*, e.g., would they recommend *FiOS TV* to their friends and relatives?

Turning in our interview to the single aspect of DVRs that Verizon likes the most, Cordero's choice is "A new way to surf for personal content, where each night the DVR folder is full of relevant content. No more flipping channels, scrolling TV listings, or searching and settling." For his Verizon subscriber clients, Cordero believes their favorite features are (1) the ability to exercise choices relating to when and how they watch TV, (2) the "smart buffer" that displays images on-screen while flipping between channels or while fast-forwarding or rewinding, and (3) the guide data from the Verizon EPG/IPG.

As for his customers' least favorite aspects of DVR usage, Verizon's Cordero has found that most would like an easy way to expand the size and capability of their hard drives and the storage of programs that those drives are capable of providing. Cordero assures would-be and actual subscribers that Verizon is working on the question of DVR hard drive expansion. Verizon is also seeking an efficient way to service its DVRs remotely, without losing content or the user's settings. Furthermore, customers have found glitches affecting the software that controls Verizon DVRs. For example, like many DVRs, if scheduled programs—such as recorded sports events—run long in time, the operational software can, in response, incorrectly substitute the wrong program. The same problem occurs when shows are incorrectly flagged as not new. Verizon is bent on alleviating these concerns.

Verizon has focused a lot of attention on its MR-DVR service and the IMG, the latter of which involves very complex software. Cordero, when speaking about Verizon's DVR set-top commitment, notes, "Overall it's a slightly more expensive set-top than the average set-top box, but a DVR version generates more money than the average box, and even slightly more if a customer purchases the Verizon Home Media service, and it increases customer loyalty so people stay with us longer." Verizon had a well-planned return on investment (ROI) model going into the first stages of the system-wide DVR deployment, based on customers' projected DVR take rates, the price of the DVR unit and service, various value-added services tied to the DVR, and estimates of whether rolling out the MR-DVR would hurt Verizon's base DVR sales. Metrics Verizon uses to measure its ROI include the number of DVRs deployed per customer, the DVR model number take rate, and the Home Media take rate.

Current marketing pitches have included ads involving NBA basketball star, Kevin Garnett. In one ad, Garnett is being instructed on the use of the Verizon MR-DVR, permitting Garnett to watch a film in various rooms around Garnett's home. Adds Cordero, "When we first started *FiOS TV*, we simply had generic commercials with voice, data, and TV. Now, we go so far as to hype MR-DVR as a full 30-second national spot." The Washington, DC market highlights Verizon's DVR service and product, at the expense of its satellite TV and Comcast cable multichannel pay TV rivals.

Moreover, Verizon only supports skipping through live and recorded video in ways that are consistent with a given content agreement, with different settings for the number of seconds a program can be skipped back and fast-forwarded. On the Verizon DVR, a customer can adjust the settings to skip back 10 seconds and skip forward 1 minute, for example.

Concluding the topic of ads and marketing, Verizon is considering the idea of keeping its ads in programs recycled, because, in Cordero's words, "Seeing an ad about an upcoming show that has already passed doesn't add any value to anyone." Cordero puts Verizon's advertiser relationship into clearer perspective by noting, "From an advertiser point of view, we at Verizon are one of the largest advertisers. And soon, we will also be one of the largest places to advertise, so we have to be friendly to advertisers. But I think we can be friendly and especially valuable to advertisers by, for example, using interactive television and highly localized ads. This way, we deeply serve customers, content providers, and advertisers, all at the same time."

Shifting to DVR regulation concerns, like the question, Does Verizon think there is a need for limitations on the ability of a DVR user to transfer content to others? Cordero, like most multichannel pay TV executives these days, walks a fine line between giving consumers what they want, while concurrently supporting content providers. "The value of our DVR is directly tied to the ability of customers to access the content they want," says Cordero. "And that content will only be produced if the creators' intellectual property rights are protected, so we have to do both. In reaching that balance, we would strive to expand options to provide more storage options and more choices for the customer."

On the legal and regulatory sides, Verizon has experienced some slowdown in its DVR development, especially as it relates to what Cordero calls "internal innovation," tied to various checks his division had to wait for before moving some of the product to market. As an example, Verizon was required to deploy new DVRs with CableCard technology tied to an FCC separable conditional access system (CAS) mandate.

Advocacy-wise, Verizon has its own blog, at http://www.policyblog. verizon.com. Its public policy positions can be seen at http://www22.verizon .com/about/publicpolicies/. Verizon's executive speeches, given at various public events discussing industry innovation, can be found online at http:// newscenter.verizon.com/leadership/speeches/seidenberg-nab-04182005. html. One particularly relevant speech of CEO Ivan Seidenberg, as it relates to DVRs and this book, notes:

"First, we recognize the importance of protecting the value of intellectual content in a digital universe. The creators and carriers of content share a common interest in this issue … after all, if we don't adequately protect the value of content, we won't have any content to provide. We believe our architecture and platform will provide opportunities to develop new ways to protect content. We are focused on working cooperatively with the entertainment industry to find the best answer to this important question."

Concluding our interview (and this case study), Cordero notes that Verizon has conducted many impact studies of deployed DVRs. These include both internal and third-party surveys aimed at discovering how customers feel about their DVR product and service, and how to improve it. As an example, there was such strong interest shown toward HD that Verizon decided to steer away from SD versions of future DVRs, and instead opted for the HD-only version for all models of the Verizon DVR. Surveys also show how important word of mouth is in helping sell the DVR product and service; how various glitches and added features affect the development and marketing of the DVR service and product; and how receptive consumers might be to additional messages emanating from data mined from their viewing of various content.

Contact Information
PR Contact: Bob Varettoni
(908) 559-6388

Stock Symbol
NYSE: VZ

Key People
Ivan Seidenberg, CEO

Key Business
A leading American broadband and telecommunications company. Core businesses include mobile phones, broadband Internet, telephony, video delivery.

DVR Connection
Verizon entered into the DVR market with the launch of the FiOS DVR. Offers multi-room capability whereby users can record and watch programing on three TVs from one DVR; today only offers as HD DVR set-top unit.

During the late 1900s, and carrying into the early part of the next century, cable companies such as Comcast and Time Warner were reluctant to commit to DVRs. Reasons behind this hesitancy included a prior decision to center on VOD, as well as concerns about being able to manage consumers' use of the new storage and content manipulation devices called DVRs. MSO hesitancy to deploy DVRs was also driven by capital budget constraints—capital was being allocated for system rebuilds, and the DVR technology was both expensive and relatively immature.

That all changed in 2003–2004, when first Time Warner together with set-top manufacturer Scientific Atlanta (today named and owned by Cisco), and then Comcast together with set-top manufacturer Motorola, jumped headfirst into the industry subsector called DVR. Since that point, neither company has looked back when it comes to its commitment to DVRs.

Indeed, as has been repeatedly recommended in this book (as it relates to advertisers and their approach to DVRs), the cable operators found that it was better to embrace the forthcoming DVR wave, rather than constantly oppose it. As such, the cable industry not only began mass deployments of integrated set-tops, home-by-home, and consumer-by-consumer, but it also made a pivotal alliance with the recognized developer and leader of the standalone and independent DVR developers, TiVo. Yet perhaps more importantly, the cable industry began a significant and near thorough integration of VODs with DVRs. Indeed, most who look at the longer term focus of the DVR industry and its future see this blending of DVRs and VOD as the most likely direction for the majority of multichannel pay TV subscribers. Notes Derek Harrar, Comcast senior vice president and general manager, video, "The unique story or spin on DVR from Comcast is how DVRs relate with a fully built out and thoughtful VOD strategy."

Noting that they are complementary technologies, Harrar further points out that DVRs are "user-controlled, time-shifting technology," whereas VOD constitutes a "network-controlled, time-shifting technology." The two work well together and can, indeed, complement one another. Comcast seeks to provide its customers with the best of both VOD and DVRs, and part of that includes making sure new subscribers understand that in their best iteration, DVRs and VOD get used together, moving closer toward one merged consumer product and service.

Comcast

Contact Information
"1 Comcast Center
Philadelphia, PA 19103
Phone: 215-286-1700"

Website
www.comcast.com

Stock Symbol
NASDAQ: CMCSA

Key People
Brian L. Roberts, Chairman, President and CEO
PR Contact: Rachel L. Cohen
410-767-8000

Key Business
Provider of cable TV, broadband internet and phone

DVR Connection
Provides DVR and HD DVR set-top boxes, as well as VOD capabilities.

Looking first to the VOD, Comcast's history began in 2003, with a mere 200 titles and "almost zero usage" in the words of Harrar. Coming five years forward, Comcast today boasts a library approaching 15,000 VOD titles, among which are more than 1,000 HD titles as of year-end 2008. Comcast data supports 300 mil. VOD views/month among the 16 mil. of its 24+ mil. subscribers who have VOD access. VOD is available to all digital subscribers, and the majority of the content is free, which understandably has a very positive impact on motivating new VOD (and DVR) usage.

"Comcast has around 25 mil. VOD-enabled set-tops among those 16 mil. digital subscribers, which means those 16 mil. VOD users go into the menu, browse, hit play, and their program pops up typically within seconds," boasts Harrar.

Turning to the DVR side of the Comcast house, Harrar has found that "The DVR user tends to be another connoisseur of time-shifted content, and each DVR sub will pay a premium to do that." Realizing that fact in recent years, Comcast focused additional energies and resources on promotions and other marketing mechanisms aimed at getting consumers to use and appreciate the DVR, together with the VOD. Thus, VOD represents the Comcast programming side of the VOD-DVR combination, while the DVR is the consumer's chance to truly take advantage of that programming and "make it his own." Harrar's idea of success in the VOD-DVR Wilderness is when the majority of his subscribers all have DVR hard drives that are constantly full, and those hard drives are constantly being aggressively managed by those consumers.

Another great moment for Comcast arose when the company and its lead set-top vendor, Motorola, began to appreciate and then supply users with DVRs that contained dual tuners. With that, consumers, especially during popular prime time viewing hours, could watch one show while simultaneously recording another—and have full pause and fast forward control of both shows, as well as rewind up to 30 minutes of that show. At the same time, using the same DVR, the consumer could store the second program for later viewing (thus avoiding the broadcasters' efforts to keep a loyal consumer from discovering another show by counter programming one show versus the other). Importantly, this function also meant more total TV content was watched by DVR consumers, because they no longer had to miss a counter-programmed show. "That was a seminal moment in the development of the DVR," opines Harrar.

A third important stage in the Comcast/Cisco development of DVRs was a Comcast focus on DVRs combined with HD. Part of the challenge here is the perennial multichannel pay TV effort to make sure that their customers actually view HD content on actual HD sets (and not on standard definition sets). This is to say multichannel pay TV providers need to make sure that customers realize that they need an HD capable set top box in order to view HD content on their HDTV sets.

For the future, Derek Harrar and Comcast are concentrating on new services and devices, such as the Anyplay hardware Comcast has developed with hardware giant, Panasonic. Announced first during the 2008 CES conference in Las Vegas, by Comcast CEO Brian Roberts and Panasonic's CEO, Yoshi Yamada, Anyplay is a DVR set top that offers the benefits of mobility—consumers can record content at home, then remove the DVR and integrated viewing screen to watch that content on the go. Anyplay is a combination of two separate hardware pieces, one portable and one not portable. This product and service is Comcast's recognition of the forthcoming trend of video mobility.

Anyplay involves a typical set-top box that sits in a consumer's home, but that simultaneously serves as a docking station that permits the user to couple a portable media device. The in-home set-top then conveys data to the portable device. This permits the consumer to take his or her favored content wherever he or she is traveling. Like EchoStar's DISHPlayer device unveiled in 1999, the new Anyplay system intends to give consumers new flexibility when viewing their content, while also restricting their ability to improperly provide copies to others. The portable side of the Anyplay system is essentially a portable DVD player, "... with a hard drive in it that functions as a DVR," describes Derek Harrar. "Anyplay is a really elegant solution allowing consumers to consume top tier content, portably, which helps Comcast answer its goal of helping its subs watch what they want and not to have to go a lot of other places to get it. Anyplay is an example of where Comcast has a lot of tools, and this one set was used to make in-home and portable work together and work properly," Harrar concludes.

1.5.5   Other DVR and DVR-Type Players

A look today at DVR and DVR-like operators and/or manufacturers includes an array of additional participants.

In a few instances, self-built DVRs have emerged in the form of hard drives attached to home PCs. Additionally, a handful of large- and medium-sized CE manufacturers strode forth into the DVR realm. These included early deployments by Philips and Sony, in the case of TiVo, and by others such as Pioneer and today's latest big-time participant, South Korean-based LG. Nonetheless, because multichannel customers are seen as the core audience for DVRs and because those operators typically already have long-established relationships with established and sometime in-house CE manufacturers, other independent CE manufacturers have steered clear of developing and distributing both standalone and integrated DVR set-top box models.

As noted above, DVRs and DVR-like functionality are finding their place in gaming devices and satellite radio devices, to name but a couple of examples.

1.5.6   DVR Industry Milestones

During the first 15 or so years of the DVR industry's development, there have been approximately three dozen significant developments worth mentioning in a top-level listing. They are included chronologically below.[20]

---

[20] The Carmel Group contributed the core of these timeline entries. They are used here with permission.

1. July 1991: Eric and Romi Goldwasser apply for the first "time-warp" patent, which is the first technological step toward the development, some eight years later, of a business selling a commercially viable consumer DVR product and service.

2. August 31, 1993: The first DVR business-related patent, the Goldwasser patent (also described in this chapter's "History" section), is issued by the U.S. Patent and Trademark Office.

3. January 7, 1999: At 1999 CES, EchoStar (DISH Network) announces integration of *WebTV's* DVR into EchoStar's (DISH Network's) satellite set-top box, the device called *WebTV. WebTV* was the first combination of a set-top that delivered Internet to the TV, was a first-generation DVR, and offered access to multichannel pay-TV signals.

4. 1999: NBC becomes the first major media and telecom company to invest in the fledgling DVR market, taking stakes concurrently in both TiVo and ReplayTV. Paul Allen also takes stakes in both services during the same basic time frame.

5. 1999–2001: TiVo receives investment from Showtime Networks, Philips Electronics, NBC Networks, CBS, Comcast, Cox, Discovery, The Walt Disney Company, Liberty Digital, Advance/Newhouse, and TV Guide Interactive. ReplayTV receives investment stakes from Turner Networks, Disney, Kleiner Perkins and numerous large advertising agencies.

6. September 30, 1999: TiVo's initial public offering (IPO) opens on NASDAQ.

7. January 6 and June 14, 2000: Both DirecTV and AOL, respectively and individually, invest in TiVo.

8. January 7, 2001: EchoStar's (DISH Network) 501 DISHPlayer series receiver, with OpenTV's and EchoStar's DVR technology, is offered free to DISH Network subscribers who subscribe to certain packages.

9. February 5, 2001: SonicBlue acquires ReplayTV.

10. September 5, 2001: ReplayTV debuts its 4000 series set-top box, with enhanced ad-skipping, show-sharing, and other controversial features.

11. March 2001: Microsoft's *Ultimate TV* product and service is unveiled by Microsoft, designed primarily for the DirecTV system, including a DVR feature, access to DirecTV programming, and an Internet connectivity feature, for DirecTV subscribers.

12. October 31, 2001: The rather substantial (and rare) combination of Paramount and other key Hollywood studios, as well as all the top TV networks, and several large cable channels together file a lawsuit, called *Paramount et al vs. ReplayTV,* against ReplayTV, specifically targeting the alleged copyright infringement aspects of ReplayTV's "Send Show" and "Auto Skip" features.

13. December 12, 2001: ReplayTV files counter lawsuit against the studios and broadcasters.

14. January 22 and May 2002: Restructuring and bankruptcies occur, the former date involving Microsoft's *UltimateTV,* in January; the latter date involving CacheVision and Keen Personal Media.

15. April 29, 2002: The U.S. cable industry unveils its first integrated DVR set-top box, the Scientific-Atlanta Explorer 8000.

16. June 2003: Comcast and Time Warner announce plans to field trial Microsoft's new multimedia software, called TV Foundation Edition.

17. October 2003: EchoStar (DISH Network) ships its one-millionth DVR set-top box.

18. October 26, 2003: SonicBlue declares bankruptcy in northern CA.

19. April 2003: SonicBlue sells ReplayTV to D & M Holdings, a U.S. subsidiary of the Japanese Marantz organization.

20. January 2004: TiVo sues EchoStar (DISH Network) for patent infringement in the U.S. District Court in eastern Texas.

21. Q2 2004: Kirkland, WA-based Digeo first deploys its dual-tuner Moxi model # BMC9012. Later that year, Digeo wins its first Emmy award from the National Academy of Motion Picture Arts and Sciences for its UI. Digeo wins its second Emmy in 2005, for its media center and multiroom features.

22. March 2005: TiVo announces agreement with Comcast to deploy TiVo services and capabilities into integrated Comcast set-top boxes.

23. Fall 2005: DirecTV launches its own in-house DVR technology from sister company, NDS. This begins the entry of NDS-branded DVRs into the DirecTV system, and the more rapid disintegration of the DirecTV-TiVo business partnership that began in the late 1990s.

24. July 2005: Forgent files patent infringement against key U.S. service providers, including satellite (DBS) providers EchoStar (DISH Network) and DirecTV, as well as the top five cable MSOs, claiming their DVR deployments violated Forgent DVR-related patents.

25. October 2005: EchoStar (DISH Network) and Apple become the first to launch a mobile DVR device.

26. November 2005: Telcos ship their first DVR units.

27. March 2006: The *TiVo vs. EchoStar* (DISH Network) case goes to trial in Texas.

28. April 2006: A trial court jury verdict awards more than $70 million to TiVo in its lawsuit for patent infringement against EchoStar (DISH Network).

29. 2006–2007: The U.S. cable industry surpasses the U.S. satellite (DBS) industry in number of DVR deployments.

30. January 2007: Microsoft announces IPTV features, including a DVR component of up to 160 gigabytes, which will be added to its *Xbox 360*.

31. May 2007: The Forgent case goes to trial; all defendants, except EchoStar (DISH Network), settle with Forgent prior to trial; jury delivers verdict favoring EchoStar (DISH Network), stating no infringement of Forgent's patents occurred.

32. June 2007: DirecTV's relationship with TiVo is minimized to the point where DirecTV, under Rupert Murdoch, no longer markets the TiVo DVR, but does, however, continue to support existing users of DirecTV-TiVo devices.

33. June 2007: DVR penetration in the U.S. reaches 26 million.

34. June 2007: Comcast, the United States' largest MSO, with approximately 25 million subscribers, accepts TiVo-branded software for deployment into the first Comcast-TiVo DVR set-top boxes.

35. December 2007: D & M Holdings sells ReplayTV intellectual property to DirecTV, as part of D & M's bankruptcy settlement.

36. January 2008: Comcast first deploys a TiVo-enabled set-top box, in its Boston, MA cable system.

37. May 30, 2008: EchoStar sues TiVo in Delaware state court, seeking a court ruling, which attempts to show its "work-around" is not a violation of TiVo's "time-warp" patents.

38. October 6, 2008: The U.S. Supreme Court affirms a patent infringement damages decision against EchoStar, in favor of TiVo, in the amount of slightly more than $100 million dollars (including interest from a 2006 $74 million jury trial verdict).

39. November 20, 2008: An Eastern Texas federal trial court judge refuses to invoke a permanent injunction against EchoStar in a "workaround" software patent infringement case growing out of the original TiVo vs. EchoStar patent infringement case, instead setting a bench trial for February 2009.

1.6 Forms

Although most people think of DVRs as being limited to devices that record TV signals, more and more video content is being delivered to and recorded by laptop and desktop computers, which arguably makes them a form of DVR, as well. Yet, the real focus of this section is on DVR hardware versions, also known as "form factors," and within that realm, the DVR set-top box is the core item. Also discussed are various forms of DVR remote control devices and the wiring behind several DVR set-top box examples.

1.6.1 Set-Top Boxes

Today, there are two clear, and some other miscellaneous, forms of DVR set-top boxes. As noted in the "Types" section of this chapter, the dominant DVR set-top versions include standalone units and integrated units.

Standalone units

Early entrants into the DVR world saw their opportunities tied closely to units that they alone would manufacture, or license for manufacture. These so-called standalone units were the early staple of companies such as TiVo and ReplayTV. The earliest versions of these TiVo and ReplayTV DVRs were analog-only, which meant that these early DVR standalone units received analog signals, and then converted those signals into digital signals inside the DVR set-top box, for display onto the monitor. Second-generation DVR units were built for (or, in the case of EchoStar, built by) the all-digital satellite providers. In the case of satellite service provider, DirecTV, it began its investment in DVRs by teaming with a first entrant, TiVo, in the late 1990s time frame. Conversely, EchoStar allied with interactive TV pioneers Microsoft and OpenTV, to design and manufacture its own DVRs. The Microsoft-EchoStar alliance, as noted, created one of the very first DVRs, the *WebTV*-titled service unveiled by EchoStar during the 1999 CES in Las Vegas, NV.

The Carmel Group has watched for years as the standalone numbers and percentage of the total U.S. DVR market declined relative to integrated set-top units (see Figure 1.10). For 2010, The Carmel Group projects that standalone DVRs will provide 2%, or one million of the total projected DVR U.S. market, from a total of 52.5 million. That means that 98%, that is, 51.5 million, will be integrated DVR set-top units. By 2015, this standalone percentage shrinks to 1%, while the number of standalone units shrinks to a mere 700,000.

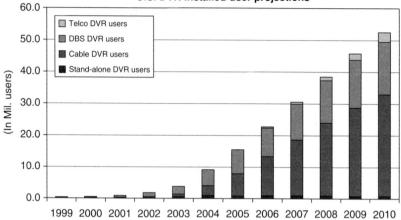

Figure 1.10 A projection comparison of U.S. standalone DVR set-top boxes to those of integrated cable, telco, and satellite (DBS) set-top boxes through the year 2010. (Copyright 2008. Property of The Carmel Group. All rights reserved.)

Integrated units

The integrated set-top box is the combination of a DVR and a receiver-decoder box that provides access to the multichannel operator's scrambled signals. Multichannel operators—be they cable, satellite, or telco—will continue to build and deploy ever-increasing numbers of these boxes, especially because these DVRs do a first rate job of retaining existing subscribers, while also attracting new subscribers. Other combinations of set-top boxes include DVRs with DVDs and the EchoStar-owned and distributed Slingbox, which delivers DVR capability via the Internet to SlingBox users tapping into their home TV and set-top DVR from afar.

Other forms of DVRs

In addition to the remote storage DVR concept discussed above, game consoles (such as the *PlayStation 3* from Sony and the *Xbox 360* from Microsoft), personal computers and laptops, and DVDs are additional devices where manufacturers are adding DVRs to make a set-top box that serves both functions. Digital audio recorder (DAR) devices have also been placed into portable satellite radios. Further, following a global and industry trend of more capacity crammed into smaller DVRs and DVR-like devices, the size and form factor of these items is expected to morph significantly. Indeed, future deployments of DVRs will hardly be recognized as such, but they will accomplish the same basic functionality of recording content for later playback and manipulation by the user. Also, as noted immediately above, the Slingbox from EchoStar delivers its own form of DVR capability for travelers on the road who want to watch their local TV signals (and home-based DVR recordings) from distant locales.

SONY®

Nick Colsey is the director of product planning and new business development for Sony Electronics, Inc., located in San Diego, CA. He has been with Sony for nearly 20 years. He has closely followed Sony's lengthy and extensive involvement with DVRs.

His view of the Sony DVR history begins more than 10 years ago, when, in 1998, Sony participated in what used to be the Western Cable Show, delivering what was then the first public showing of an HD DVR. The device consisted primarily of a cable box, which was connected to a hard drive via 1394 firewire. This was one of Sony's earlier validations of DVRs, and more precisely, the idea that "going forward, consumers would want to time shift," Colsey notes. He continues, "We liked the fact that consumers just loved it. Amongst all their gadgets, the DVR is the Number One or Number Two, year after year. In fact, it still amazes me, but they would rather part with microwave ovens than give up their DVRs." Sony found, specifically via studies of its customers, that they liked most the idea of not being tied to a linear schedule, "So they could watch in the middle of the night, or Saturday morning, or whenever it was convenient, and that took away the obligation of remembering to watch, and the stress of having missed it," Colsey summarizes. Of their dislikes during the time frame, Colsey believes it was primarily the price of the DVR, especially at retail, because, at the time a Sony DVR was in the "$399 and up range."

Asked what the other early motivators were to become involved with DVRs, Colsey believes, "Through Sony's work with the development of the 1394 standard, we did work with technology that sent digital video at high rates of speed; one application was to send digital video from a cable box to a hard disk recorder."

In the following year, 1999, Sony formed an alliance with another DVR pioneer, TiVo. Coming from that alliance, in spring 2000, Sony and TiVo launched the Sony-TiVo standalone "Series 1" line of new consumer DVRs. The "Series 1" did well, according to Colsey. "Early adopters were enthused about being able to watch TV in a new way. Customers appreciated the quality and reliability that the Sony brand brought to the TiVo product," he offers.

In the following year, 2001, DirecTV joined the mix, whereby TiVo and Sony formed an alliance to launch the first DirecTV integrated set-top DVR. According to Colsey, this product was one of the very first on the market to bring together all the convenience of multichannel satellite service and a DVR into one box.

At that point in time, Sony offered standalone DVRs with TiVo, for cable subscribers, as well as an integrated satellite DVR for DirecTV's subscribers.

Shortly after that, Sony acted to expand its DVR product line further by working with Microsoft and DirecTV to help create the *UltimateTV* product. The thinking behind the *UltimateTV* products, Colsey opines, was "Here is a DVR product that is more interactive, for those subscribers who want Internet capability, as well as dual tuners." Also, by this time, the U.S. DVR market was getting well established, and Sony was taking a significant share of that market.

In 2005, the new cable card standard was introduced by the collective cable industry, which allowed Sony to build DVRs into cable boxes. These were also cable boxes that could be sold at retail. At about the same time, using that newly developed cable technology and Sony's further expertise in HD, Sony was able to launch the first HD cable card DVR at retail in 2006.

Nonetheless, in significant measure because of the lock the cable, satellite, and telco vendors have on the DVR market, together with their exclusive DVR vendors (e.g., Motorola and Cisco for the cable industry and EchoStar and NDS for the satellite industry), Sony presently has no DVR product in the U.S. market. Nor do any of the prior vendors who participated in the early years of U.S. DVR, such as Pioneer and Philips. The so-called service operator model has figuratively strangled the competition out of today's DVR industry. Instead, any kind of a set-top box is primarily distributed directly by the operator, or it is leased. This is the model that drove CE companies, such as Sony, out of the multichannel pay TV platform. As such, Sony also no longer makes set-top boxes for DirecTV and TiVo.

The industry is changing it, but to make open standards such as Tru2way true two-way is important, so that CE manufacturers can develop DVRs that work with all cable, telco, and satellite operators. That is Sony's goal according to Nick Colsey.

Looking forward, Sony is watching carefully as the markets, technologies, and storage capabilities are changing. Adds Colsey, "We are watching; and we may see a play there soon."

Asked to look into a crystal ball that sees the DVR industry, Colsey also sees a future, many years down the road, when network (or remote) DVRs rule the roost. Moreover, he sees the average DVR hard drive "... getting bigger, with more storage, but maybe not cheaper." At any rate, he sees the value rising, so that DVRs are more accessible by more people. To get there, Colsey believes that part of the infrastructure around DVRs will involve "... using the power of the Internet, and cheap storage in the center." He also sees a steady decline, if not the total evaporation of, the DVR standalone side of the business. Colsey concludes, "Access to the network DVR function is a standard part of every set-top box, and every TV, and it works, because it is almost no cost, and just some software and a broadband connection."

Sony

Contact Information
7-1, Konan, 1-chome, Minato-ku Tokyo, 108-0075, Japan
Phone: +81-3-6748-211
550 Madison Avenue, New York, NY 10022
United States

Stock Symbol
NYSE: SNE

Key People
Sir Howard Stringer, Chairman and CEO
PR Contact: Marcy Cohen

Key Business
Multinational manufacturer of electronics, video, communications, video
game consoles, and information technology products for the consumer and
professional markets.

DVR Connection
Manufactures DVR receivers and TVs, as well as programming content.

1.6.2 Televisions

At least one large scale television manufacturer, South Korea's conglomerate LG
company, now installs a DVR at the factory into a TV monitor (as one single
unit of hardware). For people eager to eliminate the large number of set-top
box devices that surround the TV in their living or bedrooms, this should be an
attractive and popular alternative.

1.6.3 Remote Controls

Despite its small size, it is difficult to overemphasize the importance of the
remote control device to the proper functioning of and enjoyment of a DVR in
the hands of every consumer. Indeed, once installed, the consumer only interacts
with two items related to the DVR: the EPG/IPG and the remote control device
(see Figure 1.11).

Early development of the remote control is arguably a classic study of a
comparison of the different styles and strategic decisions employed by the early
DVR leaders, TiVo and ReplayTV. In addition, early development of the remote
control focused on several additional elements. One, as mentioned above, was
the concept of user friendliness, which vendors such as TiVo and ReplayTV
employed in their own separate styles. Another was the idea of the right number
of buttons, each doing just the right thing. Yet another was to find the proper

Figure 1.11 A first-generation ReplayTV remote control device (left) and a first-generation TiVo remote control device (right). (Copyright 2009. Property of Jimmy Schaeffler. All rights reserved.)

shape, so that in-hand, the consumer got the best experience. Another element involved making sure the remote worked well with the on-screen graphics and EPG/IPG.

TiVo cites the experience of relying on experts, i.e., those that knew the business of building remote controls. TiVo also worked with and relied upon so-called focus groups, whose members were taken from anonymous members of the community. As a result, TiVo's Bob Poniatowski notes that the TiVo remote control device was so unique that it eventually merited a U.S. patent and was so user friendly that it won consumer awards.

ReplayTV, on the other hand, adopted a different style when it came to early development of key items, such as remote control devices, UI, and set-top boxes. Some believe that the ReplayTV was, in fact, quite user friendly, on all levels. Many others believe that ReplayTV executives felt they were designing more for the technophile, or "early adopter," and that simplicity of use for a mass audience was thus not so critical. As such, the ReplayTV remote control device contained more buttons than did the TiVo remote control. And although a typical early ReplayTV set-top box contained few buttons on the front of the device, there were a large number of ports and functions on the back of the box that offered more connection options than did the TiVo set-top box. Additionally, early ReplayTV thinking focused on the idea of presenting quality products, such as those from similar companies like Sony, where volumes were not as high, but margins were better than the high-volume, low-margin distributors.

1.7 Software

There are really two forms of software that make up a DVR.

First is the TV programs that are displayed on the TV (or computer monitor or other screen device). This is the software content, most of which is a perfect combination of audio and video that billions of TV viewers around the world take for granted and are so used to viewing. As noted above, for a DVR to be able to manipulate and record the content, this content must be delivered in a digital—not analog—format to the TV screen or monitor.

Yet the software that is really deeper inside, and thus, more important to the true operation of a DVR, is the middleware or operational software, which makes up the on-screen EPG/IPG, and the other items the viewer sees that help him or her understand and control the content. Figure 1.12 shows a fairly typical DVR EPG/IPG, including detailed listings of various channels and their presenters, the time of the show, the current clock time, a video version of a single channel, and shows that are coming up. It is top-level EPGs/IPGs like this one that actually make sense of the ever-increasing number of programs and channels that are being placed in front of domestic and global viewers and allow those viewers to take control of the process of choosing a show, recording a show, and/or viewing a show.

The complexity that represents the so-called operational software or middleware is also worth specially highlighting. It is difficult for most laypeople to appreciate the layers of code, the mathematical algorithms, and other elements that had to be properly designed and implemented to make the early DVRs operate properly and attract additional users. Marc Beckwitt, Digeo's director of business development and industry affairs, notes, "The technical design and implementation that results in the scheduling, the control, and the organization of a DVR today, cannot be overemphasized, especially as the DVR moves into

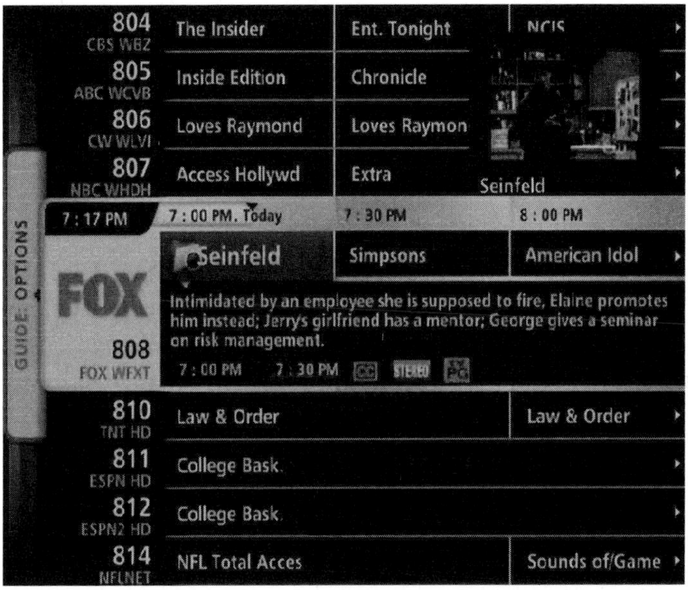

Figure 1.12 The Verizon DVR's electronic programming guide (EPG/IPG). (Copyright 2008. Property of Verizon. Used with Permission. All rights reserved.)

the future adding home networking, different media types, meta-data, and recommendation engines, to name but a few."

Indeed, early software developers like TiVo describe not just weeks or months required to create the software code behind the impressive on-screen displays on many DVRs, but *years*. They are simply that complex and sophisticated. Former ReplayTV vice president of marketing and current executive vice president and GM for Gemstar-TV Guide International Steve Shannon adds, "Especially looking at the combination of audio with video, to seamlessly record, play-back, and operate in the 'clean-trick mode' (which is a general word for the things a user might do with video while watching it, such as fast forward, rewind, pause, instant replay, and slow-motion), is just plain astounding." Michael Kornet, former top-level ReplayTV executive, today the chief marketing officer for San Antonio, TX-based NewTek, concludes, "The capability to use the remarkable software to search for any interest or person that you want to see, and have the DVR service find and record, and then have that content ready to watch, is the most magical thing of the whole system."

Turning specifically to TiVo again in large measure because its makers created such a high-level and attractive on-screen look, one of the TiVo team's early themes was to "keep the screen alive." Thus, instead of screens with flat messages and a look that was far from what the average viewer expected from his or her TV, TiVo software engineers made sure that every screen had a "live, moving, heartbeat" kind of look to it. To accomplish this presentation, TiVo built an on-screen graphics layer that was laid on top of a video background. Further, TiVo talks of its developers even stressing, at length, about whether the "bleep" sound indicating certain on-screen changes was too metallic sounding or sounding too "something else".

The DVR hard drive was another one of TiVo's challenges, as it related to the software, in part because it was used quite differently than that of a PC hard drive. Not only did the TiVo file system have to be specially designed to accept larger video files, it also had to be designed so that a user could quickly find the right data on the disk, and it had to be designed so that turning the machine off would not compromise what had already been processed. Poniatowski again notes, "One of the design goals was to be as simple to use as a toaster. Another UI design mantra was that 'There would be no tigers falling out of trees.' That is to say, we would never shock or surprise the viewer, instead offering a gentle, low stress experience. We would never set their hearts to racing. TiVo felt it needed to keep TV as a 'lean back' experience." TiVo vice president for product marketing Jim Denney, with many years of software and marketing experience, adds, "The key to TiVo software is it has to be stable, and it has to be easy to use."

1.8 Hardware

The hardware components that make up a typical DVR are threefold: first, the set-top box that houses the hard drive, chips, and other hardware elements that—together with the core software—make the DVR work; second is the remote control device that the DVR user uses to control or manipulate the DVR and its content; and third is the wiring that typically first connects the DVR to the source of the signal and then to the TV monitor.

Numerous interviews with key DVR industry personnel point out that the development of this hardware by the early pioneers—TiVo, ReplayTV, Microsoft and EchoStar—was a measure of their respect for two core elements: reliability and ease of use.

1.8.1 Set-Top Boxes

The DVR set-top box is where the true brains and muscle of the entire DVR operation reside, at least when looking at both the standalone and the integrated set-top box versions of the DVR. Figure 1.13 shows four examples of DVR set-top boxes from one satellite TV operator (i.e., DirecTV Network), one cable (i.e., Comcast), and one telco multichannel TV provider (i.e., Verizon), and one combination standalone/cable DVR provider (i.e., Digeo).

The hardware that makes up a DVR includes the elements of the hard drive, which has been discussed already, and that of the decoder chip, which captures the analog signal and converts it to an MPEG digital signal. That chip is called a media switch, which is also responsible for handling all of the so-called trafficking of the audio/video, including moving the audio and video on and off of the hard drive. In designing the chip's components, the DVR makers also had to strive again for reliability, but this time, also for affordability and efficiency (efficiency being measured by the low power processors that were implemented). Further, it is ironic that the very "super box," that was the impetus of much of the early DVR development, came back around during the first half of the 2000–2009 decade, as the DVR component was built back into so-called home media

Figure 1.13 DVR set-top boxes, top to bottom and left to right, from DISH Network (top left), Comcast, Verizon, and Digeo (bottom right).

centers,[21] which were the original vision of the networked home (and, in the case of TiVo, the vision that triggered its DVR development in the first place).

1.8.2 Remote Controls

Because the remote control is the actual piece of hardware that the customer interacts with, the remote's design and layout, including the number of buttons and what the buttons actually do, can be critical. Not only are patents awarded for design features, but also awards are given at trade shows and by trade groups for superior models. In fact, whether a consumer decides a DVR is easy to use or not can often depend on how the remote control feels and operates.

Figure 1.14 shows a DVR remote control from a standalone and satellite (DBS) DVR provider, TiVo, with the channel choice buttons on the bottom, the core DVR functionality in the middle, and additional use features on the top of the device. By comparison, Figure 1.15 exhibits a satellite (DBS) model DVR remote control. This satellite (DBS) model DVR remote control from DISH Network comprises channel choice number buttons in the bottom area of the remote, DVR functionality in the center, and similar additional use features as TiVo, in the top area.

Figure 1.16 from Comcast presents numbers for channel choices at the bottom, the core DVR functionality in the center of the device, and other miscellaneous buttons (such as channel choices, sound, and source functions), toward the top of the device.

The fourth remote control, that of Verizon (Figure 1.17), has the channel selection numbers at the bottom and the core DVR functions in the middle; however, Verizon adds a small screen on the remote to aid the viewer.

In short, all four remote control designers and operators appear to have opted for the same basic lay-out of their respective remote control devices. At the very top and on the side of each remote control device is a small light-like

Figure 1.14 The TiVo remote control. (Copyright 2008. Property of TiVo. All rights reserved. Photo used with permission.)

---

[21] "Home media center" is briefly defined as a single unit, usually housed in one central location inside the home, which contains technological capabilities enabling it to collect and distribute a large number of different signals and different functions to different devices in different locations within the same dwelling.

window feature, which sends the signal from the remote control device to the
signal reading device on the front of the DVR set-top box.

Figure 1.15   The DISH Network set-top box and remote control. (Copyright 2008.
Property of DISH Network. All rights reserved. Photo used with permission.)

Figure 1.16   The Comcast (with its Motorola-branded DVR) set-top box and remote
control. (Copyright 2008. Property of Comcast + Motorola. All rights reserved. Photo
used with permission.)

Figure 1.17   The Verizon set-top box and remote control. (Copyright 2008. Property
of Verizon. All rights reserved. Photo used with permission.)

1.8.3 Wiring

Although the wires that link set-top boxes, TV screens, and cable or satellite signals are items that most consumers prefer to never see or deal with, they are absolutely essential to the operation of most DVR devices, whether it is a standalone or integrated set-top box.

The basic elements of wiring for a DVR set-top box include input from the signal source, such as telco, cable, and/or satellite; an electrical power input; and connection to the TV screen or monitor. Additionally, because proper functioning of a DVR requires a link back to the source of the video, a telephone input line is also included. Further, for integrated set-top boxes, a slot for a user access card is almost always included.

Figure 1.18 shows a set of plugs for wires that connect to and from the Comcast integrated DVR and receiver-decoder set-top telco box. Figure 1.19 exhibits a set of that connect to and from the TiVo-DirecTV model DVR. Figure 1.20 exhibits a set of wires that connect to and from the EchoStar-DISH Network model DVR. Figure 1.21 shows a set of wires that connect to and from Verizon's Motorola manufactured integrated DVR and receiver-decoder set-top cable box.

Figure 1.18 Plugs for wires in the back of a DVR set-top manufactured by Motorola, and distributed by cable operator Comcast. (Copyright 2008. Property of Comcast. All rights reserved. Photo used with permission.)

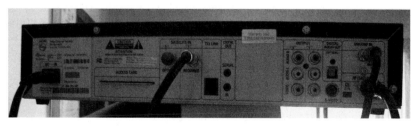

Figure 1.19 Wires in the back of a DVR set-top manufactured by Hughes Network Systems for DirecTV and for TiVo. (Copyright 2008. Property of Willy Schaeffler. All rights reserved. Photo used with permission.)

Figure 1.20 Plugs for wires in the back of a DVR set-top manufactured by EchoStar. (Copyright 2008. Property of DISH Network. All rights reserved. Photo used with permission.)

Figure 1.21 Photo of plugs for the wires in the back of a DVR set-top manufactured by Motorola, and distributed by telco operator Verizon. (Copyright 2008. Property of Verizon. All rights reserved. Photo used with permission.)

Nevertheless, despite some apparent simplicity, the stuff inside a DVR set-top is extremely complex and the result of some amazing minds (especially on the software development side). Thus, most consumers are best to simply leave the handling of the set-top box and DVR to the person who qualifies as their professional multichannel pay TV installer.

1.9 Technology

The late Sir Arthur C. Clarke's commentary, "Any sufficiently advanced technology is indistinguishable from magic," applies particularly well to the modern-day DVR. This is because the device is comprised almost entirely of sophisticated technology, and this particular iteration of that technology is also near-magical (if, for no other reason, because of what it does for consumers' enjoyment of their entire TV experience, start to finish … and even when they aren't watching, via its recording, viewer recommendation, and data-mining functions).

As its name implies, a DVR is only capable of recording digital content. This means that a DVR only processes content that is delivered in the form of ones and zeros. In the late 1990s, this technical issue presented a significant hurdle for the first DVR builders, inasmuch as almost all content carried in the broadcast and cable worlds was analog. At the time, the only real all-digital services were those of DirecTV and EchoStar. Yet, early on, from mid-1994 to mid-1999, neither DirecTV nor EchoStar had a true DVR product. Thus, the item that probably launched all three into DVRdom came in the form of a processing chip that converted the analog signal to a digital signal, called the MPEG decoder. This chip enabled the DVR hard drive to record, store, and later playback the signal. Indeed, the development of satellite service provider DirecTV and its all-digital infrastructure was the foundation for the analog-to-digital MPEG decoder that would become so important to the core of the DVR set-top box.

In the end, the real technical driver of the DVR was the combination of the MPEG decoder and the hard drive, both of which could be purchased for cheaper and cheaper sums. This combination, together with processors, tuners, memory, cooling, video outputs, and graphics rendering components, as well as a viable UI, at affordable price points, made the DVR set-top box possible.

Early TiVo DVR models in the 1999 time frame cost $699 for a 14-hour storage capacity, and $1,000 for the 30-hour version. The same models from ReplayTV cost almost the same or more. EchoStar's early units were subsidized for almost all consumers, but their production costs were in the hundreds of dollars. By comparison, examples of the cost of today's low-end DVRs are below $100, while their capacities have increased markedly. Typically, a satellite TV offers four DVR-enabled set-top boxes installed "free" in multiple rooms per household, in exchange for a customer commitment of 12–24 or more months to a minimum monthly fee programming package. Table 1.1 shows various DVR units available and comparisons of their costs and other features.

Other technological features include graphics and information that are built into DVRs for the use and enjoyment of the consumer. These include background video that gives the DVR user the constant impression that the service is "alive," such as by way of moving background images behind the EPG/IPG grid. Another feature like this is that of program offerings and recommendations, as well as various programming messages, such as those keeping customers up to date on service and programming developments. Especially for those at companies like ReplayTV, TiVo, and DISH Network, the time, effort, and thought that went into these technological solutions—which ultimately led to a great DVR user experience—is something they do not like to see overlooked.

Digeo's Beckwitt notes, "In the early days of DVRs, and to a lesser extent now, a lot of custom stuff, in custom chips, had to be mastered to make the DVR work. Early on, what went on inside that chip was an art form, practiced by guys from Sony, and Philips, and Panasonic, who had analog in their blood (which created a big barrier to entry for others). This is less so these days, as DVR development has transitioned from an art form to a science." The kind of challenges Beckwitt mentioned that had to be mastered from a technological point of view included tuning (and tuning speeds), signal-to-noise ratios,[22] and speed control.

---

[22] "Noise" is a term that loosely defines interference created from other sources to the proper receipt of video and audio signals. A "signal-to-noise" ratio helps determine whether a proper signal is being received.

TiVo's Poniatowski adds, "Service is a key piece of the technology that gets overlooked." In this, he emphasizes TiVo's creation of the DVR business based around the idea of a service infrastructure component, taking the DVR well beyond the VCR, and into a new realm of guide information, program recommendations, partner advertisements, messages from the service provider, daily software updates, and upgrades.

Former Sony Electronics senior vice president, Jim Bonan, today an independent consultant, nicely rounds out the subject of technology with the following praise for the early DVR industry developers as a whole: "Very few CE industry developers back in the late 1990s would have taken the initiative to create the kind of search and storage features for consumers that the DVR folks did. In fact, that was a consumer Godsend."

1.10 Trends

Truly, there is a plethora of technical and telecommunications trends that are behind the development of—and future growth of—DVRs.

Probably the far and away greatest trend involving DVRs is that of viewers wanting to, and finally being able to, control the content they view. This inevitably means being able to watch something other than a real-time, live, show-upon-show linear presentation of programming by the various network TV and basic cable and satellite networks. This trend of "viewer choice" was jump-started by DirecTV, via its foray into the digital delivery of television signals, in mid-1994. That is because even the first-generation implementation of digital satellite broadcasting in the United States was a huge improvement over cable, when it came to choice and quality of programming content. Satellite players such as DirecTV took the concept of more channels for less money, honed it, and the DVR followed those footsteps by allowing consumers never-before-thought-of choices, such as when to watch a program, what parts of the program to watch, and whether to jump ahead, pause, or rewind—even a live program.

Further, as noted earlier, the technical trends of more hardware for less money, and of hardware that constantly does more things, like to convert and compress signals, or store signals on hard drives, are another set of drivers behind the DVR movement. Coupled with this is the trend of putting more storage into the same item, or more capability into the same chip, both supporting the concept of what is known in the technology industry as Moore's Law.[23]

Looking into the future, several trends rise quickly to the top. These include those of the coming ubiquity of DVRs. Like the major developments that

---

[23] Moore's Law is based upon Intel co-founder Gordon Moore's famous 1965 prediction that silicon chips would essentially double in core capability—including processing speed and storage capacity, and even the resolution of digital cameras and photo devices—once every 24 months, well into the future.

preceded it in the television world, DVRs will become quite common. A good part of the reason for that is the fact that cable, telco, and satellite operators all gain significantly from their consumers' deployment of DVRs. As noted above, the core reasons for this attractiveness are the relative low cost, but more importantly, the ability of DVRs to attract new multichannel customers and their ability to satisfy existing multichannel customers, thus enhancing per customer revenues and profit, also known in financial terms as ARPU.

Another trend that is related to DVRs is that of digital and HDTV. The more cable subscribers that transition to digital cable services, the easier it is for those cable operators to offer and deploy DVRs, primarily because a DVR is made for a digital cable TV system. Moreover, DVRs do a good job of manipulating content, which makes a lot more sense when the look of that content is so much better in a HD format. This is the reason both standalone DVR providers and multichannel operators are working so hard to build HD-capable DVRs. In the not too distant future, HD DVRs will become a larger and larger percentage of the U.S. DVR base, just as more content will be digital and more of that will be viewable as HD content. Indeed, as of June 12, 2009, all over-the-air terrestrial broadcast television will only be delivered in digital format, further enhancing the growth of HD DVRs.

The trend of VOD services offered by cable and telco multichannel operators eventually incorporating and/or substituting many or all of the features a DVR offers, is one of the most important ones, in the very long-term future of the U.S. telecom industry. Chapter 8, "The Future of DVRs," offers a much more detailed discussion of this probable phenomenon. In a related mode, visionaries, such as Sony's Nick Colsey, see a future when companies such as YouTube find themselves essentially competing against what a DVR does, in that video by choice is made accessible for anyone, at just about any time, repeatedly throughout any given day. An integration of broadcast, broadband, and cable becomes yet another vision of the future that will severely affect given, traditional DVR models today.

Operators will move more to control the UI experience, placing ads and other messages within the EPG/IPG and among other on-screen messages. This management is emblematic of a greater control issue, that of the multichannel operator battling CE manufacturers for control of the hardware and software in the living room and on screens elsewhere in consumers' lives. This occurs because the entity that controls the content in tens of millions of U.S. TVHHs also then controls billions of dollars in TV-related revenues, such as with advertisements and subscription revenues. And, in a related mode, expect fierce internecine battles among the different multichannel competitors—satellite (DBS), cable, and telco providers—for that same consumer dollar.

Yet other trends will turn on the success of the telecom market and its ability to reach a balance between the right of content owners to receive fair and adequate compensation, on the one hand, and the right of consumers to have fair and reasonable access to that content (by way of reasonable prices and reasonable technological tools), on the other hand.

Global growth of DVRs is yet another expected trend or phenomenon. Thus far, the vast majority of DVRs in the world are part of the domestic U.S. landscape. Indeed, The Carmel Group estimates that DVRs located in locales other than the United States as of this printing are in the double tens of millions. As part of the same estimates and projections, this same type of global DVR growth number is expected to expand to 75 million by the end of 2010.

1.11   Key Players

To be clear, classifications of today's key DVR players include the following:

- Standalone set-top DVR developers (e.g., TiVo, Digeo, and Microsoft)
- Integrated set-top manufacturers (such as Motorola, Scientific-Atlanta, TiVo and Digeo)
- Satellite DVR operators (e.g., EchoStar and DirecTV)
- Cable DVR operators (such as every major cable MSO in the U.S today—in the order of size, Comcast, Time Warner, Cox, Charter and Cablevision—as well as more and more small-to-medium-sized cable operators)
- Telco operators (e.g., Verizon and AT&T)
- A handful of CE manufacturers (e.g., LG), as well as hybrid combinations of these classifications (e.g., AT&T in certain areas where it offers its HomeZone service, allying with multichannel TV- and DVR-supplier EchoStar)

Key DVR players in the future will include gaming device manufacturers (such as Sony and Microsoft), device makers such as Sling Media, and other yet-to-be-developed or yet-to-be-created DVR or DVR-like devices.

In addition to those players already mentioned in this chapter, other potential players include mobile device makers that will place various forms of memory, which will more and more include "flash" forms of extremely compact memory storage. In this way, storage of media eventually becomes nearly ubiquitous, whereby all media gets recorded all the time, on just about every conceivable device.

1.12   Challenges

The list of challenges tied to the DVR industry is best broken out in the form of past, present, and future obstacles that industry and consumer DVR makers, as well as users, have dealt with, are dealing with, or will deal with.

1.12.1   Past

A handful of important challenges faced the different players in the DVR realm early on. Those players include the operators, the hardware manufacturers and, of course, the consumers.

The first challenge facing the early DVR pioneers, e.g., ReplayTV's Anthony Wood, and TiVo's Jim Barton and Mike Ramsay, was just how to replace the messiness and single functionality of a VCR infrastructure with an elegant and efficient multifunctional device that was so much better (called the DVR). How could they get consumers to jettison the messiness and hassle of many VCR tape cassettes for the ease of a hard drive you never touch? In the sage words of Nick Colsey, Sony's director, product planning and business development, TV operations of America, "They had to change TV, change the way people enjoyed TV, and create something people would *really use*." (emphasis in original). Yet, having reached this vision milestone, all three of these earliest of the DVR pioneers faced many additional challenges.

Closely related to the unique and substantial technical challenges tied to developing the DVR infrastructure, early pioneers had also to grapple with the challenges of determining whether to go with a straight CE-only retail hardware sale model, or to attempt to also combine a service fee model and infrastructure. Indeed, building a model that delivered ample revenues to support the nascent DVR business was a daunting task. This was especially so because both TiVo and ReplayTV were tiny start-ups, both forced to deal early on with the seasoned giants of the CE world. These "CE Bears," as some call them even today, include companies such as Sony, Panasonic, Thomson (RCA), Philips, Toshiba, Humax, and Pioneer. Interestingly, both of the core DVR pioneers— ReplayTV and TiVo—opted in favor building two distinct company units, one focused on the hardware product and sale side, the other tasked more directly with developing the software subscription service side. In its own way, this, too, became a pioneering CE decision.

Yet, without question, the number one challenge facing the implementation of DVRs has been—and continues to be—the difficulty of educating consumers as to the benefits of DVRs and DVR-like devices and services. Getting consumers to accept and even embrace the idea of paying extra to receive and then be able to manipulate content to their liking, involves what is essentially a difficult cultural change, as well. This, then, becomes an obstacle for everyone in the DVR development chain. Until this educational barrier is overcome, nothing else that a DVR company does, or a that cable, telco, or satellite operator does, will prove effective as it relates to wanting a consumer to adopt the product and service that represents the features and assets of a DVR.

Another challenge faced by the early DVR vendors was that of raising capital to properly support growing businesses. Most believe that TiVo took advantage of the ease with which money could be raised before the "Internet Tech Crash" of 2001, which ReplayTV did not. In short, TiVo got enough financial backing early on, ReplayTV did not. And because money ran short in the early part of the new millennium, ReplayTV was doomed. "Without the bursting of the Internet bubble, ReplayTV would still be in business today," propounds former ReplayTV executive Steve Shannon. Former ReplayTV executive Michael Kornet concurs.

Beyond that basic financial support dilemma, which was focused initially on the makers of the first DVRs, industry observers note challenges such as waiting until adequate Motion Picture Engineers Group (MPEG) chips were available, choosing the proper form factors in which to place the functionality for the remote controls and the set-top boxes, finding the proper and adequate investors at the right time, and how to best protect content. There were additional concerns about getting products into the market ahead of competitors, making sure those products and services were as free from as many glitches as possible when launched, and managing the early costs for things like the chipsets and other internal components (which, like most CE products, were expected to—and did—drop precipitously in cost following initial deployment, and as additional generations of product were distributed). Yet interestingly, although the base model DVR hard drive has stayed at the same basic $40 price, rather than have its price decline, instead its storage capacity has increased incrementally through the 10 years since the first deployments.

For the multichannel operators, the decision to deploy DVRs was an easy one for the satellite operators, but a less easy one for the cable operators. The former saw DVRs as a quick and affordable way to differentiate and value their services relative to cable. The latter felt they had a superior product offering only VOD and feared legal issues and business issues that faced DVR deployment. And by the time the telcos got ready to deploy their *U-Verse* and *FiOS TV* systems around the United States, the decision of whether to include DVRs had, *de facto*, already been made for them by those same rival satellite and cable operators. In other words, to compete against cable and satellite providers, the new telco TV providers had to offer new subscribers at least equally competitive—if not more competitive—packages including DVRs (see the Verizon case study earlier in this chapter, for further discussion of this challenge).

1.12.2 Present and Future

Although the significant early costs of well near $1,000 for a better-than-average DVR are no longer common, other past challenges remain with us today. These especially include a challenge that continues to dominate the industry–consumer landscape: educating the consumer as to the whys and wonders of DVRs. Indeed, there are few in today's DVR industry who do not concede that there is still a lot of consumer education about DVRs to do, including those that have DVRs but do not know, for example, how to properly utilize the DVR recommendation engines.

Like the earliest days of the new DVR industry, DVR makers like TiVo and Digeo will be struggling to make sure that the DVR functionality is more than just another add-in inside an integrated cable, telco, or satellite box. Thus, for the future, each one of these standalone DVR companies will be focused on creating other applications that can add revenues to their business models. They will also be focused on maintaining and building the brands they have worked so hard to establish in consumers' minds.

Moreover, one of the greatest challenges for the DVR industry will be dealing with the obsolescence some predict will come from the apparent greater efficiencies offered on the VOD side of the telecom and multichannel industries.

Beyond that, experts, such as Sony's Nick Colsey and Gemstar's Steve Shannon, opine as to the decline of DVRs at the hands of the open Internet (and its services, functions, and features). These challenges come in the form of specific offerings, such as *YouTube*, *DailyMotion*, and *BlipTV*. Because these operatives already can deliver HD quality video, their ability to impinge upon what DVRs typically do is real and happening fast—especially among younger generations of Internet and mobile video users. Moreover, to the extent DVR functionality gets built into home media centers, the idea of a standard DVR in either a standalone or integrated mode also is impinged.

In its place, the home media center does permit access to a number of signals, from numerous sources, and carries those signals and content to other screens in the same house, while also serving as a VOD center, interactive TV center, and a displayer and conveyor of HD signals, as well as other functionality. As such, the ability to store content on a DVR-like device becomes less important. Digeo's Beckwitt summarizes, "The ability of consumers to receive multiple content from multiple sources via multiple methods may be the DVR industry's biggest threat, at least for DVR distributors that are putting out a commodity level DVR. On the other hand, the guys at the high-end of the DVR distribution chain are protected, because they are addressing the broad need of the end-user market. In short, the high-end guys are not building the one-trick pony device, which gives them sustainability relative to some of the other threats."

For all multichannel operators (e.g., telco, cable, and satellite alike), the *cost* of keeping consumers supplied with the latest model DVR could prove particularly problematic, as we enter the future. This could be the case for any form of new storage deployed, be it standalone, integrated, remote storage or media center-based. Beyond that concern, if the DVR industry is going to work with the free, ad-supported TV industry to create new customization and personalization opportunities, they will likely have to work together well and work together fast. This is because each new generation of technophiles is getting better and better at avoiding undesirable content, and if the new personalized ad-based content models are not rolled out well and rolled out quickly, too many of the future generation will choose instead just to ignore customized and personalized ad-based content altogether.

Note that to get the best picture of the challenges comprising past, present, and future DVR industry players, it is probably best to also read the "Opportunities" section next, inasmuch as many of the "opportunities" concurrently serve as "challenges" for this same audience. Table 1.6 shows a listing of most of the key challenges and opportunities facing those in the DVR industry today. Chapter 8, "The Future of DVRs," relates to a more specific and detailed listing and description of challenges and opportunities.

Table 1.6 The Main Challenges and Opportunities Facing those Members of the DVR Industry.

DVRs: Challenges and Opportunities[1]	
Challenges	**Description**
Abandonment of old technology	DVRs had to be desirable enough for customers to part ways with their old VCRs and VHS tapes and embrace a new technology.
Model choice	Initially, DVR companies needed to determine whether they would use a straight CE-only retail hardware sale model, or attempt to also combine a service fee model and infrastructure.
Form factor	Choosing the proper form factors to house the operation of the device was important because it was a set-top box and typically gets placed as a piece of furniture in a living room; and an attractive and easy-to-use, functional remote control device, was a key multichannel industry dynamic.
Raising capital	Finding proper and adequate investors at the right time.
Operator acceptance	Many cable operators lost the early growth opportunity to satellite because the former feared legal issues and business development issues in early DVR deployment phases.
Continued consumer education	Many consumers do not understand the difference between a VCR and a DVR. Many that have a DVR still do not know how to fully utilize its capabilities. For example, a very large number of customers do not know how to use the "recommendation engines" within a DRV's software.
Business model effectiveness	Currently many DVR makers like TiVo fear that in the future DVRs may be just another add-in inside an integrated cable, telco, or satellite box. As a result, DVR makers are spending a lot of money on creating other applications that can add revenues to their business models.
Maintaining brand awareness	DVR makers are also working hard to maintain and build the brands they have worked so hard to establish in consumers' minds (e.g., avoiding use of "let's just TiVo it" in order to protect the brand name TiVo).
Hardware obsolescence	Some industry experts predict that with enhanced VOD capabilities, and networked DVRs, individual unit DVRs will soon become obsolete.

(Continued)

Table 1.6 *(Continued)*

DVRs: Challenges and Opportunities[1]

Challenges	Description
Software obsolescence	Experts also attribute challenges to the increased efficiency of services, functions, and features of the Internet. One expert was quoted as saying, "Platforms like YouTube, Daily Motion, and BlipTV can already deliver on-demand HD quality video. The ability of consumers to receive multiple content from multiple sources via multiple methods may be the DVR industry's biggest threat."
Costs	For all multichannel operators, the cost of continually supplying consumers with the new model DVRs could prove to be particularly problematic.
Prices	Consumers balk at paying up front, especially, for DVR hardware.

Opportunities	Description
Current lack of DVR penetration	As it stands, today about 40% of TV households have DVRs. Leaves a lot of room for growth.
Global growth	A large opportunity lies in global DVR adoption. Digital pay and free TV multichannel systems are expanding rapidly throughout the world. This creates a tremendous opportunity for DVR and related companies.
Relationship with advertising and content communities	Personalization and customization of content—especially advertising related content—have the potential to engage customers like no other software has ever done.
Access to different signals	Currently DVRs are being developed with the ability to record signals from sources (like the Internet and mobile services); this means access to content beyond that provided by cable, telco, and satellite operators.
Multiroom capability	The idea of storing a program in one room, so it can be watched and manipulated in another room, presents another great opportunity for DVR makers and distributors.
Access to other devices	Additional devices can display DVR content (beyond the mere in-home DVR), meaning the value of the device is greatly enhanced.

[1] The author specially thanks TiVo's Bob Poniatowski, NewTekis Michael Kornet, and Gemstar-TV Guide International's Steve Shannon for their help with this section and this table.

1.13 Opportunities

Especially because DVRs are quickly on their way to becoming standard-issue TV-viewing hardware (and software) across America's TV-viewing landscape, the opportunities they suggest are worth determining and understanding, and perhaps also worth taking advantage of. Indeed, although well south of 50% DVR penetration is the norm in the United States today, Sony's Nick Colsey notes that going forward a huge opportunity remains, inasmuch as DVR penetration still awaits almost 60% of today's U.S. TVHHs. This is particularly important when you realize that, in his apt words, "100% of TV subscribers today would benefit from having a DVR."

Thus, today's core DVR software developers, such as TiVo, Digeo, EchoStar, and Macrovision, will necessarily continue to focus on the subscriber-supported platforms to assure their future success. Additionally, satellite, cable, and telco operators will continue to push DVRs to attract and sustain customer bases, and for revenue purposes. Two of these three, however, i.e., the cable and telco providers, will also be watching most closely as the infrastructure and capabilities of pure VOD increase and are enhanced. This is because, going forward, additional investments made by telcos and cable companies in VOD, may well substitute for investments they need not make in DVRs. Further, VOD-type offerings, such as features which allow a subscriber hooked to a central server to "look back" at or "start over" a program, make pirating those programs much more challenging for any would-be hackers.

An even greater DVR opportunity lies with DVR growth into TV markets globally. The United Kingdom's BSkyB Pay TV multichannel service has, as of its reporting dated June 30, 2008, marked success deploying its Sky+-branded DVR service in the past 3–4 years into an estimated 2.3 million of its 10+ million BSkyB digital TVHHs. Elsewhere in the world, according to OpenTV senior vice president Tracy Geist, "Wherever in the world a digital pay TV system lights up today—be it cable, telco, satellite, or digital terrestrial—it is going to give customers either a DVR or DVR-ready experience. That makes almost anywhere in the world a potential hotbed of DVR growth." Chapter 7, "International DVR Growth," offers a more focused and detailed look at this future.

Yet perhaps the most important opportunity that will ever present itself for the DVR industry is, ironically, the very thing that so threatened it during its earliest beginnings: its relationship with the advertising and content communities. That relationship is an opportunity because, if done well, personalization and customization of content—especially advertising-related content—have the potential to engage and enrapture consumers like no other software has ever done before. For DVR developers to be able to not only create attractive and relevant content, but for them to be able to educate and convince consumers to seek out that customized content, means huge strides forward not only for the DVR industry, but through licensing, for the VOD and digital signage subsectors, as well. It also means huge steps forward for consumers. Perhaps some new form of incentivizing DVR consumers to watch certain customized and personalized ads is the answer? Note also that this notion of relevant, customized, and personal ads that DVR users *want* to access also thrives, as DVRs, as noted above, reach for that 100 million U.S. TVHHs universe (to say nothing of the approximately 1.3 billion. global TVHHs universe).[24]

Further, as described earlier, another opportunity for the DVR industry is DVR access to signals from sources beyond those video and audio signals offered by traditional cable, telco, and satellite operators. For example, as high-quality audio/video is more accessible to both Internet-connected and mobile devices, savvy DVR developers will make sure DVRs are available to store content from those sources and on those devices. In the past few years, digital audio recording devices developed primarily by the U.S. satellite radio pioneers—XM and Sirius—are perfect examples of companies seizing this opportunity. Indeed, the DVR industry should be on the radar screens of every new content-related device creator in the years ahead.

Without doubt, home based multi-room DVR capability is yet another core opportunity for the DVR community, especially the idea of storing a program in one room, so that it can be viewed or otherwise controlled in another room. Digeo's Beckwitt concludes, "There's a great opportunity for the DVR to evolve into a whole new product category, as the center of a connected whole-home experience (for example, whole-home audio/video, home controls, IP content/services, etc.). That's one big road we're driving down."

TiVo's vice president for product development Jim Denney concludes this theme of future opportunities, also emphasizing the importance of a future DVR experience not only storing content, but also allowing simultaneous interaction with others through the Internet and similar technologies. He further believes the question of the limbo that companies like Time Warner and Cablevision Systems find themselves in—as they try to champion the message of a remote storage DVR-like system—will one day be resolved, and will open up an entire new realm of DVR-like potential. As part of this, Denney strongly believes that the respective Hollywood, cable, telco, satellite, network, and DVR industries will find a balance as it relates to consumer fair use and copyright concerns that currently control the landscape. And together with Denney's colleague, Poniatowski, both men still see the opportunity to make the "search and find" content feature better and better, to accommodate literally huge increases in the amount of content and files that consumers will demand in the future. "The best DVR service provider will allow you easily to stay aware, to be current, and intelligent ... in short, to get the best out of your TV experience," concludes Poniatowski.

---

[24] From among these approximately 1.3 billion global TVHHs, The Carmel Group estimates, however, that the core opportunity for the growth of DVR deployment today lies primarily with the roughly 360 million cable TVHHs.

1.14 Summary

DVRs represent the paradigm of advanced consumer-friendly services growing directly out the transition from analog to digital. As such, they pave the way for consumer acceptance of other advanced digital services and devices, such as interactive TV (iTV), HDTV, and VOD, to name but the most prominent ones today. Indeed, there are others that are less well known, and many others that are hardly known at all, or not yet a part of the public consciousness. When all is said and done, however, TV historians will look back upon DVRs, and those that are responsible for their development and universal implementation, and recognize their importance as some true pioneers of—taking the DirecTV trademarked saying—better TV for all.

2 What is a DVR?

We knew that the DVR was going to be just like high speed data. Once people made the switch, there was no going back to dial up, or, in this case, to watching TV without DVR capabilities. The choice, convenience, and control that DVR provided to consumers was going to forever change their television experience (and expectations).
—Dave Clark, Director, Product Strategy and Management for Home Entertainment Products, Service Provider Video Technology Group, Cisco (formerly Scientific Atlanta)

Without getting too technical, the sections of this chapter—the what, where, why, and when—are designed to give just about everyone a basic and complete understanding of the DVR product and service. This "everyone" includes the audiences for this book, from a major telecom techie to the ultra layperson who knows little about the technology behind a TV screen (other than that it delivers a color video program, with sound, to a TV set).

The "what" of a DVR breaks out into the hardware (i.e., the device and its components) and its software (i.e., the middleware and on-screen content), as well as the operational aspects of the DVR business. The "where" of a DVR reviews the places a DVR gets deployed; these are better broken out into current-day deployments, on the one hand, and into future deployments, on the other. The "why" of the DVR realm reflects on just what it is that a DVR does. Finally, the "when" of the DVR tries to parse through a surprisingly wide range of times a DVR can be operational.

2.1 What is a DVR?

Vudu's[1] chief operating officer and former vice president, marketing, for TiVo Ed Lichty says, "A DVR is a metaphor for the transition away from linear broadcast television." DVRs really are the beginning of the revolution away from watching television programs only when they are telecast and only on the TV to which they are first telecast. This concept of only watching live or real-time TV is called linear TV. Some also know it as real-time TV viewing. In short, DVRs give everyone an opportunity to step beyond the network control and inconvenience imposed by linear-only TV. In its place, subscribers themselves control the when, the what, and the where of their programs, also known as time-shifting.

---

[1] According to its Web site, http://www.vudu.com, the Vudu company is a Santa Clara, CA-based developer and maker of a new set-top box that instantly delivers movies and TV shows "… directly through the television, without requiring a computer or cable/satellite TV service."

The reason this definition of linear-to-non-linear TV viewing change is so important is because it focuses more on the most important element representing the DVR phenomena: what it is that a DVR *does* (rather than a definition of its hardware or software). Indeed, there is an old adage in the multichannel pay TV marketplace that, paraphrased, states, "Subscribers really don't care about *how* or *where* they get their programs, they just want to watch their shows." In other words, whether the TV signal comes via a cable, telco, or satellite, infrastructure is hardly ever the point for the average consumer, rather each just wants his or her TV.

By definition, a DVR captures the essence of a consumer going from little or no input into what and when he or she watches on TV, to a state where he or she has vast input within the realm of his or her own, personal viewing space. *Choices* as to what is watched, when it is watched, and more these days, what other devices it is watched on are becoming the norm, at least in North America.

Answering the different word parts of a DVR definition, a DVR is "digital," in that it works based upon the concept of a digital,[2] rather than an analog, technological underpinning. Although the DVR definition includes the term "video," the concept of a DVR includes capture and manipulation of all kinds of content—data, audio, video, and some other yet-to-be developed or introduced forms of content. Thus, especially in the future, it will become more commonplace for a DVR-like device to capture—by way of a portable satellite radio device like Sirius XM's Inno, as an example—all kinds of content, including some that are not video. In this sense, the video in DVR becomes more of a misnomer. Finally, the term "recorder" is the idea of the simple capture and recording of content on a device going from video and audio tape, in the earliest days, to hard drives, to a flash memory stick, to other, again, yet-to-be-developed recording forms and formats.

Chapter 3 introduces the topic of new technologies via a basic, but more technical, description of the core technical elements of a typical DVR set-top box. This technical section in Chapter 3 goes a long way toward helping any reader understand the inside hardware, and thus a purer answer to the question, what is a DVR?

2.1.1 Hardware

Because the core hardware parts of a DVR can be arranged to fit into just about any relatively moderately sized hardware box, be it a traditional cable, telco, or satellite set-top box, a gaming box, a portable device (such as the XM Satellite Radio *Inno* receiver and recorder), or in a home network box, there really is no standard hardware unit within which to find a DVR today. These core elements, which are a hard drive that stores the content and a chip that controls the digital operations of the DVR, can be placed in any number of

---

[2] "Digital" in the telecommunications context discussed here means the term used most commonly in consumer electronics and computing sectors, referring to the process whereby information is converted to binary numeric forms. Such data-carrying signals carry electronic or optical pulses, the amplitude of each of which represents a logical 1 (pulse present and/or high) or a logical 0 (pulse absent and/or low). Conversely, "analog" among the same sectors refers to a variable signal continuous in both time and amplitude.

different forms and devices. Indeed, in the early days of TiVo, their engineers and designers toyed with triangles, various tall and wide rectangles, and other form factors, before deciding on a traditional set-top box for their first generation TiVo standalone and integrated units.

Yet, realistically, most items that fit into the category of DVRs these days are, in fact, just standard set-top boxes, operated by cable and satellite multichannel TV operators. Of the total DVR set-top box base today, approximately 3% are standalone and 97% are integrated units. Among the integrated, approximately 60% are cable-deployed set-top boxes, 35% are satellite-deployed, and the remaining 5% are telco-deployed set-top boxes. The percentage of do-it-yourself customized DVRs is negligible. Figure 2.1 illustrates these data points.

Beyond the traditional set-top boxes, engineers and marketers are becoming ever more clever and are taking the basic multichannel TV DVR concept— that of being able to capture live content, store it, pause it, or rewind it live, and later play, pause, fast forward, or otherwise control it as recorded content—and moving it into every plausible platform. These include stationary or mobile, big or small, and satellite-based or terrestrial-based platforms. Indeed, as noted frequently elsewhere in this book, devices such as Sony's PlayStation 3 and Microsoft's *Xbox 360* are all over the concept of DVRs being placed into *their* devices. Home networking devices, which comprise both a basic set-top box at a main location in the home, and devices and wires to transport the content to other screens in the same home, are another example of a different DVR hardware form factor.

As also noted elsewhere in different presentations of this text's topic, "DVR Hardware," hardware for a DVR almost inevitably also includes a remote control device and the wiring in the back of the device that connects it to a signal source and

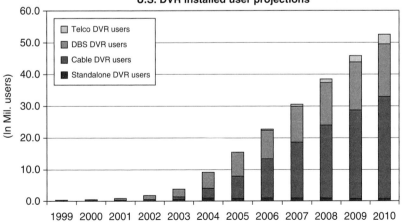

Figure 2.1 The growth of digital video recorders (DVRs) within the subcategories of standalone and integrated set-top boxes; within the latter category, notice the breakout of DVRs among cable, satellite, and telco multichannel pay TV providers. (Copyright 2009. Property of The Carmel Group. All rights reserved. Used with permission.)

to the screen on which the DVR-managed content is displayed. Chapter 1 describes the wiring and remote control and set-top box elements of DVR hardware.

2.1.2 Software

As also noted in Chapter 1, two versions of computer software—both the operational, or middleware, that makes the DVR work, and the on-screen content in the form of TV and radio programs—are the core software inside the DVR set-top box.

2.1.3 Operational

Probably worth separating and placing in its own section is the software side of a DVR, the one that makes it all work, that is, the middleware or operational hardware. Chapter 1 covers the importance and intricacies of the true "brains" inside a DVR. Added to that is the technical section of Chapter 3, where the key internal hardware parts of a DVR are discussed in greater technical detail.

2.2 Where (A DVRs Works?)

A consumer DVR works today in a handful of devices, which are part of a handful of systems. Almost every one of these is an important part of a satellite [direct broadcast satellite (DBS)], cable, or telco multichannel TV operator in the United States. Elsewhere, the same holds true, although a few free-to-air providers are beginning to deploy DVRs, in places like Europe and Australia. These devices are almost always either standalone or integrated set-top boxes, although, in a few instances, DVRs are being deployed within TV monitors. Further, in a very few, but in what will be a larger and larger number, of network systems, operator-controlled remote DVRs will become increasingly popular.

2.2.1 Currently

In the 2009–2010 world of telecom, DVRs are primarily housed inside the set-top boxes that are provided to customers of U.S.-based multichannel pay TV providers. In this particular sector, most of these are deployed by Philadelphia, PA-based Comcast cable. This has developed because of Comcast's 5–7 year effort to get DVRs into the hands of just about all of its nearly 25 million subscribers. In addition, other large distributors of DVRs placed inside most of their newer integrated set-top boxes are the other large and medium-sized U.S. cable operators (e.g., Time Warner Cable, Cox, Charter, Cablevision, Mediacom, and Insight), as well as the two U.S.-based satellite TV (or DBS) providers, El Segundo, CA-based DirecTV, and Englewood, CO-based EchoStar. Newer deployments are also being made by the two premier U.S. telcos, AT&T and Verizon, as well as a handful of other medium- and small-sized regional and local telcos and cable operators.

The next case study concerning Kansas-based Sunflower Broadband presents an interesting picture of DVR development as it relates to a relatively small, but quite well-run, cable system in Heartland America. The range of cable operators involved today points out the following message: for most multichannel providers today, if they want to compete, they have to offer a plethora of "extra" services and devices, which include not only DVRs, but also certainly HDTV and more video on demand (VOD) and interactive TV, as well as various versions of networked TV. Interactive TV is not far behind.

Standalone set-top DVRs are the kind that are offered by companies such as TiVo and Digeo, but which only offer DVR services. They are different from integrated boxes in that providing access to the multichannel platform is not one of their capabilities. Projections of future sales and deployment of these standalone boxes are relatively small, a topic which is further elaborated in Chapter 6. The real growth is going to be in integrated set-top boxes, because the operators who distribute them have the control over the subscribers they serve, and the integrated set-top DVR is the best way for them to concurrently monetize their investment and serve the subscriber.

Also, as noted in Chapter 1, other forms of DVR-like capabilities are found in gaming devices, in satellite radio devices, and in home network devices. In addition, although no longer marketed aggressively, TV and CE provider EchoStar has tried to distribute a portable DVR device, called a DISHPlayer, which travelers could take on the road and plug into a hotel TV far away and use to still be able to capture DVR functionality outside of the home. Pundits expect in the future to see more of this kind of mobile DVR functionality tied in with devices such as the Slingbox (Figure 2.2). The Slingbox is also a portable

Figure 2.2 The DISH network remote control device, which operates the sling media screen. (Copyright 2009. Jimmy Schaeffler and Sling Media. Used with permission. All rights reserved.)

device that, from afar, permits use of the Internet to tap into all of one's home programming content, including content stored on a DVR in that home (again, no matter how far away).

Lawrence, KS, is the market area for Sunflower Broadband, a cable, telephone, and Internet broadband "triple play" telecom provider, serving 30,000 subscribers; Lawrence is a suburb of Kansas City, KS. Its COO for many years is Patrick Knorr, a man who knows his industry quite well, on several levels; he is also very involved with his cable industry trade group, the Pittsburgh, PA-headquartered American Cable Association, serving as its chairman from 2006 to 2008.

Focused on his company's DVR deployment, Knorr notes, "My subscribers like controlling their video and time-shifting, and to succeed in a tough telecom marketplace, it's essential for me to like what my consumers like."

Tracking Sunflower Broadband's DVR history, Knorr recalls seeing the early promise of DVRs, but having to succumb to the slowness of the U.S. cable industry, when it came to embracing what DVRs could do: "The cable industry lagged, because of concerns over VOD, which many saw as a better technical and better financial way of achieving the same thing ... but led by cable pioneers, such as Cablevision and Time Warner, during the 2004–2009 time frame, the remainder of the cable industry quickly caught up with the early players." Sunflower Broadband began its DVR deployment in 2004.

Knorr adds, "As soon as TiVo and ReplayTV began their DVR deployments, there was no question that consumers were addicted to DVRs." He also concludes. "With IPGs like Moxi by Digeo—a fantastic product—the consumer buy-in has been remarkable." Knorr laments some early legal concerns over consumer manipulation of the content using DVRs and a lack of standardization, a set of concerns that frequently arise with the adaption of new technologies.

Moving forward, Knorr envisions the time not too far ahead, when true cable two-way interactivity will add another layer to an already robust DVR and VOD service operation. Knorr sees personalization of content as the key factor that will cause both DVR and VOD to grow and for VOD to begin to eventually supplant DVRs. Knorr adds, "VOD has time-shifting, giving subscribers control, but it's like setting them down in New York City's Grand Central Station and saying 'go talk to anyone you want,' as opposed to 'go talk to someone with whom you have something in common.'" With thousands of content choices, especially under the VOD banner, most consumers are intimidated with the common VOD—and DVR—navigation process. Whether they navigate via channel choice or via actor or actress choice, Knorr knows his VOD and DVR consumers find it tough to keep track of what they have watched.

Using Digeo, Motorola, and Pace branded set-top DVRs, Sunflower Broadband is also keen on tracking DVR growth among its peers. Knorr notes two other small cable operators, i.e., Armstrong and Cable One, as being particularly aggressive, and adept, at growing the small cable DVR–VOD pie. Cable One, in fact, these days deploys *only* set-top box units with DVRs included. Standard set-top units (i.e., those without DVRs built into them) are no longer part of the Cable One lineup.

In general, concerning his digital challenges, Knorr notes, "We are not the biggest, the most innovative, nor the most aggressive, but we are still in the lead time wise, and that has been good; that said, we have not more aggressively pursued DVRs and VOD at times because they both can be so damned expensive."

Coming back to the idea of the future growth of both DVRs and VOD, in his small-to-medium-sized cable operation, Knorr insists, "Programmers should be falling all over themselves to create personalized buckets, and working with navigation companies to get to that. It really needs to be a web interface to put together a profile for their VOD and DVR interests."

Suggestions Knorr offers the industry, to speed up and facilitate an easy and quick interface between screens, set-tops, and multichannel pay TV operators, on the one hand, and consumers, on the other hand, are (1) create a web interface to put together a profile of each user's VOD and DVR interests; (2) have cable operators work with companies like TiVo and Digeo to create profiling that leads to more recommendations, especially when a networked DVR underlies the system; and (3) reintroduce things like DVR–VOD keyboards, or voice recognition systems, which allow consumers to more readily interface to both request content choices and to also create their own content profiles.

In the end, Knorr summarizes his current view of the DVR–VOD conundrum, "You have to make it easier for people to customize—and access—their entertainment."

Sunflower Broadband

Contact Information
1 Riverfront Plaza
Lawrence, KS 66044
Phone: 785-841-2100
http://www.sunflowerbroadband.com

Stock Symbol
Privately held

Key People
Patrick Knorr, COO
Rod Kutemeier, GM
PR Contact: 785-841-2100

Key Business
An independent local cable operator that has expanded its services to include telephone and broadband Internet support.

DVR Connection
Offers DVR services

2.2.2   In the Future

Because EchoStar purchased the company Sling Media, in late 2007, the marriage of the DISHPlayer and the Sling Media technologies has already begun. Thus, industry observers expect the combination of EchoStar and Sling Media technology and engineering to create many new and advanced portable services and devices built around the idea of a DVR-like storage, together with portability. This movement will go hand-in-hand with the huge trend toward mobile devices and mobile content applications that is currently sweeping the world.

Moreover, realistically, as long as recording can be done safely, legally, optimally, and profitably, there really is a future, no limit to where a DVR or a DVR-like device can be deployed.

A study of the data from the Arlington, VA-based Consumer Electronics Association (CEA), all used with permission, shows that, in Figure 2.3, for each of 2008 and 2009, nearly 50 million units will be shipped. In both years, that represents more than four billion dollars in annual sales to dealers by CEA's core constituents, the CE manufacturers. Average unit prices for these set-top boxes come in for each of 2008 and 2009 at around $90. Note that in the past 4–5 years, the units sold and the dollar sales have just about doubled.

Many CE aficionados would call that a healthy hardware business. Indeed, the CEA, in its annual publication, "U.S. Consumer Electronics, Sales and Forecasts, 2004–2009" (costing $2000), calls the entire category of set-top boxes "a growth engine." This is in large measure because many other CE categories are leveling out. Included within this robust set-top category are DVRs, DBS receivers, cable/multisystem operator

(MSO) receivers, digital media adapters (DMAs), Internet protocol-based television (IPTV), and digital-to-analog boxes.

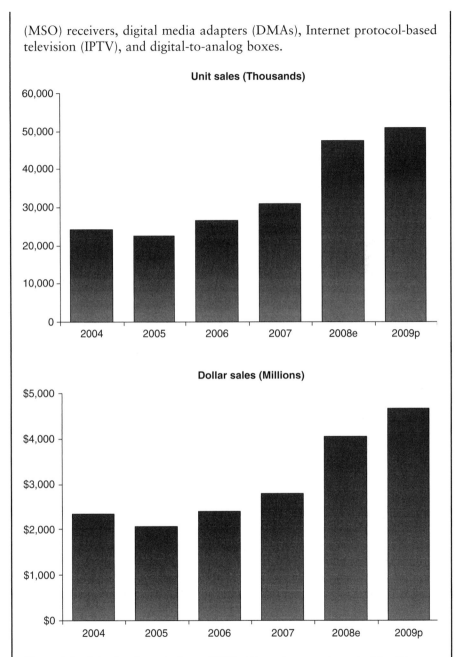

Figure 2.3 Sales by the end of year 2009 will reach approximately 50 million units of set-top boxes and dollar sales approaching 4.5 billion, according to the sales data supplied by the CEA. e = estimated and p = projected. (Copyright 2008. Property of the Consumer Electronics Association (CEA). Used with permission. All rights reserved.)

CEA's "U.S. Consumer Electronics, Sales and Forecasts, 2004–2009," cites two trends driving this growth. First would be the expanding retail market for cable set-top boxes at retail. The key to this growth comes from efforts to standardize set-top boxes, allowing consumers to buy a set-top box at retail, from a number of choices, and then take it home and insert a Cable Card that then adapts that particular set-top box to the user and to the system's specifications.

According to CEA, this attempt to more fully implement industry standardization in the set-top realm "... is expected to open up new markets for advanced cable boxes, thereby pushing shipment revenues up 20% in 2008, to $1.3 billion at wholesale."

The second major trend pushing the growth of set-top boxes through 2009 is media extension, which is also driven by advanced features inside the set-top boxes. CEA points out products such as "... Slingbox, Roku's Vudu box, and other Microsoft Vista-based media extenders ..." that are expected to greatly advance the idea of Internet-delivered and PC-based content coming to the living room and every other TV in the typical American TV household.

Looking specifically at the DVR numbers, it is important to note that the category does not break out standalone vs. integrated set-top boxes, although certainly remote DVRs are not included. CEA, in Table 2.1, points out that the DVR category includes "all set-top boxes with hard disk recording capability." Worth also noting is the growth in units sold, growing an estimated almost six times in 6 years, from 2004 to 2009. Dollar sales during the same time frame have more than quadrupled, moving from $635 million in 2004 to a projected $2.7 billion in 2009. Moreover, the average unit price during the same 2004–2009 gap has declined from $190 to $144.

Finally, note that consideration of DVR growth also needs to be made in the growth of three other set-top box categories and charts listed in this case study. These include DBS, MSO, and IPTV, all of which will offer

Table 2.1 Digital Video Recorders

| Year | Sales to Dealers | | |
	Unit Sales (thousands)	Dollar Sales (millions)	Average Unit Price
2004	3,345	$635	$190
2005	3,174	$532	$168
2006	4,980	$975	$196
2007	8,912	$1,580	$177
2008e	15,180	$2,429	$160
2009p	19,327	$2,783	$144

e = estimated; p = projected.

DVRs as standard fare in more deployments within these three sets of numbers (see Tables 2.2–2.5).

Table 2.2 Direct Broadcast Satellite Receivers

Year	Sales to Dealers		
	Unit Sales (thousands)	Dollar Sales (millions)	Average Unit Price
2004	16,250	$1,706	$105
2005	13,939	$1,366	$98
2006	13,888	$1,278	$92
2007	14,025	$1,220	$87
2008e	13,788	$1,131	$82
2009p	12,940	$996	$77

Table 2.3 Cable/MultiSystem Operator Receivers

Year	Sales to Dealers		
	Unit Sales (thousands)	Dollar Sales (millions)	Average Unit Price
2004	7,750	$574	$74
2005	8,463	$643	$76
2006	11,208	$874	$78
2007	13,235	$1,085	$82
2008e	14,780	$1,301	$88
2009p	16,450	$1,579	$96

Table 2.4 Digital Media Adapters[3]

Year	Sales to Dealers		
	Unit Sales (thousands)	Dollar Sales (millions)	Average Unit Price
2004	95	$24	$249
2005	175	$40	$228
2006	235	$53	$225
2007	634	$152	$240
2008e	2,250	$563	$250
2009p	4,500	$1,058	$235

[3] A Digital Media Adapter (DMA) is defined as a home entertainment media device that can connect to a home network to retrieve digital media files, typically from a personal computer or other media server, and play them back on a TV or home theatre system.

Table 2.5 Internet Protocol-Based Television

Year	Sales to Dealers		Average Unit Price
	Unit Sales (thousands)	Dollar Sales (millions)	
2004	75	$13	$175
2005	170	$26	$150
2006	505	$69	$136
2007	1,470	$187	$127
2008e	3,120	$371	$119
2009p	4,970	$557	$112

Consumer Electronics Manufacturer Association

Contact Information
1919 S. Eads St., Arlington, VA 22202
http://www.ce.org

Stock Symbol
N/A

Key People
Gary Shapiro, President and CEO
PR Contact: Jason Oxman
Phone: 703-907-7664

Key Business
Made up of 2200 companies within the global consumer technology industry. Conducts market research, networking opportunities with business advocates and leaders, educational programs and technical training, promotions and representation industry voice, promoting and advancing member needs and interests.

DVR Connection
Arbitrates disputes over DVR technology and capabilities. Researches impact of DVR on hardware/software manufacturers, advertisers, and consumers.

2.3 Why (A DVR Works?)

The answer to the question, "Why a DVR?" comes best from a simple response covering the concept of the viewer choosing, and being in control of, the what, when, where, and how he or she will watch every program. Being able to choose to watch, not watch, or watch later any form of content is the ultimate expansion of any business going from basic and functional to way beyond basic and, indeed, exceptional. Few would grouse at the word "exceptional" being used to describe what the functionality of a DVR does to basic TV viewing. This is another answer to the question of "Why a DVR Works?"

2.4 When (a DVR Works?)

The concept of a DVR is attractive whenever someone is observing or listening to data, music, video, or other content. In large measure, subtly, because we are a world of—and in much of the world, a culture of—*choices*, having a DVR adds a quality of life because it adds those choices to basic TV viewing. The DVR choice also usually requires no more than minimal cost and minimal effort. Just as importantly, the idea of a DVR is the idea of expanded personal control[4] over that data, music, video, or other content. These themes of *choice, control*, and *convenience* are repeated in this book, and are dominant ones that pervade the global telecom industry, now and possibly forever into the future. The quote at the beginning of this chapter from DVR hardware industry leader Scientific-Atlanta (Cisco) further elucidates this "C,C,C Concept."

Interestingly, the question of "when"—in the temporal sense—also must be addressed in this section. Thus, it is obvious that DVRs get core use when users are actually viewing content in front of their TV screens. This is the time during which live shows are recorded, paused, rewound, and sometimes fast forwarded. It is also the time when other DVR functionality, such as setting up recording shows for later access, is utilized. Thus, what is sometimes overlooked is the idea of a DVR operating when no one is watching TV, indeed when no one is around to do anything at all to the TV or the DVR. In this case, for example, shows are recorded as part of a "series recording" feature that most DVRs offer. This capability is particularly attractive because it means that if someone cannot be present to actually turn on the set or the recording device, that it will do that function automatically by itself.

Carrying this automatic-recording idea one step further, several DVR makers are deploying or planning to deploy DVR features that allow a DVR user to use the telephone or the Internet to signal the DVR at home to record a given show from any distance away from the home. Thus, if a DVR user is at work, miles away from his or her DVR in the home, this function permits him or her

---

[4] The personal control by the viewer is necessary if DVRs are going to work from a property rights point of view. This means that under the concept of "fair use," that was highlighted in the U.S. Supreme Court's 1984 *Sony Betamax* case decision, individual users of devices such as VCRs and DVRs have a limited right to record and replay for personal use, the content they receive. Conversely, individual users of VCRs and DVRs are restricted from copying and making commercial use of the content they receive. They are further restricted from conveying recorded versions of shows to others.

to use a cell phone to trigger the DVR at home to record a show that had not previously been programmed. This then becomes the idea of doing the opposite of what a Slingbox or DISHPlayer does and having the DVR receive—instead of send—a signal from a remote device.

In the author's first book in the NAB/Focal Press *Executive Briefing Series,* entitled *Digital Signage—Software, Networks, Advertising, and Displays: A Primer for Understanding the Business,* the point was made that digital signage has such great capability (and potential), that the better question became, "when should digital signage *not* be used?" The same holds true to an even greater extent for DVRs.

Nonetheless, there may come a point in the future when other devices and other technologies, such as VOD and video downloads, create a situation where in-home DVRs do not work. This is because these and other technologies may well subsume the DVR capability within their own technologies. For example, as cable operators such as industry leader, Comcast, build their VOD libraries into the tens of thousands of choices, a 90+ percentage of which are free on demand, the need of a consumer to record a desirable show becomes less and less. Accessibility trumps recordability. In addition, because true two-way VOD permits a viewer to also stop, rewind, and fast forward live content, the VOD service negates the need of the DVR for that function.

This and similar concepts are discussed in greater depth and detail in Chapter 8.

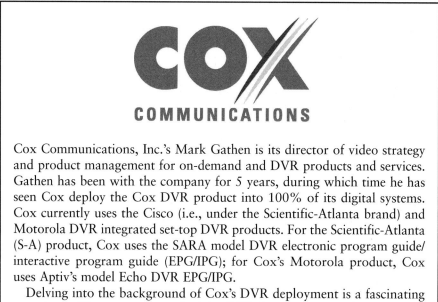

Cox Communications, Inc.'s Mark Gathen is its director of video strategy and product management for on-demand and DVR products and services. Gathen has been with the company for 5 years, during which time he has seen Cox deploy the Cox DVR product into 100% of its digital systems. Cox currently uses the Cisco (i.e., under the Scientific-Atlanta brand) and Motorola DVR integrated set-top DVR products. For the Scientific-Atlanta (S-A) product, Cox uses the SARA model DVR electronic program guide/ interactive program guide (EPG/IPG); for Cox's Motorola product, Cox uses Aptiv's model Echo DVR EPG/IPG.

Delving into the background of Cox's DVR deployment is a fascinating experience. The core reason cited for DVR involvement early on was, in

Gathen's words, "We felt that the addition of a DVR service would add value for our digital video customers," and that since then, "The DVR product has become table stakes in the video communications industry. The DVR product is a ubiquitous offering from all video providers (e.g., cable, telco, and satellite), and our customers continue to upgrade to the DVR as part of their video package."

Asked about the method behind Cox's choice of the new DVR for customers in its 19-nationwide systems, Gathen replies, "We followed the same method of discovery and due diligence as we do when determining to launch any video product. This includes market analysis, product analysis, and a focus on the potential product's business case/model." Moving to the question of measuring the effectiveness of the DVR deployment, Gathen responds, "At Cox, we measure customer satisfaction with our product through numerous internal research initiatives. This research continues to deliver positive satisfaction ratings and results from our DVR customers."

Cox's primary benefits of using or being involved with DVRs have been customer satisfaction, which in the multichannel world equates to more customers and fewer customers that leave the service or "churn." For the future, much of the development focus of the DVR product is to increase the amount of storage, in the form of larger internal hard drives. This is deemed especially relevant in the day and age of HD and customers recording HD content, which Cox supports via the offering of external hard drives and special ports, Cox calls these eSATA ports. These special set-top box connections allow transmission of content from the integrated set-top box to the external or side-car hard drive. It is worth noting, however, that still most customers today continue to record mostly standard definition linear content solely on the internal hard drive situated within their integrated set-top box receiver.

Distribution of the Cox cable service DVR is done solely through Cox's system, by shipping the DVR direct to customer's homes; providing the DVR to customers at one of Cox's customer care counters; or in the form of a truck-roll by a Cox technician, who then sets up the integrated set-top DVR (or multiple DVRs more frequently these days), within the consumer's home.

For more on Cox's future, Gathen shows solid optimism as it relates to the DVR product/service. He adds, "We continue to include the DVR as an important piece of our digital video offering. We see strong value and continued growth with the current DVR product and future DVR product offerings, such as the multiroom DVR." Looking further ahead, Mark Gathen believes, like most in the industry today, that the biggest threat to the continued growth of DVRs, specifically, is the expansion of on-demand product offerings and other time-shifted products, such as "Start-Over." "Start-Over" is an on-demand feature offered by many terrestrially delivered multichannel pay TV operators, which permits a customer to merely push a button, and then, any show presently in play will immediately start over at its beginning.

On the "opportunities" side of DVRs, Cox believes, "Customers continue to want more control over their viewing of video products ... they want to time-shift and customize, when and what they will be viewing. DVR technology enables them to manage 'what' and 'when,' then watch their television." Gathen says consumers are hugely attracted to the concept of "time-shifted live TV ... especially the ability to pause live TV." Asked about areas of needed improvement for Cox and its customers, the question of more storage is often repeated and Cox is addressing that need aggressively.

Moving to advertising and its involvement with Cox's DVR system, currently Cox is not involved with any third parties that use its DVRs for advertising purposes. This is another way of saying that, for the time being, Cox does not use DVRs to do things such as collect data and information about users and their preferences. Moreover, on a broader scale as it relates to advertisers and Cox's relationship with them, especially as it relates to staples of the TV-advertising environment, Gathen adds, "Currently Cox does not allow customers to individually skip ads—we do not support or enable a 30-second skip feature."

Concluding with thoughts about DVR regulations, Mark Gathen suggests, as it relates to transferring content to others, "As partners with our content providers, we support the protection of the high-value content distributed to our customers. We also support the viewing of content within the customer's 'trusted domain,' and are in full compliance with FCC regulations on copy protection and digital rights management (DRM)." Numerous Cox in-house DVR user studies support the opinions and data represented in this case study according to Gathen.

Cox Communications

Contact Information
1400 Lake Hearn Drive, Atlanta, Georgia 30319
Phone: 404-843-5000
http://www.cox.com

Stock Symbol
A privately held subsidiary of Cox Enterprises

Key People
Patrick J. Esser, President
James C. Kennedy, Chairman
PR Contact: Todd Smith, PR Manager, 404-269-3124

Key Business
Provides digital cable television and telecommunication services in the United States.

DVR Connection
Offers DVR and HD DVR add-ons to digital cable offerings.

2.5 Summary

This chapter provides the what, where, how, why, and when of DVRs. These basics are, in a way, the machine that runs the consumer DVR industry. It is also the chapter where key business data reside. This is information such as the number of projected sales and dollar income, as well as industry information from a key industry trade group reflecting its past, present, and future. Moreover, the three case studies—those of Sunflower Broadband, CEA, and Cox—give flavor and application to the tenets discussed in detail within the chapter.

3 The Business of DVRs

The networks and the advertisers have to talk, because [the DVR] threatens both networks and advertisers, if they don't.
— Brad Ancier, research consultant, Horizon Media, Inc.[1]

The industry still has a long ways to go, but as the DVR becomes an integral part of the digital home, I believe that the cable and satellite industries will abandon the monopolistic practices of the past and will end up benefitting more from the intense competition in the consumer electronics space.
— Davis Freeburg, "How TV Monopolies Benefit From DVR Industry Competition," from Seeking Alpha, September 29, 2006

DVR makers, networks, copyright owners, and Congress will have to work together to find a mutually agreeable path on which to take this technological revolution.
— Ashley A. Johnson, law student, Duke Law and Technology Review

The lion's share of today's global DVR industry is housed within the United States, because the United States provided the first truly fertile ground and receptive environment—both on the part of the multichannel pay TV industry and on the part of the U.S. consumer—that were necessary to overcome financial, legal, marketing, regulatory, and many other challenges during its early life cycle, i.e., 1998–2007. Nonetheless, to truly assess the current scope of the DVR industry, it is necessary to review Chapter 7, "International DVR Growth," and to appreciate the impact coming from global DVR deployments focused primarily on Europe and Asia but also on South America and Canada in the next 5–7 or so years.

As for numbers, within the United States today, approximately 40 million cable, telco, and satellite consumers daily enjoy the wonders their DVRs allow them to perform, choosing and controlling their programming. Globally, The Carmel Group estimates that there are nearly 60 million DVR households (HHs) as of the end of 2008. The U.S. DVR cumulative industry revenues for 2008 are estimated at approximately $15 billion. Figure 3.1 shows this 1999–2010 revenue growth figure. Compare these with Figures 1.6–1.10, which show one forecaster's DVR subscriber projections through the end of 2010, in the form of four separate charts.

What promises to be most interesting will be how DVRs develop in the Brave New World of Post-Broadcast Digital TV, which will begin officially in the United States on June 12, 2009. In this new environment, because of rich new

---

[1] Horizon Media describes itself as an advertising consultant. For more information about the company see http://www.horizonmedia.com

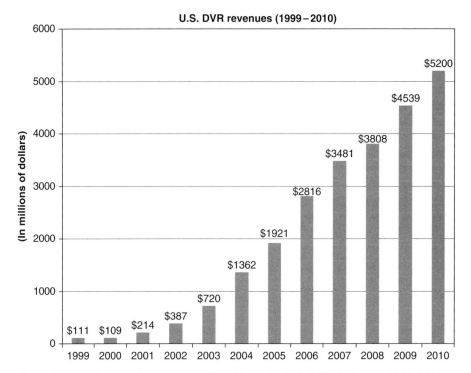

Figure 3.1 Estimates of revenues attributable to the U.S. DVR industry, 1999–2010. These are aimed at providing the reader with a clearer snapshot of U.S. DVR growth and estimates through the end of 2010. (Copyright 2009. Property of the Carmel group. All rights reserved. Used with permission.)

digital spectrum that is turned over to broadcasters, many are faced with the opportunity of becoming much more active in the future of the DVR industry, especially as many of them begin their own versions of multichannel TV services, some of which may even be pay or subscription based.

Nonetheless, looking much further out on the horizon, two technological developments stand to weaken, or completely eliminate, the DVR industry as we know it today. These would be VOD and network storage DVR systems, such as the remote storage DVR (RS-DVR) system proposed by Cablevision Systems, Long Island, NY. If these two technologies continue to grow and flourish, they can be seen logically to ultimately absorb or consume what an in-home set-up DVR does for most consumers. The original DVR function would instead be but a small part of the broader interactive user interface that is merely hinted at today, replaced what DVRs and VOD do as one system. That said, even in its most successful iteration, the combination of DVR, VOD, and remote storage networks will still leave a place for in-home, individual DVR units, at least for a minority of users who still will wish to have more direct control over and access to their own individual content.

Perhaps most important to the future of DVRs is the fact that their functionality transitions more from that of serving an elite few to that of serving mass audiences around the world. DVR ubiquity becomes the norm. Thus, ultimately, no matter what the content or the media, a DVR-like device will be there to record it and to store it, possibly forever. In this so-called future DVR world, the ultimate challenge may become not the ability to record life and all its aspects, but rather the effort to make sure it *is not* recorded in a handful of instances.

Motorola has been in the business of manufacturing set-top boxes for cable operators for decades, and DVRs for more than 5 years. Bernadette Vernon, Motorola's director of strategic marketing for video, leads marketing communications, market research, and channel programs for the company's set-top business.

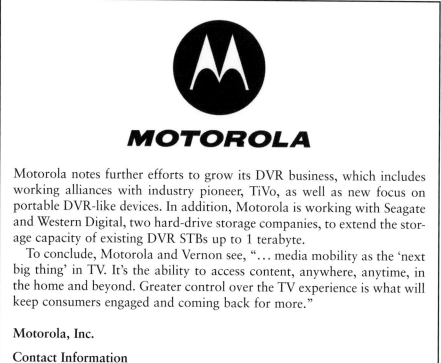

Motorola notes further efforts to grow its DVR business, which includes working alliances with industry pioneer, TiVo, as well as new focus on portable DVR-like devices. In addition, Motorola is working with Seagate and Western Digital, two hard-drive storage companies, to extend the storage capacity of existing DVR STBs up to 1 terabyte.

To conclude, Motorola and Vernon see, "… media mobility as the 'next big thing' in TV. It's the ability to access content, anywhere, anytime, in the home and beyond. Greater control over the TV experience is what will keep consumers engaged and coming back for more."

Motorola, Inc.

Contact Information
1303 E. Algonquin Rd., Schaumburg, IL 60196
Phone: 847-576-5000
http://www.motorola.com

Stock Symbol
NYSE: MOT

Key People
Greg Brown and Sanjay Jha, Co-CEOs
Bernadette Vernon, Director of Strategic Marketing for Video
Phone: (215) 323-2107
PR Contact: Maya Komadina
Phone: (847) 538-5625

Key Business
Manufacturer of wireless telephone handsets, cable, and satellite TV set-top box hardware, and wireless network infrastructure equipment HDTVs.

DVR Connection
Manufacturer of set-top boxes and DVRs used by cable and satellite service providers.

Motorola manufactured and deployed its first set-top DVR for the cable industry in 2003. Focusing on the growing popularity of HDTV, Motorola's DVR led the industry by offering a combination of HD and digital recording capabilities. Although it was not the first DVR on the market—satellite operators were the DVR frontrunners—it proved quite popular, and both Motorola and the cable industry saw significant growth in DVR revenues in a few years. Indeed, within a brief 4 years or so, the U.S. cable industry's DVR numbers would surpass those of the U.S. satellite TV industry.

Motorola and the U.S. cable industry began discovering what many had sensed early on: the combination of HD, DVR, and fast-growing VOD services was a compelling one—a differentiated package that only the landline multichannel pay TV operators, such as cable and telco video suppliers—could offer. Recognizing where consumers wanted to go with DVR technology, Motorola began focusing more and more on a completely changed viewing experience, with time-shifted television at the heart of the transition from consumer notions of "primetime TV" to "my time TV."

Current Motorola multichannel pay TV cable customers include Comcast, Cox, Charter, Time Warner Cable, Mediacom, Insight and numerous other U.S., Canadian, and Latin American operators. Vernon notes that Motorola also works closely with top national cable trade groups, including the National Cable Telecommunications Association (NCTA), the Society of Cable Telecommunications Engineers (SCTE), the Cable and Telecommunications Association for Marketing (CTAM), and the National Cable Television Cooperative (NCTC). As of the first quarter 2008, Motorola notes it had over 10 million of its HD DVR set-top boxes in the field, from a total of 16 million Motorola HD set-top boxes produced through that 2003–2008 time frame. Validating Motorola's decision to continue to hone in on HD, the company no longer produces SD DVR set-top boxes. One could argue a trend away from the manufacture and deployment of SD DVRs has materialized.

Today, Motorola prides itself on being one of the first to release an HD DVR, in the form of the Motorola DCT 6000 family, which was launched in 2003. Per Vernon, Motorola realized the riskiness of spending on the development of an HD DVR, because of the relatively small number of HD TV sets in North America at the time. Nonetheless, Motorola felt the future growth trends for HD TV were worth investing in as a competitive measure, and because "... consumers wanted the 'ultimate video experience,' which is to say HD and DVR together," summarizes Vernon. Indeed, the Motorola gamble on HD DVRs has paid off, judged, in part, by the fact that just about every major DVR provider today offers an HD DVR.

Noting additional trends it has tracked (and reacted to), Vernon cites an early Motorola focus on the cable industry—going back to the earliest days of General Instruments, the set-top box manufacturer that Motorola acquired in 2000. This is a focus that later expanded to also include the telco providers. This trend to invest heavily in cable and telco included ongoing development in VOD technology, which continues to increase consumer demand for choice and control in the TV watching experience. VOD led, quite naturally, into the deployment of DVRs. One of the prevalent trends Motorola is currently also responding to is that of "video on any device and ... multiroom DVR," as Vernon describes it. As a prime example of this trend, Motorola is assisting Verizon in rapidly filling the vacuum of demand, exercised by eager Verizon consumers, who seek to view the same video when moving from room to room. For today, Motorola touts Verizon's deployments as a model of future multiroom DVR and content distribution capabilities.

3.1 Legal and Regulatory Issues

The legal case brought by the Hollywood studios and New York City networks against ReplayTV in 2001 is probably one of the better examples of the plethora of legal questions that faced much of the DVR industry early in its life cycle. The case *Paramount Pictures Corp. et al vs. ReplayTV* grappled with a special—yet critically important—issue of copyright, that is, the doctrine of "fair use,"[2] as well as other copyright issues, such as restrictions

---

[2] Duke University law student Ashley A. Johnson's noted 2001 treatise "Hacking Digital Video Recorder: Potential Copyright Liability For DVR Hackers and Service Providers," found at http://www.law.duke.edu/journals/dltr/articles/2001dltr0029.html, places the topic of "fair use" and what might be termed DVR piracy, or hacking, in good context when she notes on page 4 (of 16), "The typical user of a DVR uses the device for time shifting, whether she records broadcasted programming to view later or pauses live TV. The mere fact that the recording is now in digital form instead of tape does not change the nature of the use. Thus, under *Sony*, private noncommercial home viewing of DVR recordings is fair use. Neither the consumer nor a DVR company is liable for any copyright violations. However, potential copyright infringement may result from making extracted video available to the public...."

on using the new storage and content control technology to create a new work.

Other legal and regulatory issues that have arisen through the years since 1998 include the two core areas of (1) patent infringement and (2) privacy. Each is discussed here.

3.1.1 Paramount vs. ReplayTV

As noted in Chapter 5, "Business Models," the two first pioneers on the standalone DVR unit side of the consumer DVR industry, TiVo and ReplayTV, were faced with significant challenges—as well as a huge opportunity—as they approached the nascent market representing the future of storing TV content. Ultimately, within a few years of their creation, one would be bankrupt, and the other would be on its way toward becoming the industry standard for many years henceforth. Perhaps as important, together they would introduce a new technology and viewing model that would, within a few months for the multichannel pay TV operators and within a few years for huge swaths of viewers, become the new "can't live without it, TV-watching norm."

Because ReplayTV chose to spend more time pushing the legal bounds of technology and because it pushed those bounds much faster than rival TiVo, ReplayTV found itself in turmoil a couple years into its official launch during the first half of 1999. As noted in Chapter 1, rival TiVo and ReplayTV were fierce competitors when it came to being the first to unveil DVR technology, and an actual DVR product, late in the millennium. Yet once released, ReplayTV quickly sought out other developmental gimmicks, which it hoped would take it ahead of its key rivals during its first years of business, that is, TiVo (and DirecTV, via the TiVo-DirecTV alliance) and EchoStar.

One key feature which ReplayTV championed, called "ad-skip," allowed users to push a button and automatically skip an entire set of commercials in a given recorded show, without having to view anything at all of the show's ad content. The other new feature, called "send show," permitted users to email to as many as 15 of their family and friends (or others?) digital copies for their own viewing, of any show desired.

ReplayTV aggressively developed and marketed these and similar features for more than 2 years following its first set-top box sale. These and similar activities distinguished ReplayTV relative to TiVo during the two companies' startup years. Indeed, inside insight suggests that because TiVo units also outsold ReplayTV at retail, ReplayTV tried to compete more aggressively on the basis of these distinguishing features, such as "send show" and "ad-skip." Yet, because the television and Hollywood studio companies sensed great actual and/or potential damage to their respective business models, they joined together through their trade group, The Motion Picture Association of America (MPAA), and sued ReplayTV in 2001. Additional plaintiffs joining the case included Paramount, Metro-Goldwyn-Mayer (MGM), Columbia Tri-Star, Fox, Orion, Time-Warner/Turner, Disney, ABC, NBC, Showtime, and ABC, as well as Viacom and CBS. The plaintiffs' complaint argued that the "send show" feature allowed unauthorized and uncompensated copies of shows to be improperly distributed[3]; the "ad-skip" complaint argued that taking the ads from a show essentially permitted ReplayTV (and the consumer) to unilaterally alter the original content of every show in a way which the law would not permit.[4]

The *Paramount et al vs. ReplayTV* case eventually settled and resulted in an order in 2002, shortly after Japanese tech company SonicBlue bought ReplayTV. The settlement compelled plaintiff ReplayTV/SonicBlue to cease permitting the controversial "send show" and the "ad-skip" features.[5]

Ultimately, in some significant measure because of the TV and motion picture company resistance to ReplayTV's aggressiveness, and the resultant law suit they filed, ReplayTV's business model was fatally harmed, and ReplayTV was sold to Japan-based SonicBlue in 2001. Unable to right the ReplayTV ship, SonicBlue itself sought bankruptcy protection in 2003. Thereafter, the company was again sold to D & M Holdings, another Japanese entity, in the same year, which was again sold to DirecTV in 2007.

3.1.2 Patent Infringement

Because of the creativity and newness represented by the DVR business, both on the software and the hardware sides of the business, and because this process is managed by sophisticated businesses and the basis of the inventions represents big dollars, many patents have been filed in and around the DVR industry. And, many continue to be filed, as the technology is further developed, morphed, and refined. This goes as far back as the pioneer "Goldwasser" patent of 1991, which is discussed more thoroughly in Chapter 1. Indeed, because of its closeness to the interactive TV business, going back to such seminal cases as the *Gemstar-TVGuideline*, there have been an inordinate number of DVR patent litigations.

Key among these have been two sets of DVR patent litigation. One involves TiVo as the plaintiff, it having sued the multichannel pay TV operator EchoStar

---

[3] ReplayTV's send show technique was also claimed to be a violation of the "fair use" doctrine that was established in the seminal U.S. Supreme Court *Sony Betamax* case.

[4] See *DGA vs. ClearPlay* for the basis of this argument and this line of cases.

[5] TiVo offers a way to skip through advertisements in a program using a "30-second skip" function in its set-top DVR boxes; however, TiVo decided to make it a more subtle offering, one which TiVo calls an "undocumented feature." This means the "30-second skip" in TiVo set-top boxes is a functionality that can be removed by TiVo anytime it wishes, without prior warning to the consumer, because it is not officially part of the TiVo product and is not marketed as a feature. As part of its business analysis, TiVo realized early on that the 30-second skip feature would upset the TV networks (several of which became DVR company investors). TiVo also decided that it was better to compel users to actually fast forward through the ads (rather than to have them automatically skipped), because the user then actually viewed what was being skipped—albeit at speeds many times that of normal viewing. Today, TiVo offers its own advertising solutions that depend, in part, on viewers not completely skipping TV ads.

successfully for the violation of TiVo's multimedia time-warp patent. The other involved another company that claimed it created or acquired core early DVR patents, called Forgent.

The first TiVo case against EchoStar was filed at the instigation of former TiVo president, Marty Yudkovitz, and then CEO of TiVo, Michael Ramsay, in 2004. This case was litigated for several years and resulted in a jury verdict for TiVo, with damages amounting to more than $70 million, in 2007. That verdict was appealed all the way to the U.S. Supreme Court, where, in the Fall of 2008, it was upheld in favor of TiVo. TiVo has since received a damages check, including interest, of more than $100 million from EchoStar. Almost concurrently with this case, EchoStar and TiVo brought other claims against one another, one of which involved the question of whether a "work-around" EchoStar is claiming allows it to keep using DVR software in its set-top boxes, without paying TiVo and/or without violating TiVo's patent (and without having to replace hundreds of thousands of set-top DVR units).

In the case of Texas-based Forgent, it brought its case to the point of settlement with just about every defendant (including satellite TV vendor DirecTV, and cable TV vendors Charter, Cox, Comcast, Time Warner and Cable One), to the tune of nearly $30 million collectively. Nonetheless, this time legal matters went in favor of EchoStar. EchoStar successfully convinced a jury to invalidate the Forgent patent claim, emerging victorious in 2006. Many legal observers note rather ironically that EchoStar used the Goldwasser patent owned by TiVo—the same one it had earlier disputed—to make its winning claim in the Forgent patent case.

In yet another litigation involving TiVo, a 2001 patent infringement case titled *Pause Technologies vs. TiVo*, TiVo again emerged victorious. Pause Technologies' patent purportedly covered a way of pausing live television, replaying portions of a program while it is being recorded and fast forwarding through recorded segments to "catch up" to a live broadcast being recorded. A Massachusetts U.S. District Court found that TiVo had not violated the plaintiff's "Time Delayed Digital Video System Using Concurrent Recording and Playback" patent, which covered both video and audio systems. Earlier in the same year, Motorola became the first company to license the so-called Pause Patent for its forthcoming line of PVR-enabled set-top boxes.

3.1.3 Privacy

From the earliest days as a flashy new technology, DVRs have evoked visions of George Orwell and his "Big Brother," i.e., a super government controlling entity that, for example, can collect information about the number of pornographic or revolutionary shows a viewer watched, and turn that over to law enforcement or the media, with obvious results. Yet, fully appreciating that concern about privacy from the start, executives at TiVo and ReplayTV were quite circumspect when it came to which consumer data were collected (if any at all), which user it was linked to, who received and who used it, and when it could be used for what.

Industry pioneer TiVo, for example, openly states that it uses, or "mines" its customers' use data. Yet, to be certain, TiVo insists that it makes use of these data only according to the "stringent policy guidelines" it maintains. For example, TiVo consumers are given three important options as it relates to their data: (1) by default, TiVo only collects anonymous viewing information (i.e., it cannot be traced back to the viewer); (2) viewers can opt out completely, not permitting any viewing data to be gathered from them and their DVR usage; or (3) they can purposely opt in to make their data "identifiable" (to them) for certain uses. TiVo goes to great lengths to point out that the "opt in" is required in the form of an intentional act by the consumer and that TiVo is, as a company, a "privacy fanatic."

Super Bowl XXXVIII, which was broadcast live on February 1, 2004, from Houston, TX, highlighted TiVo's data-collection abilities, as critics were bothered by the ability of TiVo to gather the number of TiVo subscribers playing back and viewing again Janet Jackson's and Justin Timberlake's halftime performance that involved baring Jackson's breast. This was not the first time that concerns had been raised about TiVo's data-collection capabilities. In 2001, the Federal Trade Commission conducted an inquiry into TiVo's privacy practices, which resulted in TiVo authoring a top-level, 26-page white paper, which quelled future possible legal and governmental regulation of DVR companies (see http://www.tivo.com/abouttivo/policies/index.html).

3.1.4   Other Legal Matters

DVRs, from a legal and regulatory standpoint, make for fascinating developments and discussions. For example, early on in their life cycles, both TiVo and ReplayTV were greatly concerned by the prospect of legal and/or regulatory guidelines requiring them to obtain hundreds—indeed thousands—of individual content licenses to run their businesses. Early on, and perhaps even today, such restrictions would likely have killed their respective business models. For their part, counsel for these two companies instead turned to U.S. case law in the form of the *Sony Betamax* U.S. Supreme Court decision from 1984. That decision, supporting the concept of time-shifting, allowed TiVo and ReplayTV not only to avoid threats of early license and related requirements, but also to take several of the TV networks and studios so far down the road of DVR acceptance, so to speak, that several actually became significant investors in TiVo and ReplayTV in their early years. In the case of Time Warner/Turner, it had insisted on a license with TiVo as a condition to investment; when TiVo refused, Time Warner/Turner turned to ReplayTV, which agreed to the license, and the investment by Time Warner/Turner in ReplayTV was completed.

Other DVR legal regulatory concerns have had to do with how large the hard drive on a DVR could be (i.e., how much capacity to store content could be built into DVR set-top boxes); the legality of RS-DVR systems; the *Grokster* case, establishing again at the U.S. Supreme Court level that the *Betamax* decision had on-point applicability to future technologies; and various questions of trademark control and ownership coming from icons being displayed during on-screen programming.

Another unique DVR-related legal and regulatory matter arose in Lincoln, NE, in 2007, when the city challenged the local cable franchisee, Time Warner, over recurring problems consumers were having with the company's integrated set-top DVR. The matter points out greater concerns the DVR industry has relating to the limited choice consumers have within the cable, telco, and satellite industry subsectors, when it comes to choosing a DVR product and service. This topic will be covered in more detail in Chapter 5, "Business Models."

Moreover, as was the case with technological predecessor Xerox, TiVo (the only successful one of the two U.S. DVR pioneers), confronted problems of "overuse" and "misuse" as it related to its brand name. That brand name, TiVo, stood to lose its meaning as a brand and thus enable others to call their products TiVo, as well, had TiVo not resisted such use and promoted the generic term of digital video recorder or of DVR. Thus, for example, TiVo's in-house legal department has a long track record of reminding a reporter who stated he "TiVoed so-and-so-show," that what he needs to say is that he "used my [TiVo] DVR to record so-and-so program."

3.2 Financial

One way to look at the financial scope of the DVR industry is to look at the average revenue per unit (ARPU) represented by a satellite TV or cable or telco video customer. As an example, for the third quarter of 2008, DISH Network reported ARPU of $69.82, and rival DirecTV reported same period ARPU of $83.59. For EchoStar, with 13.8 million subscribers, which amounts to a gross monthly subscriber revenue of $963,526,000; for DirecTV with approximately 17.1 million subscribers, the same gross subscriber revenue per month sum comes to $1,429,389,000. Combining these two multichannel pay TV satellite providers, their ARPU for Q3 2008 amounted to $2,392,905,000. Importantly, a comfortable part of these revenues is attributable to DVR installations, DVR lease fees, and/or DVR-related purchases.

Financial data for several large, publicly traded companies are available online from each of those companies, typically by clicking on the link to "Investor Relations," followed by a link to a specific government filing and/or a link to a press release summarizing a particular result. Occasionally, such a document will mention in greater detail a company's DVR developments and/or results. Appendix B of this book includes the Web site addresses of more than 60 companies in and around the DVR industry today, each of which typically includes additional financial information.

Taken just one step further, add in DVR-related revenues from U.S. cable and telco DVR providers, and the billions noted above for the multichannel satellite pay TV providers quickly morphs into several billions of dollars more per month.

Add in the chip makers, the silicon providers, the hard-drive manufacturers, and all the other players in the DVR life cycle, and the revenue numbers truly amaze.

Another way to look at the financial scope of the DVR industry is to look at the millions spent on litigating certain technical and copyright aspects of the DVR industry, as well as the more than $100 million payment TiVo received in 2008 as a result of a jury verdict against EchoStar, as but one additional example.

Yet another way to view the DVR industry's financial scope is to look at the hundreds of millions of dollars that have been spent on developing and implementing DVR technology by the standalone companies like TiVo, Digeo, and ReplayTV; by the DVR hardware manufacturers, such as Panasonic, Sony, Cisco (formerly Scientific-Atlanta), and Motorola; and by the amounts spent by the cable, telco, and satellite TV companies—just to involve themselves in the DVR side of the business.

Furthermore, Figure 3.1 again offers a snap shot of actual annual revenues and forecast annual revenues through the year 2010, for the U.S. DVR industry as a whole. This chart and its data come from The Carmel Group, which has been studying DVR growth since 1998.

Looking specifically at a couple of publicly traded companies, to attempt to understand DVRs from their point of view, TiVo and DISH Network make for fascinating examples. TiVo has used the DVR Revolution to build its own unique place on the playing field that is DVRs, circa 2009. For third Q 2008, for example, TiVo noted the following exact highlights in its press release of November 25, 2008:

- [During 3Q '08] TiVo received compensation in the amount of approximately $105 million in initial litigation damages from EchoStar.
- Net income for the third quarter was $100.6 million compared to a loss of $8.3 million in the year-ago quarter. Excluding the EchoStar damages award net loss would have been $0.9 million.
- Adjusted EBITDA for the third quarter was $95.3 million, compared to $0.2 million in the year-ago quarter. Excluding the EchoStar damages award, adjusted EBITDA would have been $7.5 million.
- TiVo partners with Netflix to stream its library of over 12,000 videos directly to the TV.
- Comcast announces roll out of TiVo service to additional markets.
- TiVo extends distribution agreement with DirecTV; TiVo is now partnered with three of the top five television providers.

3.3 Marketing

There are truly six definable classes of DVRs for marketing purposes. One is that of DVRs placed, mostly in businesses globally, for security purposes. As noted elsewhere in the book, because this book, *DVRs: Changing TV and*

Advertising Forever, writes about consumer DVRs, the focus on commercial/ enterprise/business use of DVRs for security purposes is minimal.

The second truly definable DVR class is that of a standalone DVR. The third is a DVR that is part of a multichannel TV or other video provider's set-top box. A fourth is the equivalent of a DVR, in the form of a RS-DVR, where the storage is done by the multichannel TV operator at a remote locale. The fifth class is that of DVRs that are actually a hodge-podge of the core DVR concept, such as storage devices in flash form, or those intended for other devices, such as Slingboxes, or mobile satellite radio devices. The sixth class of DVRs involves custom home-made do-it-yourself DVRs.

For the DVR pioneer, like TiVo, it has two different DVR messages, for two distinct audiences. One is aimed at the standalone DVR purchaser, who is someone typically walking into a consumer electronics (CE) retail store, and looking for a DVR that is not necessarily tied to any one multichannel TV service provider. The message for this person is of all the functions that certain DVR models can perform, often beyond what might be offered by the local multichannel TV service provider.

On the other hand, with some overlap, a would-be TiVo DVR user (in a Comcast service area) interested in what his or her multichannel TV service provider might offer in the way of a TiVo DVR, might go to the Web site http:// www.comcast.net, for the cable service provider Comcast and seek out the latest on a TiVo set-top DVR co-developed by TiVo and Comcast, and distributed by Comcast. From an August 2008 TiVo press release, TiVo proudly states, "TiVo service on Comcast now available in Connecticut; Comcast will also continue to fund development work for the TiVo product to expand the feature set and add support to the Tru2way [cable] infrastructure." Other highlighted elements of the same press release include the following:

- Adjusted EBITDA for the second quarter was $10.6 million, compared to a loss of $11.2 million in the year-ago quarter, exceeding guidance.
- Net income for the second quarter was $2.9 million, compared to a loss of $17.7 million in the year-ago quarter.
- TiVo and *Entertainment Weekly* join forces to connect TV viewers with their favorite shows on an automatic basis.
- TiVo successfully launched in Australia by Seven Networks.
- YouTube videos now available on the TiVo service; TiVo now provides access to more television and broadband content choices than any other offering in the world.
- TiVo's recent research deals with media marketing research firm TRA, ties anonymous viewing behavior to product purchases in millions of homes, significantly changing the quality of information available to marketers.

For TiVo rival, Digeo, marketing comes via a dual message: First is the overall message of the Digeo service tackling the whole home media integration issue, with a focus on the TV experience, Diego uses digital cable as the primary constant source, but supplements that cable source with Internet video, music, photos, and information (such as news, weather, and sports). Another, more subtle message comes to the consumer in the form of a value message, assuming that the consumer has done his or her homework. Comparing the composite pricings of the hardware and the fees, Digeo believes it has created a quite competitive offering compared to its rivals in the standalone side of the DVR business. More about these kinds of marketing vis-à-vis business model discussions is covered in Chapter 5, devoted to the discussion of various sample business models (or sets of business models).

Marketing for a typical cable, satellite, or telco multichannel video service provider comes in the form of two messages. First would be that aimed at potential subscribers, and the other would be a marketing message aimed at getting existing subscribers to spend more, upgrade their services, and thus enhance the multichannel TV service provider's ARPU. These two messages aimed at these two audiences achieve the service providers' main goals as it relates to DVRs and related advanced service, that is, to bring in new subscribers and to keep those subscribers happy (and spending more).

Looking at the cable example of privately held Cox, headquartered in Atlanta, GA, its Web site, at http://www.cox.com, has a home page link to "Digital Video Recorders (DVRs)" under a heading of "Favorite Services Links." Appropriately, this DVR link resides between similar links such as "High definition services," (sic) "TV Listing," and "On Demand." Once on the Cox DVR page, a "View DVR demo" link is also offered, along with an "Order DVR" link, and between these two links, the site lists the following typical DVR features:

- Automatically record your favorite shows
- Pause and rewind live TV
- Record two programs at once
- Record an entire series
- Even record in high definition

Looking on the satellite TV side at DirecTV, for example, the online site, http://www.directv.com, has a "What To Watch" video window on the home page, which has a clip featuring the DirecTV "DVR Scheduler" functionality. Under the heading "Program your DVR using your computer or mobile phone," a spokesman tells consumers specifically how the free service works. Clicking onto the DirecTV Web site's site map, a category called "Receivers" offers links to view information about five DirecTV set-top boxes or similar receivers, two of which include DVRs. A Web site listing of the features of DirecTV's top-of-the-line HD DVRs includes the following:

- High definition (MPEG-2, MPEG-4) and standard definition (MPEG-2) enabled. View the best in both HD and SD programming.
- Record up to 200 hours of SD programming, and up to 50 hours of HD programming. Watch your favorite shows on your own schedule.
- DirecTV on demand capable. Enjoy 24/7 access to over 4000 movies and shows with DirecTV on demand. (Internet connection required.)
- Record two shows at once while watching another recording.

- Series Link feature: Automatically record an entire season of your favorite shows, even if they change day or time.
- One-touch record, auto record, manual record, and bookmarks.
- Pause and rewind live HD TV for up to 90 minutes. Control what you watch—back up, slow down, or use instant replay.
- Media Share capable: Listen to music and view photos stored on your Intel® Viiv™ processor technology-based PC.
- Two satellite tuners for access to SD and HD DirecTV programming.
- Take advantage of DirecTV interactive features like DirecTV Active™. Get weather information, lottery results, and horoscopes onscreen.
- 14-day Advanced Program Guide®. Search the channel guide for shows up to 14 days in advance.
- Dolby Digital 5.1 Surround Sound capable. Listen to superb theater-quality sound with additional hardware.
- View and log caller ID info provided by your local phone company.
- Parental controls/locks: Enjoy peace of mind over what your children are watching by locking out objectionable programming.

In print, in the form of a DirecTV startup kit for new users, called "The DirecTV Experience," probably the best marketing feature is an inside fold-out pamphlet that highlights all the programming channels on one side and all of the remote control features on the other side. The "Remote Reference" separates DirecTV's HD DVR remote control buttons into equipment controls, DVR controls, navigation controls, and interactive controls.

A third example of multichannel TV DVR marketing is Verizon's Web site at http://www.verizon.com, showing DVR marketing from a telco video provider. The home page offers a "Home Media DVR Upgrade" under the "Residential" service category. Clicking on the Verizon home page's "TV" link takes the Web surfer to another heading, "Free 90-day upgrade to our Home Media DVR." Beyond that, little more is said on the Verizon Web site about DVRs.

Marketing for RS-DVR type systems is quite limited in a public sense, inasmuch as the very theme and concept these types (of remote storage DVRs) remain under significant legal attack in the U.S. courts. Marketing for Slingbox, for example, is featured more specifically under the Slingbox discussion in Chapter 4 and via the Internet Web site http://www.slingmedia.com/. Slingbox Web site entry categories include "Products," "Support," "Downloads," "About," "Contact," and "Buy," Marketing for the XM/Sirius portable storage "Stiletto" brand satellite radio is displayed via the Internet at http://shop.sirius.com/edealinv/servlet/ExecMacro?nurl=control/StoreDirectory.vm&ctl_nbr=2640&catLevel=1&catPa rentID=7874&scId=7874&oldParentID=7870

Note, too, that each of these company's Web sites offers links to press releases and sometimes video ads highlighting DVR features, and these companies typically display ads for DVRs on TV, the Internet, and at various tradeshows and conferences. Digital signage—in cinemas, airports, outdoors, at retail and in elevators, for example—is another advertising source for DVR company marketing. Of course, other media, such as newspaper stuffers, magazines, and newspapers, are also used for DVR marketing purposes.

At the end of just about every DVR marketing discussion DVR-related companies and agencies have had, there is a specific challenge of convincing people who have never had a DVR that it is something worth obtaining. Many in the marketing community attribute this concern to the arguable mediocre growth of DVRs—especially relative to what they do and who has been involved in that—during the past 10 years. A September 6, 2005, article in *Mediaweek*, citing a study by researcher Magna Global, notes that many marketers also believe that vendors' decisions during these years to charge consumers for the DVR have further limited its growth potential. Media researcher, Nielsen, juxtaposes these rather mediocre marketing messages by noting 3Q 2008a 52% year-over-year increase in the average number of hours viewers watched time-shifted TV, going from under 3 hours to 6.

3.4   Programming Content

The fact that DVRs, in some studies, cause people to watch more TV and to watch TV programming that they never would have watched without the DVR is a quite telling message.

Yet, beyond those types of "DVR epiphanies," DVRs are also responsible for (1) getting content moved from one room to another, (2) getting content moved from one device to another, and (3) getting content moved from one physical location to another. Remarkably, thus far, DVRs have been able to do that while successfully walking a gauntlet of actual and potential legal and regulatory pitfalls. Indeed, it is not inaccurate to surmise that DVRs have also given the legal term "fair use" a whole new meaning (and will continue to push the technical envelope while they do so).

That the multichannel TV providers need to continue to work closely with those on the programming creation, production, and distribution sides of the business is quite clear from the example of how TiVo has run its business versus how ReplayTV ran its business. The latter is out of business, while the former continues to lead new DVR developments.

3.5   Other Content

Specific types of new content finding its way into new environments include photos, music, games, data (such as stock information), home videos, and other peripheral and yet-to-be developed and/or implemented forms of content.

3.5.1   Data Mining

The issue of obtaining DVR users' data, such as what they watched and when they watched it, creates a classic dilemma: it has huge potential (much of it positive), yet its misuse can also be terribly troubling.

On the "positive potential" side of so-called data-mining, those with access to a DVR user's data can take that information and, especially when added to and compared with that of many other DVR users, use the data in it to determine many things that help consumers. These would include more programming that they like, and better configurations of programming, both from a program and an advertising point of view. Or these data could be tied back to use of the EPG/IPG to determine not only which EPGs/IPGs consumers prefer (and for what parts or reasons) but also how much advertising (if any) they would react to or tolerate.

Especially in league with the advertising community, the controllers of DVR user data have a great chance to not only increase the measurement level of viewer data but also, if done correctly, to create a win-win-win for all. In this scenario, the viewer opts in to receive commercial messages of pointed relevance to him or her. The DVR data collector then mines the data to determine what products and services are on point for that particular consumer. This information is then gathered in conjunction with the "right" agencies and advertisers, and upon delivery, if the consumer buys within a given time frame, then additional rewards are offered to those that are a part of this commercial data mining chain. If the proper guidelines are established and, more importantly, followed, by all members of this commercial DVR chain, then data mining in the DVR World of the Future is maintained.

Even for those who do not accept the optimum opt in to exchange and interact with advertisers, they still stand to benefit greatly from viewing and use data gained in the aggregate, and then used to make better the DVR and programming experience. Positions CNetNews.com writer, Ben Charny, in a February 6, 2004, article entitled, "TiVo Watchers Uneasy After Post-Super Bowl Reports," states "Since they let consumers jump quickly over ads, DVRs have been in the spotlight as a potential thorn in the side of network TV. However, the networks have been tantalized by the devices' ability to track viewer behavior, intelligence that could ultimately be used to improve the effectiveness of marketing campaigns and so forth" (see http://www.news.com/2102-1041_3-5154219.html?tag=st.util.print). Indeed, the future of DVRs cuts both ways.

The "bad" side of data mining is that some entity, for example, a governmental agency, would acquire viewing data and use it in such a way that the entire concept of individual or family privacy would be lost. The problem with these parties obtaining and using data without appropriate checks and balances is their ability to take legal content (such as adult programming in most parts of the world, or various other topic material, which if judged in a vacuum, could be harmful or fatal to the viewer), and turning that into illegal or socially derelict behavior. Charny continues in the same CNet article, "Most consumer data collection is done for marketing purposes, resulting, at worst, in more junk mail for those whose name winds up on a given list. Still, some privacy advocates worry that intimate data—once collected—may take on a life of its own, either by mistake or through malicious behavior. Such information could be damaging, if it would come up as evidence in court proceedings or in other unexpected contexts."

Note that some critics have questioned the real anonymity of DVR user data collected by "DVR hosts," such as standalone DVR providers, and cable, telco, and satellite DVR providers. These observers note that, very often, information about the specific user remains inside the thread that represents the collected data (see David Martin, Assistant Professor of Computer Science, University of Denver, "TiVo's Data Collection and Privacy Practices, March 26, 2001, at http://www.cs.uml.edu). Professor Martin summarizes his topic coverage as follows: "TiVo's later privacy policies (including those available in 2001) no longer claim that 'all of your personal viewing information remains on your [TiVo] in your home.' This is important, because the report below shows how that statement was (and perhaps still is) not true. But in no longer making that claim and instead promising not to misuse any personal information they might encounter—as well as intentionally not perfectly separating the viewing data from subscriber identity—TiVo is doing just fine. In light of these changes, it seems appropriate that the Federal Trade Commission (FTC) to (sic) declined to undertake viewing a full investigation in 2001. By the way, I love my TiVo."

In the end, what this discussion concludes, is that DVR companies in place to mine data have rich treasures of useable information; however, they must constantly and forever cherish and protect the access to that data, if they are to do the best for their companies and consumers in the long term, and if we are to remain a privacy-protected society. CNet's Charny adds, "Once one-way receivers, televisions and even radios are becoming two-way devices capable of sending information back to service providers. The shift promises to fundamentally change the ground rules for media, which increasingly must adhere to standards to ensure that new technologies aren't abused in the name of demographics or the like."

3.6 New Technologies

On November 11, 2008, DISH Network took the wraps off of its DTVPal DVR, a digital-to-analog converter box with digital recording capabilities. The box was made available for preorder nationwide starting November 19, 2008, with sales projected to begin in mid-December, the company said. Also, DISH Network said its ViP211 and ViP211k DVR conversion feature would be available at the end of that month. The feature offers customers the ability to convert a single tuner ViP211 and ViP211k set-top box into a DVR, by simply attaching an external hard drive. More recently, at the 2009 Consumer Electronics Show, EchoStar unveiled its HD-DVR model 922 with Sling Media built into the new integrated set-top box.

As noted extensively in Chapter 7, "International DVR Growth," some fascinating developments are occurring in the area of DVRs being created inside computers, such as PCs and laptops. German-based Nero has recently unveiled its partnership with TiVo to allow TV viewing and DVR functionality within the standard computer. This development also has relevance to the subtopic of "Distribution" in this chapter, because Nero's LiquidTV branded technology is also an additional way to distribute DVR content. Together with "on-the-road, I can see my TV devices," such as the Slingbox (discussed more thoroughly in Chapter 2), and the "multichannel TV provider does your DVR storage for you, at our facility" (proposed by Cablevision Systems, and discussed more thoroughly in Chapters 1 and 8), new examples of impressive new technology are constantly arising, involving new DVR and DVR-content distribution models and methods.

As a single, yet quite explicit, example of the steady march of new DVR technology, one need only look to the relative DVR newcomer, the traditional telco provider, Verizon. Verizon has recently morphed itself into a "quadruple play" provider of wireless, telephone, Internet broadband, and TV services, DVRs being part of that impressive package. As part of a press release dated October 23, 2008, Verizon claimed, "Among the new *FiOS TV IMG* features now available in New Jersey are: Return to paused programming—Customers can pause live programming, change channels, and then return to the paused program and pick up where they left off. No part of a program will be missed with this new feature." Expect many more such DVR technological feature improvements, from not just Verizon and the telcos, but also from most or every one of the other "DVR family members" identified in Appendix B of this book.

Chapter 8, "The Future of DVRs," handles this topic of new technologies in much greater substance and detail. Of particular importance is the future of new DVR technologies, as it relates to VOD and RS-DVR-type infrastructures.

3.7   Distribution

Like most set-top boxes for use in consumer video applications, DVRs are available from various outlets. These typically include CE retailers, online, and from the multichannel TV service provider.

Standalone DVR providers, such as Digeo and TiVo, design and have DVRs manufactured for them by reputable third party set-top box manufacturers (often based in South Korea or China, where technology is plentiful, yet labor and manufacturing costs are relatively low). Those boxes are then shipped and delivered to CE retailers, such as Radio Shack, for retail sale to walk-in consumers. Costs for these boxes are typically in the range of $300–800, depending on the maker and characteristics of the standalone DVR box. Once purchased, consumers bring the set-top standalones home and set them up according to maker and service provider specifications. Inevitably, this "buy-a-standalone-DVR-at-retail" method of distribution (and consumer purchase) is more complex and complicated for the parties involved; however, the results can also be much more pleasing. This is because the consumer has a much wider choice of DVRs and DVR capability to choose from, and thus can tailor the DVR to his or her liking.

Online distribution of DVRs is similar to shopping at retail; however, online usually offers much less in the way of human contact, and thus, much less in the way of instant supply of needed information.

Also, worth noting are do-it-yourself DVRs in the form of software kits and some hardware parts (such as tuners installed in PCs and hard drives for PCs or "side-car" DVR storage devices). These types of devices can be obtained at some business locations, but more frequently, they are obtained by going online and ordering a mail shipment.

Further, what has been and continues to likely be the dominant distribution model is that of multichannel TV operators distributing set-top DVR boxes to individual consumers inside their homes. This distribution allows for self-installation; however, the vast majority of today's and tomorrow's consumers are going to leave the technical chores to the multichannel operator's "guys in the trucks."

3.8 DVR Executives' FAQs

Questions frequently asked of executives in and around the consumer side of the DVR industry are of themselves quite telling, to say nothing of the various answers. The section of Q & A below presents a hypothetical bunch of questions asked of (1) a United States-based advertising agency/advertiser type of executive, and (2) an executive from a United States-based supplier of DVRs for consumers.[6] The hypothetical responses are those of the author.

3.8.1 Advertisers and Advertising Agencies

Is the ad model dead? The ad model is unlikely to ever die, not as long as there is room for creativity and room for compromise. It is hard to see a time when people do not consume and when people do not rely on information for that consumption, and thus, where they do not need advertising.

If it is not dead, what shape is it in? Right now, the ad model in the United States and greater parts of Europe and some small parts of Asia is troubled. DVRs have done that and continue to do that.

Can DVRs and advertisers for advertiser-supported programs coexist? DVRs and advertisers will have to coexist, because it is unlikely—now that the DVR Genie is out of the bottle—that the number of consumers using DVRs (or DVR-like devices) will ever decline. Thus, solving the dilemma of coexistence turns to those among agencies, advertisers, networks, studios, regulators, and others in

---

[6] This hypothetical supplier of DVRs for consumers is intended to represent a combination of a standalone, an integrated, and a remote storage DVR supplier, which could hail from a cable, satellite, or telco multichannel TV operator.

the DVR life cycle, to combine, coordinate, and create a place at the table for everybody, especially including the consumer.

What are some alternatives being considered that help resolve the difficulties? Four very good ones quickly come to mind.

- The potential of something like the remote storage DVR, owned and maintained by the faraway multichannel provider, yet controlled almost entirely by the in-home consumer, is significant.
- Data mining is another tool of great merit.
- New content and ad creation schemes, such as those involving ads built around the idea that people will skip them, have promise.
- Better audience measurement tools.

Within what time frame are we looking at to make progress toward these goals? It is certainly already happening, but it sure could use some help from one or more of the more important trade groups and some of the larger media concerns—sort of a "get us all on the same page" mission for the industry, like what is going on right now with the analog-to-digital transition. With help like that, new models could be built and implemented within a matter of a few years, instead of half or more decades.

CBS◉

A remarkable set of DVR-related data points, many of them quite attractive to advertisers, are the product of research undertaken by David Poltrack, who is the chief research officer for parent CBS and president, CBS Vision. "Effective, relevant, interesting, and compelling commercial messages are the Holy Grail of life within the DVR Era," according to Poltrack.

When telling his (and his company's) DVR story, Poltrack begins by noting that the DVR is the device that switched TV from a linear to non-linear service and that TV is clearly no longer constricted by place and by time. With its own research facility, one that runs 365 days a year, CBS Television and its other divisions are in a unique position to study and, ideally, intimately know, how DVRs impact, influence, and otherwise change the business of TV in North America. Indeed, according to Poltrack, "Any new technology gets tested."

Following the deployment of the first DVRs in 1999, an awful lot of doomsday predictions accompanied a view to the future of all traditional TV. Notes Poltrack, "At that time, the point of view was that DVRs would be this dramatic altering vehicle, that they would essentially change the way folks watched TV, and eliminate the viewing of ads." Yet early testing, by CBS and others, challenged that assumption from the beginning (see Chapter 8, "The Future of DVRs," for a description of NBC Universal's studies concerning user receptivity to and cognition of fast forwarded ads).

To begin with, CBS, backed by similar research coming from industry research leader Nielsen, noted that the DVR was increasing the amount of TV people viewed. The study found that the DVR freed their ability to watch TV of their own choosing and, as a result, they would be watching more TV (once they had a DVR). However, the greater question arose: Will people watch more TV, but, at the same time, skip (and thus miss) the commercials? Again, the given presumption was that no rational person would watch ads if he or she could fast forward through them. Moreover, most assumed that people would simply record and rearrange all their programming, ultimately avoiding the viewing of live TV altogether.

However, such was not the case, according to CBS. The reality comes down to the fact that a majority of the TV that people watch is still live TV. Poltrack and his research team found early on that DVR users displayed anywhere from a 50–50% to a 45–65% range of live vs. recorded viewing practices, indicating that the viewing of live programming remained a staple of DVR users.

Then came the focus on advertisements. Because the earlier days of research involved users, self-reporting, CBS believes that research suffered from the politically correct impulse of DVR users to simply state, "I skip all the commercials," and leaves it at that. Yet, the updated CBS research indicated that this was simply not the case.

Indeed, the implementation of more sophisticated research infrastructure, methods, and technology, brought in a remarkable set of new data points. New forms of electronic measurement showed that people with DVRs actually zapped or fast forwarded the ads in their shows no more than 60% of the time. This meant that 40% of the ads in the recorded shows were actually viewed at a normal play speed.

Yet, perhaps most importantly of all, CBS and others' research of DVR users noted that the extent to which a person starts using his or her DVR to fast forward through an ad *varies substantially with the appeal of the commercial*. Moreover, tied in with this finding was a similar discovery that where an advertisement is placed within a group of ads (the group also being known as a "pod" of ads), is an important measure of that ad's likelihood of being viewed, as well.

In sum, Poltrack opines, an important message faces Madison Avenue: *deliver quality advertisements, because the majority of the program audience today is still watching your ads (even in fast forward mode).*

Further, a debate rose as to the value of recorded programs' advertisements. Advertisers, on the one hand, felt that ads shown on shows that were "DVRed," and then watched many days afterward, had limited or no value. Broadcasters, on the other hand, suggested that most ads had value within several days following their original airing. A compromise was reached whereby payments were made for ads shown within 3 days following the original airing of the TV show. Reaching this middle point was particularly important for the broadcasters, because if a determination was made that only live audiences would be valued (a number and percentage of which was expected to decline every year, because of DVRs), the networks would consistently lose income year over year. Also, the fact that studies showed that the programs that were most frequently "DVRed" were concurrently the most popular, worked to the advantage of both broadcasters and advertisers. Poltrack concludes on this point, "The greater quantification of the ad model has opened the door to a more intense qualitative analysis of commercial content on the networks."

Poltrack also adds, "The beauty of this capability is that it will offer consumers access to all programming, on their own schedule, with advertising targeted specifically to them; and, it will offer advertisers the means to measure the impact of that advertising through a census of millions of consumers, as opposed to surveys of a small subset of these consumers. Today's DVR will eventually evolve into tomorrow's virtual DVR."

CBS Corporation

Contact Information
51 W. 52nd Street, New York, NY 10019-6188
Phone: 212-975-4321
http://www.cbscorporation.com

Stock Symbol
NYSE: CBS

Key People
Sumner Redstone, Chairman
Leslie Moonves, President and CEO
David Poltrak, Chief research officer
Phone: 212-975-4321

Key Business
Leading TV and production company

DVR Connection
Has attempted to study DVRs and the DVR impact on CBS proprietary programming content

3.8.2 DVR Providers

Why is supplying DVRs to consumers so important to multichannel pay TV providers? DVRs make money. They add subscribers in large numbers, and once those new subscribers are on board, they do not churn out, and they spend more on DVRs and DVR-related products and services. And, they just make a lot of sense within this whole new digital telecom world, linking smartly together with other advances services, such as HDTV, VOD, and interactive TV.

Are others offering DVRs these days? Sure, competitive forces mean that any multichannel TV service provider is going to have to go digital and have to offer the full range of advanced digital services to maintain or grow market share. It is simply a fact of life.

Who will be offering DVRs in the future? Every device maker and every service provider will offer a DVR or something that acts like a DVR. Ubiquitous storage of all data is that trend we are all following. It gets cheaper and cheaper, and consumers like it more and more, we just need to make sure there continues to be a sensible and profitable place for the other important players, such as the advertisers and the networks.

What are the downsides of offering DVRs for DVR providers? They cost money to create, to implement, to distribute, to maintain, and even to remove. They are not inexpensive pieces of software and hardware, and they are getting more sophisticated and sometimes more expensive, for example, when you add and combine an HD with a DVR. Moreover, installation and repair mean people and truck rolls, which cost more money. And, there continue to be questions about potential liability, such as what we have seen since the earliest days of the *Sony Betamax* line of cases and related governmental concerns. Many DVR consumer users, in fact, still the majority, domestically and globally, have not used DVRs, and educating them on the topic presents a continuing challenge.

When do DVRs become ubiquitous in America? In 2020, DVRs will be like color TV, very few devices will exist, and very few consumers will watch TV without utilizing the service, and without knowing full well what a DVR is and what it does. At that point, DVR use will also be a clear case of going from point to point and from locale to locale, expecting continuous and fluid DVR functionality to move there with you.

What needs to happen to get U.S. consumers there? Stepping away from specific self-interest, and looking at a frank answer to that question, little doubt remains that a more competitive DVR environment needs to be created. I am not sure how that comes about, but for the overwhelming majority of the U.S. cable industry, with some 65 million TV consumers, to have their multichannel service operator offer them only one choice of a DVR service provider, remains a concern. Strong competition is the model that America knows best and under which it best operates.

ECHOSTAR

EchoStar Corporation's Dave Kummer, its senior vice president of engineering and manufacturing, has led EchoStar's efforts in creating and engineering digital video recorders for the company's largest customer, DISH Network.[7] Kummer has been with the company for nearly 16 years, during which time he has helped EchoStar deploy millions of DVR set-top boxes throughout the United States, Canada, and in Europe. DISH Network also utilizes the EchoStar-designed user interface for its DVRs, the development of which Kummer also oversaw.

EchoStar introduced the first DVR at CES in Las Vegas in January 1999. Looking at the original business plan, and how best to achieve the hoped for ROI, EchoStar made a wise decision: Build DVRs made for longer term subscribers, which made for more ARPU for the company. DVRs also kept those subscribers from going over to the competition, be it DirecTV or a cable company. At the same time, a little known company called TiVo introduced a similar device. At that time, EchoStar partnered with Steve Perlman, founder of *WebTV* Networks (*WebTV* was later purchased by Microsoft). Perlman's company implemented software enabling the innovative on-screen guide (i.e., the EPG/IPG) and hard-drive operating system, while EchoStar designed the hardware and software integration for access to DISH Network's programming. The hard drive model called the Model 7100, and later renamed the "DISHPlayer," was a hit among videophiles looking to rid themselves of the messy inconveniences of VCR tapes. The DISHPlayer was a combination computer/Internet terminal/satellite receiver/hard-disk recorder/video-system controller. With a 6-hour recording time, the DISHPlayer promised "to revolutionize the TV-viewing experience, by integrating EchoStar's DISH Network digital satellite television programming with an Internet TV experience from *WebTV Networks*."

EchoStar's motivation to deploy DVRs came from the early realization that high-power satellite (DBS) signals were, from inception, transferred in a digital format, which lined it up nicely with DVRs, which were also a digital service. Thus, for those in and around DBS, it was natural to want to record those signals digitally, as opposed to doing it using an analog VCR tape. And although DISH Network's first effort in this arena was actually a digital VCR, the company soon realized the future was in internal hard drives. This was especially the case as the costs of hard drives declined, and the technology around them was enhanced. Looking ahead,

---

[7] DISH Network spun off its engineering and satellite-leasing divisions in January 2008 to form EchoStar Corporation.

DISH Network executives suggest that the only thing that might end their focus on DVRs would be "... increased costs or their replacement with new technology" (perhaps something in the future such as flash memory).

Although other companies, like TiVo and ReplayTV, had introduced hard-disk video recorders, EchoStar's new DISHPlayer offering was touted as a "smart home-entertainment device." The DISHPlayer's built-in ultra-fast 8.6-GB hard drive was capable of simultaneously recording and playing "full-quality" digital video. At the time, one of its most alluring features was labeled "TV Pause;" this function allows viewers to walk away from a show for up to 30 minutes and yet later resume watching. Much like a search engine on the Internet, the DISHPlayer lets viewers search for programs or actors as part of the IPG. Moreover, using *WebTV*, viewers could send and receive emails from their TV, using the DISHPlayer's telephone line connection for dial-up Internet.

"We looked to the future, and believed the DVR would become the core of the twenty-first-century television receiver that all households would have," said Kummer. "Today, EchoStar places hard disks in a large number of the set-top boxes it produces."

According to EchoStar's communications director, Marc Lumpkin, its DVR models today far surpass their predecessors in terms of functionality, reliability, and performance. With more than a dozen models of DVRs deployed in the last 10 years, today's top-of-the-line EchoStar DVR records close to 350 hours of programming in standard definition, and more than 110 hours of high definition TV shows. Unlike its competition, EchoStar implemented a 30-second skip button, which allows viewers to skip commercials—or huddles during the football game—a half minute at a time. And to allow DISH Network to deliver video to multiple rooms in a house, EchoStar includes a large hard drive in its DVRs, one that can record and play up to five high-definition programs at one time from the satellite or from an over-the-air digital tuner. Some other more subtle advantages to a DVR for EchoStar include customer retention, and enabling the downloading of advertising and the downloading of a satellite version of VOD, as well as enabling more customer training.

"We're to the point now that we're satisfied with our experience and successes in developing DVRs," says Kummer. He added "We were putting computer hard drives into a set-top box for the first time. So, in the early stages, we had to overcome heat problems from spinning hard disks, noisy fans, and chassis vibrations. We've solved these issues, allowing us to create DVRs that have won CES Innovations awards and CNET awards numerous times, while delivering a highly reliable DVR to our largest customer today, DISH Network."

Asked to identify the greatest threat facing DVRs today, EchoStar suggests "content providers giving programming away via the Internet for free." Yet ironically, the biggest opportunity was identified as, "Internet content delivered to the set-top box and capable of being recorded onto the DVR." And asked to label the single aspect of DVRs that the company likes the most, the answer came back, "To record what you want, when you want, and watch it anywhere: mobile, home or around the house." Finally, asked if EchoStar could change any aspect of DVRs, Lumpkin opines, "We'd like to reduce the remote control's number of buttons, making it easier to operate the DVR."

In the realm of legal and regulatory concerns, EchoStar states firmly that it adheres to copyright and other proprietary rights limitations that prevent content from being distributed digitally from its DVRs to other unauthorized devices. On the legal side, Echostar's DVR usage and deployment had been influenced by several actions involving DVR industry pioneer, TiVo. A patent infringement suit was brought by TiVo against EchoStar in 2005; TiVo received a more than $100 million verdict in 2007, and a final payment from EchoStar in 2008. In the meantime, EchoStar has designed what it calls a "work around," which would permit EchoStar to continue to use its own software to operate its DVRs, without making further payments to TiVo for patent infringement, which is also in litigation. In another DVR patent infringement suit against EchoStar, nearly a dozen defendants settled with the plaintiff, Forgent, while the sole remaining defendant, EchoStar, took the case to trial and was victorious.

Over the years, EchoStar has employed an army of software engineers to develop and help enable the hundreds of functions of its DVRs. Kummer expounds, "I believe we are the only company feeding as many as five incoming video signals to a hard disk at one time. We had to overcome difficult software challenges to enable a hard drive to manipulate multiple video SD and HD signals from the satellite, as well as from an off-air antenna." EchoStar also implemented a multiroom DVR, giving customers access to their DVR content from any TV in the house.

Looking at its prime audience, DVRs were initially targeted to the videophile or high-end (i.e., wealthier) customer. Today, DISH Network offers an advanced DVR free, with a lengthy DISH Network subscription, or at least at a low entry price. Analysts have suggested that DISH Network in 2008 has somewhere between four million to six million customers using DVRs. "DVRs are not only a retention tool, they've become a primary selling tool to lure new customers," said Kummer.

Further, DVRs have provided operators with another tool: advertising. EchoStar's DVRs have the capability to receive a show streamed to the DVR via satellite or broadband, greatly enhancing viewers' choices of on-demand movies or video entertainment. Interactive TV also gets a technology boost with DVRs. Although interactive TV functions were once downloaded via satellite using "push" technology to a flash drive inside the non-DVR box, today such interactive TV capabilities can be downloaded to the hard drive, allowing for greater amounts of features to be delivered to the set-top box.

EchoStar notes also that it has worked with its partner, DISH Network, to enable triggers that take viewers from a brief commercial to a long form, a 2-minute commercial that resides on the hard drive or on another channel. EchoStar states that it can place advertising on the hard drive and allow viewers to view it at any time. Also, DISH Network's channel 100 portal permits its viewers to access a menu of interactive features, including the ability to find a local pizza franchise and view more information, such as photos, when researching the purchase of a new automobile. Parties using DISH Network DVRs for advertising purposes include EchoStar's own advertisers, such as Ford and Papa John's Pizza. Moreover, DISH Network collects data about its users and their preferences, but with strong assurances that it is done only in the aggregate, and only "to improve our systems and identify technical problems," adds Lumpkin. This includes data targeted to specific audiences at specific times. Further, although EchoStar does not, in general, feel that there is a need for limitations on the ability of a DVR user to skip ads, if a programming provider requests that the DVR's ad-skipping device be disabled, EchoStar might consider disabling that ad-skipping feature.

In 2007, EchoStar purchased Sling Media, a company that goes beyond EchoStar's ability to time-shift using DVRs. Instead, Sling Media's Slingbox allows users to place shift their programming. For instance, using a Slingbox connected to a satellite receiver, viewers can watch their content via their PC or laptop or on some cell phones while traveling. EchoStar is working to integrate this feature into its future set-top boxes, to allow consumers to "sling" their content around the house (or around the world).

Figure 3.2   The Sling Media Slingbox by EchoStar enables users to view programming anywhere.

EchoStar says it continues to remain on the forefront of DVR technology and, based on numerous real-life customer "human factors" sample testing, EchoStar is currently redesigning the look and feel of its DVRs in a whole new way. EchoStar claims its engineers are creating a stylish, simplified, visual user interface, which is capable of integrating multiple functions in an easy-to-understand format, while taking strides to bridge language and usage barriers. "These new DVRs provide easy navigation and recording capabilities, with a cursor-type pointer for selection and animated graphical elements (to simplify menu navigation), as well as fast scrolling through long lists of information such as program guide, recorded content, DVR timers, or 'favorites' lists," concludes Lumpkin.

EchoStar Technologies LLC

Contact Information
90 Inverness Circle E., Englewood, CO 80112
http://www.echostar.com

Stock Symbol
NASDAQ: SATS

Key People
Charles W. Ergen, Chairman and CEO
PR Contact: Marc Lumpkin
Phone: 303-871-2741, E-mail: B2B.PR@echostar.com

Key Business
Set-top box hardware provider for direct broadcast satellite, as well as cable and telco, service providers

DVR Connection
Provides DVR and HD-DVR add-ons to its set-top box hardware portfolio.

3.9 Summary

This chapter points out all of the key elements behind the consumer side of the DVR business, focused primarily on the United States; however, most of the information in the different sections of this chapter is clearly attributable to DVR deployments overseas (see Chapter 7, "International Growth of DVRs"). The three case studies here, those of DISH Network, CBS, and Motorola, have shown the reader three key aspects of "The Business of DVRs," that is, those, respectively, of a very large multichannel pay TV operator, a very large hardware manufacturer, and a very large video programmer.

4 DVR Uses and Applications

As far as DVRs, Buy a TIVO, or rent a DVR from your cable or satellite people, or build your own if your a geek (sic), but get one. It will change the way you watch TV forever. You'll never miss anything, never race to get home, pass an invitation, and never ever almost pee yourself waiting to for a commercial (sic).
—Unidentified commenter on Captimes.com, October 2008

Typically, there are two main uses for a DVR. One—that of content storage devices inside consumers' homes, permitting the greatly enhanced enjoyment of audio and video programs—is well known to most people these days. In this chapter, this first use will be highlighted and discussed under the heading, "Consumer Uses and Applications." The second use, in security deployments, is much less well known and will be discussed under the heading "Security Uses and Applications."

Further, as noted in numerous other chapters in this book, analysis of trends suggests that within as little as a decade, and perhaps within a more lengthy period of time, the function of the in-home DVR set-top box unit will be replaced partly or perhaps entirely by a remote storage-DVR (RS-DVR) device. The RS-DVR is a form of storage built inside a building, owned and controlled by the cable or telco multichannel TV operator, and typically located far away from the customer's home, which uses many servers to deliver and store just about any content the customer desires to view. Further, eventually the operations and components of the RS-DVR are expected to merge with those of the cable and telco operators' VOD services, creating something quite different from an infrastructure involving scores of millions of individual in-home DVR set-top units that populate U.S. TV households today.

4.1 Consumer Uses and Applications

In the same way that while reading a book, the reader can stop and review a page read earlier, a DVR permits a viewer of video content to stop and review, pause, and even fast forward that same content. This means that content can either be seen again, when otherwise it would be lost forever to most consumers. Or it can be avoided altogether, which many consumers welcome as it relates to annoying and irrelevant advertisements. Like its predecessor video cassette recorder (VCR), the DVR does a wonderful job of allowing many shows to be stored and saved indefinitely for later viewing. In the case of the DVR, however, it stores all the content inside the set-top unit, on a hard drive, rather than on separate handheld cassettes that must be individually and separately handled and stored. This, then, is the core use and application of today's (and tomorrow's) in-home set-top DVR.

4.1.1   Single Room DVR

In the earliest days of DVR development in the United States, that is, during the 1999–2004 time frame, the idea of networked DVRs and TVs in other rooms and content that could be passed and manipulated from room to room was not yet ready for prime time. Thus, if a consumer wanted DVR functionality in another room, he or she had to buy or lease a second, third, or fourth individual DVR set-top unit for each separate room. This additional DVR set-top unit would then be placed in the second, third, or fourth room inside the same house and could be used to choose and control content on that TV—and only on that particular TV. No connection with other TVs or DVRs in the same house was typically provided.

This model was a good one for standalone DVR manufacturers, such as ReplayTV and TiVo; however, for consumers, it required large sums of additional spending, planning, and hassle to add additional DVRs, in additional rooms, within the same household. The different DVRs within the home also did not "talk" to one another. This model begged for a better solution.

During the millennium's first decade, the multichannel pay TV industry provided that answer. The implementation of a single home DVR and infrastructure that would permit viewing of the same recorded program in other rooms within the same home was a more elegant answer, which had the potential to revolutionize the way content was managed inside the home. New systems led by software developers such as Microsoft (allying with cable and telco operators) permitted the development of single DVRs, which could deliver content to other TVs in other rooms, permitting users in those other rooms to similarly manipulate that same content on the centrally located DVR, wherever they find themselves in the home.

Although today most multiroom-DVRs (MR-DVRs) are a system of individual DVRs purchased or leased and placed in each separate room—where they operate separately from the other DVRs in the same household—within years, this model will change to the point where the single DVR in a main room controlling content on TVs in other rooms will become the new standard.

4.1.2   Multiple Room DVR

The idea of the single DVR in a single room, which then sends a recorded program to another TV in another room of that same home, for additional viewing, makes great common sense. It also makes good deployment and good economic sense. It links content together in the same household, meaning all one needs to continue the viewing process is another TV screen in another location. It also eliminates the need for the purchase and set-up of additional DVR set-top units for every TV screen in the home, which, if done, still means that each DVR operates separately from the others, and does not allow sharing of programs from one hard drive inside one DVR to that in another.

In addition to the DVR, which typically is placed in the living room of most homes, there is also a wireline or wireless connection between the DVR and small receiver units located beside the other TV screens in other rooms. Today, most MR-DVR systems are connected via wires, however, with the expanding growth of wireless services, expect wireless transmission of signals to become the new norm in households across America. Nonetheless, numerous bandwidth-related issues, especially with high-definition (HD) signals and the number of megabits involved, remain a concern.

Telco

New York, NY-based Verizon offers a multiroom, single home DVR content solution it calls the MR-DVR service. As noted in the Verizon case study featured in Chapter 1, connection from the main DVR to outlying TV monitors is made via wireline, specifically via coaxial connections. Two standard definition (SD), or one SD and one HD, TV combinations in other rooms can be accessed off of the one main in-home DVR in the Verizon MR-DVR system. Verizon serves as good example of the future of MR-DVRs as it relates to landline multichannel pay TV operators, especially those in the telco arena. In addition, the MR-DVR from Verizon permits a user in another room to watch recorded content, live TV content, or VOD content emanating from the MR-DVR hub.

Dallas, TX-based AT&T also has begun offering its consumers MR-DVR functionality, in the form of a new service it calls "Total Home DVR." In the words of an AT&T press release of September 9, 2008, the new AT&T system "…allows its users to record and playback multiple programs on different TV sets around the house." AT&T states that up to eight TV sets in a given home will be able to access recordings from a single DVR and can also record up to four shows simultaneously. Continues a Reuters article about the AT&T DVR sharing service, "The free upgrade will be deployed to all AT&T *U-Verse* customers by the end of year 2008. It needs no visits from technicians or any new hardware, as the advanced Internet protocol television (IPTV) system allows AT&T to upgrade its software remotely."

Satellite

DirecTV (NASDAQ: LMDIA), one of two U.S. Satellite [direct broadcast satellite (DBS)] TV providers, has software that is under development that will enable the customer to share DVR-recorded content in any room in the house. The software for the new DirecTV version of a home media center will be beta tested and released during 2009. As such, the software will not necessitate the replacement of existing HD DVRs, but rather will work with existing HD DVR set-top boxes.

For its part, DISH Network, the second largest of two U.S. satellite TV providers, has its own version of a MR-DVR device. Using existing in-home wiring, DISH Network has, going back to 2005, offered its customers the option of viewing shows "DVRed" on one room in second and third rooms inside the same home. DISH further envisions a time when signals not only are conveyed via wires, but also wirelessly, inside the same home. What is particularly interesting in the case of DISH Network is its multiroom system reliance on *cable* wires, which are installed in the majority of U.S. homes. Thus, from an output on the back of the DISH Network DVR, the DVR remodulates the signal, sends it through the typical RG-59 type of cable wire, and then into the back of the distant TV. This saves DISH Network and/or the consumer the cost and hassle of getting an additional set-top box for the additional TV set(s) in the second or third room(s). DISH Network states that it charges no extra fees per box per month to send the signals to additional sets in the same home.

Cable

Like its cable brethren, Cox has not yet unveiled a MR-DVR product, yet it is "... closely studying the opportunity to provide a product customers are interested in, extending their DVR experience from one into multiple rooms, without having to buy an additional DVR, and allowing customers to move around the home and resume a show off the main DVR's hard drive ... we are looking to have that multiroom opportunity for both HD and SD applications," notes Cox's director, video strategy and product management, for on-demand and DVR products and services, Mark Gathen (see Cox case study in Chapter 2; see also Comcast case study in Chapter 1). Cox's current goal is to perfect the multiroom vision and strategy, bring it to trial in 2009, and deploy it as soon afterwards as feasible. Part of Cox's experience also involves technological plans and implementations with Cox's hardware vendors, Cisco/Scientific Atlanta and Motorola.

Others

Well into the future, it is probably not too far afield to suggest that other telecom operators may well seek and be granted access into people's homes as TV and related telecom providers. This could, for example, eventually include electrical utilities. Nonetheless, to maximize their competitive chances, it is likely that future DVR deployments will have to hit the ground running, so to speak, which is to say they will be expected to begin service to consumers with all the DVR and DVR-related bells and whistles possessed by the existing cable, satellite, and telco rivals. This will certainly include uses and applications such as an MR-DVR functionality. Verizon's entry into the delivery of video services is a perfect example of a new DVR provider faced with this conundrum. The Verizon case study in Chapter 1 describes this difficult transition in more detail.

4.1.3 Mobile DVR

The combination of the Internet and the DVR has resulted in devices that permit localized, home-based video content—including content recorded on DVRs—to be conveyed just about anywhere around the world for viewing from distant locations.

Sling Media

Sling Media, now wholly owned by EchoStar Corporation, headquartered at Englewood, CO, is a Foster City, CA-based company that has patents and other intellectual property supporting a set-top-type box that acts to permit delivery of TV signals and content from a user's home TV and DVR to a computer (typically a laptop), typically located in a distant and often faraway location. This in-home set-top box, called the Slingbox, is ideal for frequent travelers and displaced nationals who want to be able to continue to access and view their home-based content in distant lands. EchoStar purchased Sling Media in 2007.

The Slingbox device has the ability to carry live local signals from a TV in one's home to a computer just about anywhere else in the world where it can obtain an Internet connection. In short, the Slingbox uses the Internet to connect between the two locations and to deliver whatever content a user might enjoy normally at home, either live or using the DVR. The Internet also operates to convey signals from the distant computer to the DVR itself, thus permitting the user to manipulate his or her content on the DVR, even though he or she is nowhere near the device. In short, the Slingbox permits its users to use DVR functionality for local, home-based content, viewed on a screen, at another point around the world.

In fall 2008, Sling Media and EchoStar Corporation launched an HD version of the Slingbox, "slinging" Internet-delivered HD quality shows to users' laptops globally.[1] This was followed by the 2009 CES announcement of the new 922 HD-DVR set-top box, with Sling capability embedded. Also, the small, portable SlingCatcher device permits users to send signals directly from the Internet connection in a wall to the monitor in the room, such as a TV screen in a hotel room. Indeed, no laptop is needed when using the SlingCatcher, and, like all the content that is accessible from afar, the user of the SlingCatcher can utilize the home's on-screen interactive programming guide (EPG/IPG) menu from any locale anytime.

In late 2008, Sling launched its http://www.sling.com service, which permits subscribers to access old TV shows (where agreements are already in place with content owners). This is a service similar to those offered by Internet content rivals Hulu and YouTube. Sling is further positioned to send signals to portable personal digital assistants (PDAs), such as Blackberry devices, meaning one's local TV content and DVR content can be viewed on that ultimately portable device, anywhere in the world where Internet content is accessible. This would also include use inside vehicles, such as passenger cars, which is another future trend that is literally and figuratively just around the corner.

---

[1] Note that the Slingbox also allows both SD and HD content to be carried from one TV source to another TV within the same home (and not just to locales far, far away). Sling Media calls the device that features carriage of HD content a Slingbox Pro-HD. This device also helps consolidate content in one source and then distribute it for later viewing or manipulation to other TVs within the same home. Note, too, that at the "other TVs" within the same home, in order to receive signals, a computer (such as a laptop) or a SlingCatcher device will have to also be installed in addition to the Slingbox located at the "host" TV set or the "host" TV/DVR set-top unit.

EchoStar's Dishplayer

The PocketDISH was a small, portable media player that allowed an EchoStar DISH Network subscriber to download content from his or her DISH Network DVR to the PocketDISH recording device and then use a built-in screen on that device to later view the downloaded content. In short, the PocketDISH was a portable DVR storage device. Unfortunately for DISH Network (and for a lot of actual and would-be consumers), the original PocketDISH, manufactured by a French company, called Archos, never gained the kind of traction as that of the Slingbox. The PocketDISH was discontinued in 2007. Nonetheless, Archos continues to make these types of units, which still have a unique high-speed connection for downloading (meaning users can turn on the units and start watching as soon as the downloading begins). According to an EchoStar spokesperson, these portable media players continue to work "seamlessly" with most DISH Network products.

Sprint's Pivot

Like the PocketDISH, the joint venture between Sprint and four major cable TV operators, called Pivot, also ran into distribution and sales problems before being terminated in April 2008. Pivot was the telco Sprint's effort to remain competitive with its telco brethren, Verizon and AT&T, in the provisioning of a so-called quadruple play, that is, an offering by a telecom provider of the four elements of (1) voice, (2) video, (3) wireline telco, and (4) wireless telco and the Internet. Cable operators Cox, Comcast, Brighthouse, and Time Warner were the key partners relying on Sprint to deliver quality wireless spectrum and services. Related to DVR, the Pivot plan was to allow video content to "pivot" from the in-home DVR to a mobile phone, wherever the latter was located. Early deployments of Pivot included Comcast in Boston, MA, and Portland, OR; and Cox in Raleigh, NC, Austin, TX, and Cincinnati, OH. At one point, the Pivot wireless service was scheduled to be available in 40 U.S. markets.

4.1.4 Related DVR Uses

As noted elsewhere in this book, the *concept* of a DVR and what it does is probably the most important message a DVR delivers. That is because the actual application becomes less and less important, as other competitive DVR uses and applications become prevalent. A perfect example is the use of DVRs and their applications originally presented in the form of the TiVo and ReplayTV products and services; these were later supplemented by DVR products and services and uses and applications developed by companies such as Microsoft, EchoStar, Motorola, Cisco/Scientific-Atlanta, Time Warner Cable, and Cablevision Systems, be they in either individual set-top unit or RS-DVR forms. It is widely expected in the future that DVRs will be subsumed on the cable and telco sides of the telecom world by all-encompassing VOD systems, which will present content in such prolific forms that costly in-home, individual unit DVRs will no longer be attractive to most consumers.

Nonetheless, as noted above, on the mobile side, the concept of a DVR begs deployment in every kind of imaginable device and with every form of content. Thus, all forms of radio, listened to in the car or at home on the Internet, become instantly recorded and stored for later playback. Indeed, even telephone conversations, be they on landlines or via mobile phones, will offer instant playback to check what was said. In addition, expect content to be much more legally and much more easily distributed from one individual user to the next, once content holders have worked with technologists and regulators to find that perfect balance between monetized distribution and free or "fair" use by consumers.

Also worth noting are DISH Network plans to build future set-top boxes without hard drives, but which can be made into DVRs via (1) attachment of a "side-car" type hard drive box, and (2) downloading of software to the non-DVR set-top, which will enable it to become a DVR set-top. This scheme has the potential to save huge sums of money for manufacturers and those consumers not wanting to pay for a set-top box in advance that contains an unwanted hard drive. Nonetheless, if that same consumer later changes his or her mind and decides to add the side-car unit that can easily (and relatively cheaply) be accommodated, without having to obtain and switch-out a still expensive existing set-top box.

RENTRAK
multi-screen media measurement

Portland, OR-headquartered Rentrak Corporation describes itself as "an industry-leading information management company, providing content measurement and analytical services to some of the most recognizable names in the entertainment industry." As an example of its mission, Rentrak measures television across multiple platforms, from traditional linear viewing at the second-by-second level, to on-demand consumption and the impact of DVRs on television viewing.

With an estimated more than 25% of television households using a DVR today, DVR technology has already made a significant impact on advertising, helping to spur the movement to commercial ratings, and challenging networks and advertisers to become more creative in their efforts to engage the consumer. The evidence of the impact of the DVR can be seen with the introduction of content wraps, minisodes, and shorter commercial "pods," attempting to keep consumers tuned in through commercial breaks and to stop them from hitting the fast-forward button. Rentrak feels that accurately evaluating consumer viewership of programming and advertising, on a second-by-second level, in this "everything on demand" world, is the key to unlocking the potential of new and existing media distribution platforms.

To do this, Rentrak has developed what it calls "TV Essentials," which is a linear television measurement system currently processing data from more than two million set-top-boxes, collecting data from multiple network operators across multiple markets. The question of how consumption of linear television content and advertising are affected by DVR viewing has been, and continues to be, a focus for Rentrak. Indeed, where the industry is headed and what standards need to be in place for the proper measurement of DVR usage, will continue to be debated in the coming months and years. The set-top box data within "TV Essentials" will allow users to truly understand how consumers use DVRs to view programming, that is, important data such as (1) what programs are most likely to be recorded, (2) what percentage of viewing is spent time-shifted, (3) when time-shifted content is played back, (4) the differences in time-shifting behavior across demographics, and (5) how time-shifting behavior changes over time.

For Rentrak, a key question is not only how should the impact of DVR viewing be measured, but also by what standard? Rentrak believes there are not currently enough data about consumers' interaction with DVRs to permit a definition of an industry standard. "TV Essentials" was designed by Rentrak to help its clients answer the questions posed above and to permit flexibility in measuring.

For example, DVR playback may not have a standard number of days within which it must be played back, in order to be measured. Furthermore, these playback parameters may be different for each advertiser, agency, or media buying unit. Rentrak seeks to give its operator partners, content providers, and advertiser clients the ability to negotiate their agreements based on their data needs. Experience shows that a standard for one client is not necessarily the same standard for another client. A department store with a one-day sale may not be interested in the "Live + 3" measurement, where a movie studio opening a film in 3 weeks may be interested in seeing just how many time-shifted viewers watched their trailer or promo any time before the movie opened, requiring as much as a "Live + 21" metric. Therefore, Rentrak has incorporated incremental metrics, starting at "live shift." This term is defined as viewing that takes place during the linear airing or shortly thereafter, as well as hourly breakdowns within the first day and live viewing, plus one day of delayed playback ("Live + 1"), measuring all the way through live viewing plus 30 days of delayed playback ("Live + 30"). These different parameters allow Rentrak's clients to define the measurement.

The role of the DVR in the media marketplace will only increase during the next few years. For multichannel pay TV operators, networks, and advertisers to unlock the insights into these audiences and to leverage them for more effective campaigns, it is necessary to understand how consumers are interacting with their DVR, sometimes more minutely than most could ever imagine.

Rentrak

Contact Information
1 Airport Center, 7700 NE Ambassador Place Portland, OR 97220
Phone: 503-284-7581
http://www.rentrak.com

Stock Symbol
NASDAQ: RENT

Key People
Paul A. Rosenbaum, Chairman and CEO
PR Contact: Sallie Olmstead, Rogers & Cowan
Phone: 310-854-8124

Key Business
Telecom audience measurement company

DVR Connection
Measuring the use and effectiveness of DVRs

4.1.5 Consumer DVR Services: What a DVR Does

Beyond the realm discussed earlier in this chapter of "what and where," there are questions of just "what" the DVR does to make it so special. The sections immediately below are intended to be a clear and concise summary of just what it is that the typical DVR does.

Record

Any way you stack it, the main thing a DVR does is record content.

In addition, because DVRs are usually accompanied by a multichannel pay TV operators' EPG/IPG, this guide works quite well to allow the consumer to simply find a future show on the EPG/IPG, highlight it, push a "record" button, and the show will then be saved to a hard drive in the future. Most DVRs also allow another couple of buttons to be pushed during this process, allowing all future showings (or all new showings) of the same show to be automatically recorded for later playback.

Marc Beckwitt, Digeo's director of business development and industry affairs, notes, "The core time-shifting record function must always be bullet proof, and if it does that reliably, consumers will continue to need and pay for it."

Beyond the core record function, different companies battle to find computing and technologies that surround the record function and make it work that much better. Beckwitt concludes, "Very few get it. A good DVR needs the right features, the right usability, and the right extendability."

Pause, Rewind, and Fast Forward

As was true of just about any VCR (the device that preceded the DVR in the realm of record, rewind, pause, and fast-forward applications), the DVR also performs these standard applications. Yet, a modern-day DVR can be used for much more. Most importantly, today's DVRs automatically begin recording every show that is accessed (or turned on) by the consumer. The DVR does not need to have its "record" button turned on to record what is showing. The importance of this feature is in allowing consumers to rewind all of what they have watched, typically, and to also then pause and fast forward that recorded content. In addition, if the consumer decides, upon watching live TV, to then record it permanently to the hard drive, that, too, is possible.

Transfer

Getting content to and from the DVR is a third important feature and will become more so in the future. On the typical DVR device today, content that is SD (both that is transferred from analog to digital and that is originally carried in SD) and content that is carried in HD, can be delivered to the DVR and recorded.

Yet, understandably, a good part of the concern by developers of the DVR world, including content owners and distributors, is that proper rules and guidelines be followed. This is because these players in the DVR arena want to be fairly compensated for their efforts to provide users with content. Thus, there is great pressure to set-up and abide by rules and regulations—at state and national and international levels—intended to ensure that a viable content delivery, storage, and display business can be maintained.

Also, once the content has been delivered legally to the DVR, additional steps are necessary to make sure the same rules of distribution and compensation are followed. These steps include allowing consumers to reuse and replay that legally obtained content, on other devices, and for other limited purposes. The U.S. Supreme Court has termed this additional limited use by consumers "fair use." Yet, as distribution grows well beyond that by standard multichannel pay TV video operators (e.g., cable, satellite, and telco), moving well into wireless- and Internet-delivered content, the rules, regulations, and guidelines, as well as the technology, are further stressed and challenged to keep up. An example would be DVR maker EchoStar's efforts to build DVRs that do not feature digital output ports, which, in turn, would promote the making of digital copies of copyrighted content.

nielsen

• • • • • • • • •

In the words of Anne Elliot, Nielsen's vice president of communications, "Nielsen's commitment to measuring time-shifted viewing is a natural extension of the company's core principle of providing its clients with the most reliable information about how people watch television."

Nielsen began working with manufacturers of DVR equipment several years ago and developed data collection solutions, including one that could reside on the TiVo box and would be activated only when a TiVo household became a Nielsen home. Yet, the technology was only one part of the equation, the two discovered.

New York-headquartered Nielsen spent a good deal of time working with its advertiser and agency clients to determine what metrics would meet their needs. In fact, the company delayed national implementation to add capabilities based on specific client requests. In Q1 2006, Nielsen began to report time-shifted viewing in two data streams, "Live and Live + 7 Day" playback, for local clients in the spring of 2005, and in three data streams, "Live," "Live + Same Day," and "Live + 7 Day," for national clients. As clients began to see the impact, they then asked for another metric, that is, commercial minute ratings. Much of this data is presented and described, with numerous charts, in the Nielsen publication, "Audience Insight: U.S. DVR Penetration and Usage," in Appendix C (reprinted with the permission of The Nielsen Company).

Elliot continues, "As advertisers and agencies understood the use of DVRs, they wondered how much commercial time was being skipped. Thus, in spring of 2007, Nielsen introduced a data file that reports viewing of only the commercial minutes in a given program." This file includes six data streams, all of which Nielsen continues to provide its clients.

During the 2007–2008 upfront season, Nielsen's clients seemed to line up in agreement: the data stream representing "Live + 3 Days" of playback became the time-shifted interval of choice. Elliot explains "That is their choice and we continue to provide all data streams for analysis, buying and selling."

Perhaps most importantly, Nielsen also continues to provide clients with in-depth analyses of how people are using their DVRs. This is part of the full understanding Nielsen seeks to provide as to how people watch television.

Further in this vein, Nielsen recently released the first report on "Three Screens," which include (1) traditional television, (2) Internet, and (3) mobile. This was done to begin to better understand the connections between these technologies.

Moreover, Nielsen states that it is constantly looking ahead to new technologies—many of which may never come to market or reach a significant number of homes—to be sure it can measure and report that potential future usage.

Elliot concludes "That is always connected to our clients' requirements, which create a never-ending balancing act. Susan Whiting, the executive vice president of The Nielsen Company and Chairman of Nielsen Media Research, clearly set this course when she pledged—we will 'Follow the Video,' to provide audience measurement. And so we will."

Nielsen

Contact Information
770 Broadway, New York, NY 10003-9522
Phone: 646-654-5500
http://www.nielsen.com

Stock Symbol
Privately held company

Key People
David Calhoun, Chairman & CEO
PR Contact: Ed Dandridge

Key Business
Supplier of marketing information, media information, TV ratings, online intelligence, mobile measurement, trade shows, and business publications.

DVR Connection
Nielsen conducts measurement of statistical analysis as to how DVRs affect TV viewership.

4.2   Security Uses and Applications

On what is almost entirely the business side of DVR usage, DVRs are highly prized for their ability to efficiently and relatively cheaply store and manipulate content that can later be used to assess employees', customers', and others' actions within a store, factory, or similar commercial environments. DVRs in these instances are utilized because they can do a lot to satisfy the needs of their users. For example, a DVR can be equipped with numerous tuning heads, allowing numerous video feeds from numerous camera locations to be recorded on the same DVR unit simultaneously for later playback and review. DVRs can also be set-up inside moving vehicles, such as police cars and busses, to permit viewing and permanent recording of action in and around the vehicle.

Using just about any browser and typing in the acronym and words "DVR + mobile" delivers a long list of security-related applications. A similar search for the acronym and words "DVR + security" produces listings in the millions.

Typically, a DVR in a security setting is part of a closed circuit TV (CCTV) system, meaning a TV system that is private and controlled by the owner/operator. Although in older days a VCR tape would be used to track and document movement within a facility, modern-day DVRs are a step ahead of that technology. This is because the modern-day DVR adds features, such as video searches by event, time, date, and camera. Quality and frame rates can also be adjusted on a DVR, permitting the hard drive's disk space to be optimized. Further, when the disk approaches full capacity, the DVR can be set to automatically overwrite the oldest security footage. In some DVR security systems, remote access to security footage using a personal computer (PC) can also be achieved by connecting the DVR to a local area network or to the Internet.

On the technical side, security DVRs are categorized as either PC-based or embedded. A PC-based DVR's architecture is that of a classical PC, with video capture cards that are created to capture video images. An embedded type DVR, on the other hand, is specifically designed as a DVR. The embedded DVR has its operating system and application software contained in firmware or read only memory (ROM).

All this said, the combination of consumer and commercial uses (in the form of mostly security applications and uses) begs the question: what about combining the two? Actually, because the DVR is so adept at tracking and documenting movements, that capability can be featured in just about any space, including private homes. Thus, more in the future, in-home DVRs are expected to include security tracking and recording features as part of their core functionality. This trend represents a natural progression in the life cycle of DVRs.

Research of online companies that provide DVRs as part of security offerings includes the following from a random company advertising itself and its products, called 2M CCTV (see http://www.2mcctv.com/index-CompleteSystems .html?gclid=CMq68NG4zZYCFRIcawod92qt3A): "And finally the 16 CCTV camera surveillance systems are top quality CCTV CCTV security surveillance system you are looking for! (sic) These include Dell and Geovision packages that consist of 16 Day/ night/ infrared security surveillance cameras, 380 TVL, 16 channel DVR capture card, and Dell PC. The other package includes 16 Samsung 480 TVL cameras, GV-1000 Geovision 480 fps DVR, and Dell server."

4.3 Control

Control of just about all DVR functions comes in the form of the DVR user pushing the buttons on a hand-held remote control device. Some DVRs, however, can also be controlled via a computer keyboard. The latter would be true in the cases of both (1) a Slingbox and (2) a do-it-yourself home-built DVR or DVR-like device.

4.3.1 Remotes

Various designs of DVR remote control devices populate the market place today. Just about every single one features channel-changing buttons in one area of the hand-held device and a set of buttons in another area dedicated exclusively to operating the DVR. Among TiVo-DirecTV, EchoStar-only, and DirecTV-only remote controls, for example, all three feature the ten numbers (i.e., 1–10) for channel changing on the bottom half of the remote, with the actual stop, fast forward, and replay buttons located just above that in the middle of the remote. Power, video input, and miscellaneous other buttons reside at the tops of the standard DVR remote control device. Figures 1.15–1.18 show four different remote control devices that control the uses and applications offered by a DVR.

4.3.2 Other Forms

As noted at the outset of Chapter 1, because the DVR today is truly just another form of a sophisticated computer, it comes as no surprise to many computer sophisticates that the DVR can be part of a real PC and/or that it can be controlled by the keys on a PC or laptop. Today, both the Slingbox and related devices, as well as a DIY home-built DVR inside a PC, are controlled via a keyboard. Although not as elegant as the average remote control device, for basic functionality, the keyboard works just fine.

In the future, more DVR functionality will be done via something like a cell phone and/or a PDA. In fact, it is not too far afield to envision a set of future cell phones that have DVR functionality built into them. The traveler will push a button on his or her cell phone inside a hotel, and the device automatically substitutes for the remote control device used at home. Turn on the TV in the hotel room, make sure it is connected to a device such as the SlingCatcher (which plugs into the Internet port in the room and then into the back of the hotel room TV), and with that push of a special application button, your cell phone becomes any traveler's on-the-road remote control device. From there, certain assigned buttons on the cell phone will permit fast forward, rewind, pause, and recording of all content from one's home TV, including local, network, cable, satellite, telco, and DVR-recorded content.

4.3.3 Transferring Content

Content can be transferred from a DVR to a side-car device, that is, one that is intended to act as a mere hard drive that simply adds more storage for an already full set-top box unit DVR. In other words, the side-care is comparable to a flash memory stick, yet it is larger and storage is in the form of a hard drive disk rather than flash.

Another form of content transfer using a DVR occurs when the DVR is used as the main set-top unit within the home and content gets transferred through wires to other TVs in the same abode. This is an example of a new trend within the DVR and multichannel pay TV worlds called "multiroom" or "home media center," for example.

Using a device like a Slingbox, as discussed earlier in this chapter, is another way to convey content stored on a DVR to another device, be it a TV in another place, or a cell phone.

Note that in each of these transfer implementations, the developers have been careful to build in technology that allows control of the content, well within the range of "fair use" discussed earlier in this chapter. This is important because, ultimately, distributors will not be encouraged to continue distributing content if they are not adequately compensated for their efforts.

4.3.4 Other Applications

As offered, for example, in the software from satellite TV operators, i.e., EchoStar's DISH Network and DirecTV, below, numerous on-screen software applications are typically available to DVR users.

When pressing the DISH DVR remote control upon turning on the DVR, the first screen features:[2]

*   My Recordings: Gives list of content we have recorded
*   Movies and More: Lists of all HD movies on demand
*   TV Entertainment: 11 miscellaneous short features
*   My Media: Features a multimedia device that gets connected to the DVR's USB port
*   DishONLINE: Go to http://www.dishnetwork.com/DishONLINE for info on movies and other programs using broadband Internet connection
*   Cancel

In addition, pushing the "Main Menu" off of the DISH Network remote brings up:

*   Program Guide
*   Themes and Search
*   Customer Support
*   Multimedia
*   Locks
*   System Setup
*   Daily Schedule
*   Preferences
*   DISH on Demand

[2] More specifics concerning the uses and applications of DISH Network DVRs can be accessed online at http://www.dishnetwork.com. In addition, other DVR company listings can be seen by turning to this book's Appendix B.

When pressing the DirecTV remote control upon turning on the DVR, the first screen features the following applications:

- Now Playing List
  - Lists what the consumer user has recorded
  - Once that program has been clicked-on, next screen presents (1) title and description of that show, (2) length, rating, time, type of program, plus, (3) choices of (a) play, (b) keep until, (c) delete now, (d) save to VCR, or (e) do not do anything

- Watch Live TV
  - Clicking goes right to a live TV show on the channel previously chosen
  - Screen shows title and description and length, etc. of that show for several seconds

- Showcases: Offers coupons for products

- Pick Programs to Record
  - Searches by title (e.g., movies, sports, news, kids, family...alphabetized listings)
  - Searches using a "Wishlist" (e.g., pick an actor name by keying in the name)
  - Offers suggestions
  - Records by time or channel
  - Offers a season pass manager
  - Offers a to-do list

- Read New Messages and Setup

- Standby

4.4 Summary

This chapter is intended more as the "insides" of the engine that drives DVRs. The Rentrak and Nielsen case studies provide additional insight into an important view to successful DVR applications, that of measuring how they are succeeding or not. Although there are a number of DVR uses and applications, this chapter also shows that this number can also be described within a few pages of a book.

5 Business Models

DVRs will impact viewer behavior and thus ultimately the TV industry value chain and the business models. The increasing use of DVRs puts the current programming choice models and the implied business models of TV stations and of cable/satellite service providers in jeopardy.
  —Loebbecke and Radke, Business Models and Programming Choice: Digital Video Recorders Shaping the TV Industry[1]

As advertisers lose the ability to invade the home, and consumers' minds, they will be forced to wait for an invitation. This means that they have to learn what kinds of advertising content customers will actually be willing to seek out and receive.
  —Henry Jenkins, Advertising Age Magazine[2]

We do think the DVR is an inelegant solution to recording programming for consumers, and that it could be done on a network basis more efficiently.
  —Tom Rutledge, COO, Cablevision Systems

Because this book is about television, which is primarily a consumer medium, there will be little or no discussion, within this "Business Models" chapter, of DVRs used for security (other than to mention that it is a thriving business globally). Indeed, in most countries globally, especially because of post 9–11 security concerns, the security side of DVRs is way more popular (and prevalent) than the consumer side. Thus, for most business and commercial entities, their knowledge of DVRs is going to be mostly on the side of security devices.

That said, there remain several fascinating stories of consumer DVR business models—past, present, and future. This chapter seeks to identify and make sense of a handful of the important ones.

When all is said and done, a business model is about building a structure, typically with the goal of making money and being profitable. This, then, is the focus of this chapter.

5.1 Standalones

Because they are the U.S. (and, in many senses, the global) pioneers in the development of consumer DVRs going back to 1998–1999, TiVo's[3] and

---

[1] See, *Proceedings of the Eleventh Americas Conference on Information Systems*, Omaha, NE, August 11–14, 2005, which is a good review of various business models in the new world of DVRs.

[2] Jenkins, Henry. "Convergence Culture: Where Old and New Media Collide. Buying Into American Idol." (pages 66–67).

[3] The original name of TiVo was Teleworld; it was changed by TiVo co-founders Jim Barton and Michael Ramsay in 1999.

Replay's were the first DVR business models. Yet, it is rather interesting, indeed, fascinating, to observe how different the two models were created and grown, and, as a result, how differently the two companies turned out.

5.1.1 ReplayTV

ReplayTV, like TiVo, grew out of the Silicon Valley, and a group of technology developers who had seen the prospects to turn hard drives into storage for more than just basic computer content, instead using those hard drives to store video, in the form of digital ones and zeros. ReplayTV's founder, Anthony Woods, fought valiantly in a pitched battle to be first to market and to be first to many other things against the rival Silicon Valley team of Jim Barton and Mike Ramsay at TiVo. In the end, he and his company were far from successful, although they did accomplish some remarkable things.

Like TiVo, ReplayTV sought outside funding to grow its operation. Ironically, Microsoft cofounder and current charter cable controlling owner, Paul Allen, was approached by both TiVo and ReplayTV in 1998. At his lavish home in the Pacific Northwest, Allen listened to proposals from both providers and ultimately chose to invest in both.

Similar to TiVo, ReplayTV sought investment from Hollywood studios and TV networks, and both TiVo and ReplayTV were relatively successful in their early days. Nonetheless, some insiders believe that the real demise for ReplayTV came because of its inability to quickly grab timely and all-critical financing, where months before TiVo had been successful.

Further, perhaps where success was most important, in the goal to obtain a working relationship with a major U.S. multichannel pay TV operator, ReplayTV was again unsuccessful, while TiVo was successful. Many today believe that this failure and ReplayTV's aggressive efforts to quickly push the DVR technology limits (and thus more quickly push the demise of the TV advertising and copyright systems) were the two real reasons for the collapse of the ReplayTV business models and the company's subsequent bankruptcy.[4] Publicly, at least, this ReplayTV "technology push" came primarily in the form of ReplayTV's "ad-skip" and its "send show" features. Both features were well beyond what TiVo had offered and were apparently offered by ReplayTV in an effort to better challenge TiVo, which already in its first couple of years had chalked up a retail sales advantage over ReplayTV. But the new ReplayTV features backfired, in the sense that they occasioned the *Paramount* lawsuit, which helped to lead to ReplayTV's demise.

---

[4] Note that ReplayTV was sold in 2000 to SonicBlue, which itself went bankrupt shortly after settling the litigation brought against ReplayTV by the Hollywood studios and by the TV networks, called *Paramount et al vs. ReplayTV.*

As to its core initial business model, both ReplayTV and TiVo asked consumers to expend hundreds of dollars on the standalone set-top box unit and then asked them to also shell out monthly lease fees to access the proprietary interactive programming guides (EPGs/IPGs). The consumer, however, under both business models, had the choice also of paying several hundred dollars up front for a lifetime electronic program guide (EPG/IPG) fee, thus completely eliminating the pesky monthly (EPG/IPG) fee.

ReplayTV is mentioned again further in this chapter under the subheading "Software," inasmuch as ReplayTV shifted its business model from that of being a hardware and software DVR provider to that of being exclusively a software DVR provider in 2001. Ultimately, the standalone side of the DVR business proved simply too competitive for ReplayTV (and SonicBlue) to survive.

5.1.2   TiVo

Like Digeo, headquartered at Kirkland, WA, TiVo, based in Alviso, CA, also straddles the lines between a standalone and a cable-focused business model. Both companies, in fact, offer both. While TiVo, in its earliest days, tracked the early business model of ReplayTV, it met considerable additional success in the 1999–2001 time frame in its deal with satellite TV provider, DirecTV.

Realizing that a better long-term business model involved (1) access to a large, single-company audience, (2) significant monthly EPG/IPG lease revenues, and (3) set-top box lease revenues, TiVo entered into a multiyear agreement with DirecTV, allowing TiVo-branded DVRs to begin to be installed into millions and millions of DirecTV TV Households.

This arrangement worked quite well for TiVo until DirecTV's controlling ownership was sold to Rupert Murdoch's News Corporation in early 2004. The new management at News Corporation/DirecTV acted quickly to begin terminating the DirecTV–TiVo relationship, replacing entry level DirecTV–TiVo boxes with those from News Corporation-controlled set-top and technology vendor, NDS. Yet, like many other newcomers to the DVR space and many other multichannel TV providers, the News Corporation–DirecTV combo quickly discovered how difficult creating and building and installing quality DVRs could be. Early models of the new DirecTV NDS-built XTV brand set-top DVRs met considerable resistance from both consumers and critics. Following the sale by News Corporation of its DirecTV interest to Dr. John Malone's Liberty organization in 2008, DirecTV reactivated the relationship with TiVo, however, at a much more limited level than before.

Yet, very likely, most important to TiVo's long-term health is the status of the part of its business model that relies on relationships with other multichannel TV vendors and with new vendors overseas. In the former category are cable operators, such as Comcast. Although slow to develop, and still difficult for TiVo to manage, access to nearly 25 million potential Comcast subscribers makes for interesting—indeed, possibly enticing—financial results. Further, as described in more detail in Chapter 7, "International DVR Growth," TiVo has begun tapping markets in Europe and Asia.

Yet another important potential financial and revenue vehicle for TiVo lies in relationships it has created with companies such as Amazon.com, YouTube, and Nero. These allow not only access to new content and new purchase opportunities but also new forms of DVRs for users beyond TV, i.e., those using PCs and laptops. Another realm is that of transferring content to mobile devices for use while traveling.

Perhaps the granddaddy of all business models for companies like TiVo, including other standalones, as well as other service operators who control or have access to a user's viewing data, is that of data mining. As noted in Chapter 3, data mining is so attractive because of its potential to not only please advertisers who can get to specific, welcoming consumers, but also to please those very consumers with the helpful and relevant on-demand content they are getting.

5.1.3 *Digeo*

Like TiVo, Digeo has a long history that traces back to its owner, Paul Allen, and his earliest investments in TiVo and ReplayTV. Today, Digeo mingles both with large and mid-sized cable operators, and with retailer customers, in the form of its new standalone set-top DVR box.

Digeo's main venture into multichannel pay TV America received a rather significant head-start because of Paul Allen's controlling interest in top 10 U.S. cable operator, St. Louis, MO-based Charter Communications. Featuring its Moxy brand set-top box and EPG/IPG, Digeo has had success in this market, which has led it to reach additional agreements with smaller sized cable systems, such as Bend, OR's Bend Broadband.

In the standalone market, Digeo's late 2008 unveiling of its new set-top box model, the Moxi MR-1500T3, is based upon a unique value proposition. Rather than pricing its first model in the $300 range (as standalone competitors do), and then charge another (1) $12.99/month, or (2) $199 for 2 years, or (3) $299 for 3 years, or (4) $399 for a lifetime subscription, Digeo has chosen to instead charge a higher, one-time only fee of $799 up front for the set-top box and lifetime service together. Digeo prides itself on noting that it seeks to avoid almost every future additional fee, excepting perhaps some later fees that it has not yet recognized or envisioned.

Further, Digeo prides itself on its 500 gigabyte hard drive, which is quite competitive in today's marketplace, and on what it claims is a much faster competitive processor. In addition, Digeo states that it has spent a good deal of time creating and enhancing its Emmy Award Winning EPG/IPG.

digeo™

Greg Gudorf, chief executive officer of Digeo,[5] is his company's—and one of the DVR industry's—top executives and a chief cheerleader, especially when it comes to the future prospects for DVR technology. With Digeo since 2005, when he began as the company's president and chief operating officer, and, prior to that, with Sony Electronics, as a senior vice president on the TV side, Gudorf describes Digeo today as "... a CE manufacturer that provides innovative solutions for the connected media environment. Digeo solutions are implemented by service operators, such as multisystem service operators (MSOs), or directly to consumers via the retail channel. Digeo's core product is the Moxi brand user interface and application software stack. Moxi runs on a variety of hardware platforms, under both a Windows and a Linux operating system. Some of the hardware products are designed by and built for Digeo directly. Additionally, Digeo has a unique connected portal service that communicates with each Moxi product, in a two-way manner, on a daily basis, enabling content and software updates, as well as diagnostic, billing, and usage data to flow, on a near real-time basis."

More specifically, Digeo's Moxi brand hardware and software technology and services for digital media recorders provide users with a wide range of home entertainment features and services, including DVRs; HDTV programming; digital media management of photos and music; content sharing with PCs; interactive data services, such as the Moxi SuperTicker; Moxi games; and web scheduling. Digeo's flagship product—the two-time Emmy Award-winning Moxi Media Center—serves as a hub for whole-home distribution of digital entertainment. The Moxi Media Center was first commercially deployed in 2004, with total unit shipments now in the range of 500,000, involving partnerships with nine U.S. cable operators.

According to Digeo, it continues to innovate with a next generation Moxi cable solution and several retail products currently under development. Digeo also has a strong patent portfolio, it reports, related directly to its Moxi products and services, with approximately 125 patents awarded and 150 patent applications pending.

---

[5] Readers will note that this Digeo case study is longer than the average case study in this book. This is a result of (a) the value of the information provided by this company and its top executive and (b) the cooperation and attitude of Digeo in this regard.

Looking into Digeo's past, its motivation to involve itself in DVRs began in the early 2000s, when the Kirkland, WA-based company saw a significant market opportunity in the area of DVRs being developed for U.S. cable MSOs. Looking at the direct broadcast satellite (DBS) providers, cable operators were loathe to see their satellite-delivered rivals grow their subscriber base, largely at cable's expense, by aggressively deploying integrated satellite/DVR set-top box receiver decoders. To compound the problem for cable, satellite (DBS) providers were successfully using DVRs to attract and retain high-end, high-margin customers. Gudorf notes that there was an obvious need for cable operators to deploy a DVR solution, so as to compete with their satellite rivals. Without DVRs, cable operators stood to continue losing subscribers and revenues to their satellite TV rivals.

Digeo saw a significant market opportunity for a media center product, with an intuitive user experience, and the potential to serve as the hub for all digital media in the home, without the setup and use complications or "usability hassles" of the PC. What's more, Digeo foresaw that the cost-performance curve of silicon platforms and the cost-down curve of mass storage disk drives would enable truly unique and engrossing user interface experiences at set-top box prices that were the near equivalent of the run-of-the-mill legacy set-top boxes. Against this backdrop and driven by consumer responses to the Moxi experience, Digeo's market analyses showed the potential for a strong business, in both the system operator and retail channels.

Gudorf goes on to note that most major cable operators were in the final stages of a significant plant upgrade during the early 2000s time frame, which enhanced the potential for two-way communication and increased bandwidth utilization. This massive system-by-system upgrade positioned cable to provide VOD, high-speed data, telephony, and more video channels (including HDTV). Yet, in spite of all the improvements in the cable plants nationwide, the legacy consumer premises equipment (CPE) in the home was still a bottleneck—unable to fully leverage the system-level advancements. More powerful set-top box hardware/software, and a better user experience, were sorely needed. According to Digeo, this was the impetus for the original Moxi line of products.

Further, today Digeo sees DVRs offering a compelling consumer value proposition, and significant continued strong growth is expected over the next several years. Market trends—such as the transition to digital video, the growth in HD content, and HDTV price reductions—are all further spurring consumer adoption of DVR technology, opines Gudorf. He also concludes that, "At the same time, the growth in home networks, digital audio/photos, and the proliferation of online video content have the potential to expand the role of the DVR. The DVR has the potential to serve as the hub of a whole-home media center, accessing content from various sources (including traditional linear cable broadcast, cable VOD, Internet services, and home network-stored content), and lawfully distributing that content to multiple display devices inside and outside the home."

For the more distant future, Gudorf and Digeo believe that this whole-home media center concept will continue to be a core component of all Moxi-brand products. Market trends are now lining up to support this vision, Gudorf believes, positioning Moxi well for the next wave of growth in the digital home.

The dialogue turns most interesting when Gudorf was asked about future concerns, as Digeo looks at its future vision of DVRs in the whole-home environment, and future impediments to that result. Gudorf notes, "Digeo's products are intended for sale through two primary channels: service operators (e.g., cable MSOs) and retail channels. On the service operator side, many MSOs often place greater emphasis on the cost than on the ultimate power and experience of a product. While Digeo strives to develop a superior product with a compelling value proposition, cost-only focused solutions can result in the good blocking the great." He goes on to note, "Similarly, MSOs often prefer to deliver a consistent user experience on a familiar platform. While this may not provide the absolute best user experience, it offers the MSO operational efficiencies. This 'familiar platform' theory means that an incumbent vendor advantage in both hardware and software is an obstacle for any company, like Digeo, that looks to expand sales to new cable operators, well beyond legacy DVRs. It is an obstacle to consumers who want a selection of best-in-breed DVRs from their cable operators."

Turning to challenges on the retail side, Digeo believes a large challenge lies on the side of effectively communicating the DVR's value proposition to consumers. Given the vast amounts of information (and misinformation) in the consumer electronics space, Gudorf notes, "This can be a task as challenging as it is fun." Moxi DVRs are available in the retail channel via key distributors, such as on-line retailers (including direct sale from Digeo) and national retailers.

Turning to the criteria Digeo uses to assess the effectiveness of its deployment of DVRs, like any business, Digeo notes that it uses standard financial metrics to evaluate the economic returns of its business. At the same time, Digeo notes that it also believes it is critical to evaluate the effectiveness of the Moxi products from its partners' perspective. In other words, Digeo states it is critical that it ensures its solutions deliver a compelling value proposition to its partners. Toward that goal, Digeo has engaged in studies to evaluate additional key financial drivers in areas such as customer churn, VOD usage, feature usage, and overall customer satisfaction.

Some data points from these studies include the following:

- Digeo VOD usage that is up to three times greater than that of other DVR competitors[6]
- Customer retention that is one of the highest in its category, for example, 37% lower churn vs. industry standard DVR churn[7]
- Average Revenue Per Unit (ARPU) that is one of the highest in the industry, for example, $2–$5 monthly increment vs. the industry standard DVR ARPU[8]

Further, Digeo states that the feedback, both objective and subjective, from consumers exposed to the Digeo Moxi product indicates the potential value is, indeed, real value, in the eyes of consumers.

Going deeper into the DVR benefits found and offered by Digeo, Gudorf reasons, "DVR functionality is generally well understood and can act as a starting point in communicating Digeo's suite of features and consumer value proposition. What's more, being involved with the DVR market, in the form of the Moxi Media Center (as opposed to a DVR-only product), has taught Digeo unique and valuable lessons as to how consumers think about their content types, and how they wish to enjoy them throughout their home. This experience, and the reality of the two-way, connected home—the world the Moxi Media Center resides in, along with its customers—is a key portal into the future of home entertainment."

Zeroing in on the types of DVRs Digeo currently deploys (e.g., stand-alone, service operator's set-top box, home media center, gaming device, and PC-based) the company has DVR-based products positioned both in the MSO and retail consumer electronics spaces. On the MSO side, Digeo sells its solution to the specific MSOs across the United States, which, in turn, lease the product to their subscribers. An incremental monthly fee of a few dollars is the typical model utilized by the multichannel operators. When working in this model, the product development and implementation is based on Digeo's ability to create an innovative value proposition for both the consumer, who uses the product, and for the service operator, which distributes and leases the product.

At retail, Digeo also develops products for sale directly to consumers. Digeo's products are primarily targeted at customers who receive their programming from MSOs. Digeo's DVR solutions are also available to consumers who receive broadcast programming from the Advanced Television Systems Committee (ATSC) digital standards-enabled over-the-air TV tuners. These retail offerings are offered on standalone Digeo set-top hardware, as well as software for use with Media Center PCs, along with the unique device offerings these retailers offer. According to Gudorf,

[6] Per study of all DVRs in certain Adelphia markets between February 5 and March 5, 2006.
[7] Per reports from certain MSOs in 2006.
[8] Per study of more than 300,000 DVR subscribers in certain Adelphia markets, over 11 months, from January 2005–November 2005.

looking into its own version of a crystal ball, Digeo believes that "... our flexible and dynamic architecture would also allow us to easily develop solutions for service providers in the IPTV space." This would possibly include large telcos, such as Verizon.

Focus on the Digeo whole-home solution reveals that Digeo's DVR solution is based on a multiroom design, which allows customers to have products located in multiple locations within the home. The products are networked together, utilizing the home's internal wiring, which may be in the form of coax-, Ethernet-, or powerline-based solutions, or, as the technology continues to improve, wireless connectivity. Each product within the multiroom design has a core capability to maximize the customer value proposition. For example, the main Moxi DVR includes the digital cable tuning capability and primary storage. Within the other rooms, a customer can place a client device, called a Moxi Mate, which can independently access any of the content or services of the main Moxi DVR. Yet, concurrently, each Moxi Mate device can also access the customer's broadband Internet access, and thus could receive content from a remote content service, such as Netflix, YouTube, etc.[9] Gudorf summarizes, "The key to Digeo's multiroom approach is that all content, whether it is DVR content or broadband accessible content, can be enjoyed by the consumer throughout the Moxi home, in a secure manner, with all the same features and functional abilities available at each Moxi end-point."

Digeo's design of its user-interface and seamless integration of items such as EPG/IPG, search, etc. is also worth noting. Gudorf continues, "The key difference of a Digeo DVR begins with the unique and Emmy-award winning user interface. The Moxi interface provides an innovative approach to keeping every feature available to the user, just a click or two away, while being simple enough, so that users can readily learn of the system's power, while also never getting lost in the detail. This is accomplished via Moxi's center-focus interface, which places all the key categories of features across a circular horizontal band, and the detail of each feature across a circular vertical band. As a result, the user can never get lost. This is because one can always readily return to where the journey began."

Supplementing and maximizing the Digeo customer's user interface, the list below indicates its core features:

- Picture-in-graphics: This feature means the TV's video content is ever-present, even while accessing the menu, or while playing a host of parlor games.

---

[9] In several instances, this case study uses examples of potential third-party providers of online services or content. These are intended only for illustration purposes and do not imply endorsement by these third parties; nor are they intended as statements that Moxi product(s) will provide those specific services/content.

- Merging cable content with Internet content: This feature permits the vast video content available from a cable provider to be mixed with the ever-expanding amount of content available on the Internet. Thus, premium movies, music from favorite artists, or personally-created content can be made available from providers, such as Flicker or YouTube, via the Moxi service.
- Expandable hard drive storage options: Involving expandability on the level of multiple terabytes, Digeo states the Moxi home's DVR capability can be increased substantially by simply adding a standard off-the-shelf external hard disk drive purchased from the local electronics store.
- Accessible content: Easily accessible content (e.g., video, pictures, or music) from any network-connected device [e.g., a PC or a network-attached storage (NAS) device] can be delivered to the DVR or Moxi Mate portable device via Digeo's Digital Living Network Alliance (DLNA)-enabled services.
- Remote scheduling: This is a feature whereby DVR access can be delivered from any Internet browser, to schedule a recording, and then know instantly if there are recorded scheduling conflicts so the viewer/user can make the correction and be assured of catching that show.
- Search engine: Digeo claims its Moxi search engine is "blazingly fast," when delivering on-screen content stored on the Moxi DVR or on network-connected devices.
- A device that permits users to instantly touch the remote and receive weather, news, sports, and entertainment content: this feature, called the Moxi SuperTicker, displays ever-changing on-screen Internet video content and plays beneath standard video content. According to Gudorf, SuperTicker is "... fully interactive, allowing the user to skip between headlines, updated throughout the day, or see more information, without ever leaving the on-screen TV program."
- An HD interface in a 16 × 9 aspect ratio: this feature allows every pixel and every color on the palette to be utilized; Gudorf notes, "... thus creating the most visually-stunning, innovative and user-friendly experience of any DVR product on the market."

A closer look at the content sources that Digeo can record on its DVRs includes the three primary categories of video, audio, and photos, as described below:

- Video: Since the current Digeo business focuses primarily on interaction with the cable community, the video content includes the complete channel listing that the customer subscribes to. Additionally, Digeo says it is able to directly integrate access to the pay-per-view and VOD content that a customer can purchase. Further, in the case of the retail Moxi products, because the Moxi DVR is connected to the customer's broadband Internet access, Moxi enables access to video content, such as NetFlix, YouTube, or other video content providers. Last but not least, the customer may access video content stored on connected, video-enabled devices on his or her home network, via Digeo's DLNA service, and then stream that content onto either the Moxi DVR or the portable Moxi Mate.

- Music and Pictures: Music and still picture content can be enabled in much the same manner as video, via (1) the cable provider, via (2) Internet services (such as Rhapsody for music, or Flicker for pictures, or via (3) the customer's home network-connected DLNA devices.

Turning to the consumer's operational control of Digeo's DVR product, the company reports that its Moxi products utilize an operational software architecture designed by Digeo. Part of that includes control of Digeo's DVRs via infrared signals delivered from a remote control or directly from an Internet protocol (IP) connection. The software is hosted on the DVR product, but it is designed to communicate via IP connectivity with the Digeo Network Operations Center, in order to receive updates, allow for customization, or even enable the customer to communicate with his or her product, from any Internet browser to set up a recorded event or provide other directions.

Further focusing on Gudorf's opinion of the biggest threats facing the future deployment of DVRs, he begins by identifying the fact that serving approximately 110 million U.S. households are three primary providers for the reception of multichannel pay TV services today, i.e., cable, satellite, and telco. Within each segment, each major service provider, e.g., Comcast, DirecTV, and Verizon, treads a fine line between cost control and innovation, with cost control always being the key issue. For example, within the cable community, there is a vast legacy of set-top box products, which have only the most basic hardware capability by today's standards. Such legacy products often prohibit many innovative software solutions from being deployed, due to hardware incompatibilities.

Additionally, a key hidden cost, within each of these provider's models, is the customer service costs to address customer questions, technical issues, etc. To best control these costs, the most economical path is to *limit differentiation in hardware and user interaction*, so that a customer support representative does not have to spend time determining what product or version of an application is deployed within the home or at the network level, as they attempt to maintain and deploy different versions of the then-current software stack. Consequently, the pace of innovation is naturally slowed by the lowest common denominator and that means what currently is deployed everywhere. In the opinion of Gudorf, "The resulting homogenization challenges the very foundation that Digeo was created upon, i.e., user interface excellence that pushes the innovation envelope forward."

Turning to the top DVR opportunities, Gudorf notes that the same threat mentioned above can also be the source of the greatest opportunity. In a homogenized world, the smallest implemented product innovation can create a ground swell of adoption: As an example, Gudorf cites the Apple iPod, which, in turn, forces the entire marketplace to rise or be swallowed.

In the realm of the single aspect of DVRs that it likes the most, Digeo claims that, "DVRs offer the consumer a compelling value proposition for navigating, recording, managing and watching, and simply enjoying, vast amounts of audio and video content. The consumer can now enjoy what he or she wants, and whenever. The DVR value proposition may also serve to educate and entice consumers toward adoption of a whole new wave of home entertainment products/services. This would include items such as whole-home audio/video distribution, access to IP-based content services, and home controls."

As for Digeo's two key clients—which would be consumers and the multichannel pay TV operators—the aspects of the Digeo DVR implementation that Gudorf believes the MSOs favor the most are in the form of what he calls "monetization." Specifically, under the *operator* side of this heading, Gudorf lists the following:

- With the seamless integration of pay-per-view and VOD into the interface, Digeo's MSO clients find triple the usage over other DVR competitors.
- As noted above, there is a 40% lower churn vs. industry standard DVR, and MSOs get the highest ARPU, that is, $2–$5 monthly increment vs. industry standard DVR, using Digeo.
- Innovative and user friendly user interface (i.e., the EPG/IPG).
- Advance feature sets, including full-featured multiroom support.

Focused, on the other hand, from the *consumer* perspective, Digeo lists the benefits as follows:

- The simple-to-use innovations of the Moxi user interface (i.e., the EPG/IPG).
- The ability to easily search across vast amounts of content choices to discover what is desired.
- The unified approach to multiroom access of all Moxi features and content.
- The convenience of great connectivity between products, enabling constant up-to-date access to the latest content choices and technical improvements.

Yet, with a view toward improvement, asked about what aspects of DVRs Digeo's clients or customers identify as their least favorite, Gudorf admits that some operators cite the additional operational support (e.g., call center training and installer training) as a challenge. Moreover, if Digeo could change any aspect of DVRs, what would that be? Gudorf adds, "The typical DVR's 'grid guide' approach is way too limiting in today's world of rapidly proliferating content (with hundreds of linear channels and thousands of VOD titles, for example). As previously discussed, Moxi's Emmy award-winning user interface avoids what we call 'grid-lock,' and provides an intuitive paradigm for accessing content and services, and thus we believe it's the interface all DVRs should strive to utilize."

Summing up in the area of advertising, Digeo, via Gudorf, describes its advertising model as follows.

"Digeo has worked with partners to develop test versions of advanced advertising applications. These include such ad forms as telescoping, which enable the user to select a long-form commercial, while pausing the current program; and 'speed-bumps,' which display an image while the user fast-forwards through a commercial. Digeo's experience in this arena dates back to 2001, and, when coupled with the constantly-connected Moxi approach, is readily enabled, as operators desire to be fully deployed."

As it relates to Digeo and its ability to work with third parties to use DVRs (and the user data they can gather) to display user-specific targeted ads, Digeo is not yet working with any specific third party to achieve this goal; however, the Digeo platform and backend portal is reportedly capable of readily supporting ad delivery and measurement, as the market size warrants. In that vein, Digeo currently uses—within the guidelines of the appropriate privacy policies—its DVRs to collect data and information about users and their preferences. Anonymous usage logs can be delivered to the Moxi portal from all Moxi devices, on a daily basis. In addition, users can set preferences for certain applications via the Internet and the Digeo website, http://www.My Moxi.com. Analysis of anonymous usage logs is used to evaluate how users interact with the product, helping Digeo make informed product design decisions as to features and functionality. In addition, usage data is also used to generate audience measurement reports, including Moxi's "Time Machine" report, which provides a forward-looking view of shows that will be recorded in the upcoming week. In addition, usage data is used for other aggregate measurement purposes, such as VOD purchases, service message viewing, and use of the "SuperTicker" product, described earlier in this case study.

Lastly, consumer privacy-controlled preferences, set via http://www.MyMoxi.com, allow for a customized user experience, such as auto sign-in for integrated third party applications and remote recording. In the end, Digeo has designed its platform and backend portal to provide the ability to leverage usage data ad/content targeting. According to Gudorf, "This will need to be done in a manner that provides real value to the end-user, and is highly sensitive to the end-user's privacy requirements."

Turning to the question of operators or others implementing features that give operators control over consumers' use of features—such as blocking the ability to skip through a commercial—Digeo believes that while that control is technically feasible and currently available within Moxi (should the operator desire to activate this item), such a limitation is not necessary. Gudorf concludes "Yet, that said, the proliferation of DVRs, and their ability to fast forward through television content, may require advertisers to evaluate new advertising models/form factors. Digeo's platform can and will support the delivery, implementation, and measurement of such advanced ad applications."

On the final topic of the dialogue with Digeo, when asked about the ability of content owners and distributors to restrict users' use and reuse by others of the same content, Gudorf states, "Digeo believes that the content owners, who expended the financial resources to create the entertainment material, should be compensated fairly for their effort. The key challenge in this conversation is how to define 'others'? If it refers to devices within the customer's home, then limitations to prevent this could be contrary to what consumers feel is fair. If it refers to sharing content with friends, neighbors, and more people, then there should be a mechanism available to the content holders to limit this, if they wish." In this vein, Gudorf thinks that savvy owners will embrace these challenges as part of the opportunity to create new business models balancing consumers' expectations together with the importance of the content owners' bottom lines. On this topic of sharing data and other content, Gudorf philosophizes, "We are at a critical stage in how 'fair use' will be defined in the digital age. As an example, the Motion Picture Association of America (MPAA) and its studio constituents have proposed to allow multichannel video programming distributors, e.g., cable companies, the ability to control which digital and analog outputs are available for devices to use—as they so choose. While this is not to suggest doom and gloom, such broad ability potentially changes what consumers can do with the consumer electronics equipment and content they have purchased or otherwise legally procured."

Gudorf believes that there needs to be a new definition of what "fair use" constitutes in the Digital Age. This would be a definition that protects the content rights holders, but does not eviscerate consumers' rights or breach the balance of interests between content creators, technology innovators, and consumers.

Finally, Gudorf was asked about studies Digeo has deployed to better understand the deployment of DVRs. Gudorf concludes, "As of this moment, all Digeo DVR products have been sold to MSO customers, who, in turn, deploy the product into consumers' homes. While Digeo maintains all these products, only anonymous usage data is collected for use with our partners in compliance with their individual privacy policies and none of that analysis is available for general release." For its upcoming retail product releases and in keeping with Digeo's consumer privacy policy, Digeo will have the ability to conduct more user-specific studies, as are decided to be appropriate.

Digeo

Contact Information
8815 122nd Ave. NE
Kirkland, WA 98033
Phone: 425-896-6000
http://www.Digeo.com

Stock Symbol
Privately held

Key People
Paul G. Allen, Chairman
Greg Gudorf, CEO and COO
PR Contact: communications@digeo.com

Key Business
DVR hardware and software company.

DVR Connection
Sells Digeo branded DVRs, as well as third-party Digeo-enabled DVRs sold through retailers.

5.2 Multichannel Pay TV Operators

Three main groups make up the cadre of multichannel pay TV operators in the United States. These include, by size, cable, with approximately 65 million video subscribers; satellite, with approximately 30 million video subscribers; and telco, with several single-digit millions. Although currently not a single major U.S. multichannel operator is even close to opening up the DVR side of its business to competition—competition that will, for example, create lower prices for DVR hardware and software contracts, savings of which would then be passed onto consumers—some argue that the industry appears to be heading in that direction. An industry observer Davis Freeberg argues that, "The industry still has a long ways to go, but as the DVR becomes an integral part of the digital home, I believe that the cable and satellite industry will abandon the monopolistic practices of the past and will end up benefitting more from the intense competition in this consumer electronics space."[10]

5.2.1 Satellite

First among the U.S. multichannel pay TV operators to unveil a DVR was Englewood, CO-based EchoStar, through its DISH Network subsidiary, in 1999. DirecTV followed soon after, with its first TiVo-based set-top DVR.

EchoStar

DISH Network's first DVR was created and implemented in conjunction with computer software giant, EchoStar, in the form of the now defunct *WebTV*

---

[10] See, Freeburg, Davis, "How TV Monopolies Benefit From DVR Industry Competition," *Seeking Alpha*, September 28, 2008.

service. The original business model, and the one still in place today, was that of using low-cost DVR deployments to not only entice new subscribers, but also to make those new subscribers so happy with the overall DISH Network service that they would never want to leave and would constantly want to spend more on other digital products, such as HDTV, interactive TV, and VOD-like functions. This early business model was later implemented quite aggressively by EchoStar rival DirecTV, and later again by the core of the U.S. cable and telco industries.

As noted and highlighted in Chapters 3 and 8, EchoStar and its DISH Network have expanded this business model to include many new elements. One of those was the 2007 purchase of the remote TV viewing provider Sling Media. Another is the unveiling of HD DVRs. In Q4 2008, EchoStar unveiled a new analog-to-digital broadcast TV converter box (costing $249 after rebates and credit), which contains a built-in DVR with a 150-hour standard definition (SD) recording capacity, called the DTVPal DVR. Yet another is EchoStar Technology Corporation's long talked about $39.99 external box, which allows DISH Network customers to convert their single tuner set-tops into DVRs, by attaching the ViP211- and ViP211K-model set-top external hard drive devices. The most recent EchoStar DVR advance is the 922 set-top model, which combines Sling with an HD-DVR.

DirecTV

Not far behind EchoStar in its recognition and implementation of its own DVR strategy and business model, the first high-power satellite TV provider in the U.S., DirecTV, unveiled its first DVR product late in 1999. This was a base-model DVR, developed and manufactured in conjunction with TiVo, as well as CE manufacturers, like Sony and Philips.

Years later, in 2004, with the acquisition of DirecTV by News Corp., DirecTV began phasing TiVo out of the DirecTV set-top box operation; however, following News Corp.'s sale of DirecTV in 2008, TiVo was permitted to rejoin the DirecTV team, yet in a greatly reduced role. Today, DirecTV's main set-top supplier remains News Corp.-owned and -controlled NDS; yet, many believe that DirecTV will be much more aggressive in opening DirecTV to more DVR competition. Many DirecTV consumers and critics have been rather adamant about seeing that happen. Indeed, the same could be said about just about all of today's U.S. multichannel pay TV operators: they need to open their DVR businesses to more competition, and hopefully use that competition to provide better DVR-related products and services to their subscribers.

5.2.2 Cable

A short version of the cable industry's development of its DVR business model begins in the late 1990s, when the cable industry's more than $100 billion investment in digital infrastructure upgrades prompted it to first look at both DVRs and VOD. Because of concerns about viewer control of in-home DVRs (and the content those DVRs stored) and because of concerns about damage to advertising models, the leaders in the cable industry chose VOD almost exclusively over DVRs. Yet, as DVRs grew out successfully under the shepherding of satellite pay TV providers EchoStar and DirecTV, the big cable operators looked over their shoulders and noticed those rivals taking cable's subscribers away and in large numbers. This occasioned those cable operators to also consider what many thought (and still think) is the superior business model: that of combining VOD and DVRs, which only terrestrial, two-way signal providers can truly do.

Note also that whenever something like a DVR can be used to bring in a new customer, which also sets up the opportunity for the cable service operator to offer something the satellite TV providers cannot: the full "bundle" or "triple play" cable services, that is, video, telephone, and Internet broadband services. In short, digital advanced services like DVRs, HDTV, VOD, and interactive TV have special value for cable operators, because if they help to deliver a new subscriber, it is just that much more likely that the cable operator has more digital services to sell them.

Historically, first Time Warner and then Comcast led the cable charge into DVRs, together with their respective lead set-top box manufacturers, Cisco (Scientific Atlanta) and Motorola, in the 2003–2005 time frame. Although they started several years behind the satellite TV operators, by 2007, the cable industry's DVR deployments nationally had surpassed those of the satellite industry. This was a remarkable achievement.

Today, every level of cable operator finds itself not only having to offer digital services to its subscribers, but also digital services such as DVRs and HDTV. Indeed, these two are an essential part of multichannel pay TV business models, because, without them, few providers can compete.

Although they are not often the true pioneers, expect cable operators to be among the more aggressive leaders, as DVRs and DVR-like functionality move into Internet-delivered broadband, content to mobile devices, and similar future technological developments.

5.2.3 Telcos

Coming late to the video service and advanced digital video service parties, the two key telcos, Verizon and AT&T, have had expensive lessons in catching up. This is true especially as it relates to Verizon's and AT&T's own in-house video services, *FiOS* and *U-Verse*, respectively. Thus, wherever their new digital infrastructures permit, these telcos choose to bypass agreements with satellite providers, agreements aimed at delivering satellite TV (and DVRs) to the more rural of the telco's subscribers. In short, to avoid "splitting the pie," Verizon and AT&T instead are forced to spend to deploy their own digital video services—including their own DVR set-top boxes—as much as they can these days. Even though deploying a digital line and hardware into someone's home for the delivery of video may be more expensive in the short run, for these telcos, it is worth the cost. Like the satellite providers and the cable providers before them, the ultimate reward for the telcos is in enticing new subscribers to join telco video and then making them so happy that they spend more and more on telco video services (and never leave). After all, even though they have agreements with the satellite providers, those satellite guys are still their competitors.

One more thing worth specifically pointing out as it relates to telcos as multichannel pay TV providers; may be the cable providers have their so-called triple play (i.e., video, Internet broadband, and telephone service), but the telcos take that business model one step further, with their so-called quadruple play (i.e., video, Internet broadband, telephone, and wireless). When the telcos can use DVRs and other digital services to entice hordes of new subscribers, better still, good, strong, ARPU paying subscribers, then it is just a short step from there to get them to buy a "bundle" of the other services (at a special discount, per service taken, of course).

Verizon

As noted in the case study in Chapter 1, Verizon has been aggressively deploying its new *FiOS* fiber-to-the-home video, broadband, and telephone service. This deployment also includes remarkable deals on set-tops with DVRs for new *FiOS* subscribers. In addition, in areas where *FiOS* is not yet offered, satellite TV is offered to video users. Thus, even if they have to share some revenue with a satellite TV rival, these new guys on the multichannel TV block, the telcos, must have DVRs not only to bring in subscribers who have never had multichannel TV, but also to bring in ones from their satellite and cable competitors. In other words, even if the telco has to split the additional revenue, it is still an additional revenue, which would not then go to a competitor. If the telco can get the new subscriber to sign up for satellite TV today, maybe tomorrow that same subscriber will switch over to one of the telco's new FiOS SD/HD DVR set-top units. After that, maybe he or she signs up for the entire "quadruple play," as well as numerous advanced services, and keeps paying the telco remarkable monthly APRUs for decades.

AT&T

AT&T terminated a video supply agreement with EchoStar in summer 2008 and replaced that with a new DirecTV agreement months later. Thus, wherever AT&T determines customers are not yet ready for AT&T's *U-Verse*-branded digital to the node service (with a set-top DVR included), the company will deploy DirecTV's model of set-top box with a DVR inside. Further, like

Verizon, AT&T also has a set-top unit with DVR inside, which is offered as part of its *U-Verse* service.

Qwest

Denver, CO-based telco Qwest has yet to develop and implement its own digital service plan like that of Verizon and AT&T. As such, it remains tied to its own version of a telco-satellite TV deal. Like in the other telco-satellite TV deals, this agreement requires that the two providers split the monthly ARPU, which greatly diminishes the value of the business model.

5.3 Software Only

A handful of DVR software-only companies have populated the DVR landscape since its earliest days. One of the earliest was ReplayTV, when it jettisoned its set-top box product, and instead focused on the software side of the business. DVR software is typically sold to individuals seeking to buy and download their own DVR functionality onto a computer, which then often will be connected to a TV for better viewing. Nonetheless, many DVR users continue to view most of their DVR content from a computer.

5.3.1 ReplayTV

As noted in the beginning of this chapter, ReplayTV was not only a true pioneer in the set-top box DVR business model phase, but also one in the DVR software phase. After selling itself to SonicBlue, what was once ReplayTV morphed into a software-only service in 2001. Even as what was once ReplayTV sold itself to DirecTV in 2007, it remained as a software-only service. In a 2007 iteration, ReplayTV's software-only offering is described as costing $99 at retail and requires only that the user have a computer with a TV tuner card. After the first year of use, the program guide then costs $19.95 annually. Users can watch the recorded content on the computer monitor or on a TV if there is suitable video output from the computer.

5.3.2 OpenTV

San Francisco-CA-based OpenTV is another DVR software provider whose roots go back to early EchoStar affiliation, as EchoStar began creating its own version of the DVR in the early 2000s. As noted in Chapter 7, "International DVR Growth," OpenTV today is deployed among numerous multichannel pay TV operators globally.

Microsoft®

Jim Baldwin is Microsoft's (NASDAQ: MSFT) director of product development, one of those responsible for the Redmond, WA-headquartered company's DVR deployment through most of the past 10 years. Looking back at its DVR history, Baldwin turns first to Microsoft's partnership with Englewood, CO-based EchoStar (NASDAQ: DISH) and their joint development of the first *WebTV* DISHPlayer branded DVR, which also included an Internet connection. Baldwin notes the early success of the *WebTV* DVR, which in its launch during the 1999 time frame, meant it was "nearly three times as popular as both ReplayTV and TiVo units combined."

The Microsoft-EchoStar *WebTV* combination dissolved among disagreements about the automatic deletion of content and its affect on consumers, as well as accusations of ineffective marketing a couple of years later, setting the foundation for Microsoft's alliance with EchoStar rival, DirecTV (NASDAQ: DTV), in 2001.

The DirecTV-Microsoft alliance created the *UltimateTV* set-top DVR, which was widely and aggressively sold to DirecTV's millions of subscribers, up until 2004. One of the first of its kind to be marketed, the dual tuner on the *UltimateTV* DVR permitted users to both record a TV show and watch another show being broadcast at the same time, simultaneously. Like *WebTV* before, *UltimateTV* also permitted Internet access. Baldwin notes, "*UltimateTV* had a great run, in part because the dual tuner device reduced—or better, completely eliminated—conflicts over the notion of what to watch and what to record."

Yet, *UltimateTV* and the DirecTV alliance, like the *WebTV* EchoStar alliance before it, also ran into problems, causing the software giant to cease marketing the service in 2002–2003. Baldwin and others at Microsoft feel strongly that the two prior separate alliances with both large satellite multichannel pay TV vendors set an important stage for Microsoft's DVR business today, wedded deeply inside *Microsoft Mediaroom* and *Windows Media Center*, which are Microsoft's answers to the whole-home media distribution challenge.

Microsoft describes *Windows Media Center* as a "TV on your terms." Included with the Microsoft products, *Windows Vista Home Premium* and *Ultimate*, the *Windows Media Center* turns a PC into a quite capable DVR. With the addition of an inexpensive TV tuner inside the PC, a viewer can watch, pause, and record live TV to enjoy at his or her convenience. Baldwin notes the free online programming guide makes it easy to find the shows desired and to schedule recordings of programs up to 2 weeks in advance. Further, the *Windows Media Center* means there is no extra cost or monthly fee to enjoy TV, TV which can be enjoyed according to the user's (not the programmer's) schedule. Access to Internet TV shows and movies, photos, music, home videos, and more is also available.

Add an Extender for *Windows Media Center*, like the *Xbox 360*, to your home network, and Microsoft notes you can access your PC's digital media on the big screen in any room of your home. You can also bring your favorite TV shows and movies with you when you sync *Windows Media Center* to your *Zune* or *Windows Mobile* device.

Baldwin quickly labels *The Windows Media Center* as a "... great combination of the PC and the DVR, it brings media into the PC world." Recent additions include a modern tuning system with open cable, cable card support, and Advanced Television Systems Committee (ATSC) tuning. Baldwin adds, "*Mediaroom* is essentially the product marketed toward giving a broadband provider a full-blown TV services platform."

Microsoft *Mediaroom*, on the other hand, attacks a different market than the PC, instead tying in with the homeowner's TV experience. In the words of Microsoft, "The Microsoft *Mediaroom* is an Internet protocol-based television (IPTV) and multimedia software platform that enables the best, most personalized, TV and entertainment experience, so our individual consumers can easily find and watch what they want, when and where they want it. Broadband service providers who license Microsoft *Mediaroom* can deliver superior experiences to their subscribers with advanced digital TV features and media sharing capabilities, to successfully compete in the television market."

DVR Anywhere, a feature within Microsoft *Mediaroom*, gives consumers the flexibility to watch their recorded programs on any TV in their home. For example, viewers could begin watching a movie in the living room, resume it on the kitchen TV during dinner, and finish watching the same movie from the comfort of a bedroom. *DVR Anywhere* gives consumers the ability to watch the same or different recorded programs, from multiple TVs, in the home simultaneously, while at the same time recording others to be viewed at their convenience.

DVR Anywhere is software-based, so no TV tuners are needed. It also requires that only one set-top box in the home have a hard drive, thus lowering the expense for service providers and consumers. The service, which will support standard and high-definition TV, is the first whole-home DVR offering available today from an IPTV provider.

AT&T, which is using the Microsoft *Mediaroom* platform to power their *U-Verse TV* service, is also using *DVR Anywhere*, branded as

U-Verse Total Home DVR, giving *U-Verse TV* customers the freedom to playback SD and HD recorded programs on any connected TV in the home. AT&T is the first provider to rollout Total Home DVR on the Microsoft platform.

The chart below from Microsoft indicates comparisons between *Windows Media Center* and Microsoft *Mediaroom*.

Baldwin sums up Microsoft's optimistic view of DVRs, across numerous platforms, claiming, "From scratch, Microsoft treated the DVR as a first class citizen, and we understood the DVR as a core part of all TV, which is now also a core part of *Mediaroom* … as result, we can do some compelling things, such as record and keep track of media, ID and track it, and build the idea of the DVR into core of security ahead of time, as well as live TV. We also believe in what we call the '*DVR Anywhere*' concept, for both our cable and telco clients."

Turning to its plans to help telco digital subscriber line providers, such as AT&T, in their TV ventures, Microsoft sees one of its greatest opportunities as that of getting the IP package distributed to all the sets in the house, in the form of a home network. As detailed in Chapter 4 and in Microsoft *Mediaroom's DVR Anywhere* feature, in this model, the recording device in the home acts singly on behalf of all the TVs in the home to distribute to and allow control of the main DVR set-top unit from other rooms in the home. In this model, the DVR became "… the primary way to manage the system (instead of just a piece of it)." With its *Mediaroom* channel surfing speeds and live TV tuning speeds of a fraction of a second, Baldwin believes Microsoft *Mediaroom* is "better than any digital TV system out there today." Summing up, Baldwin believes, "Our success happened because we approached the problem differently."

Table 5.1 Microsoft Media Center vs. Microsoft Mediaroom

What	Windows Media Center	Microsoft Mediaroom
What the consumer buys	Device	Service
Hardware platform it runs on	PC	STB/CE
Primary sales channel to consumer	PC retailer	Service provider
UI controlled by	User	Service provider
User profile and core experience	PC	TV
Supports full PC functionality	Yes	No
Runs Windows apps (Office, Dig Imaging, etc.)	Yes	No
Consumer controls what runs on device	Yes	No
Consumer has full access to Internet	Yes	No

Looking toward its future relative to its specific DVR view, roughly 80% of Baldwin's Microsoft peers believe there will always be a notion of storage device as part of the TV-video infrastructure, Baldwin adds "But more and more, the on-demand world takes over." Baldwin also believes it will take a long time to get to the point where on-demand substitutes for DVR functionality, and Microsoft will, in the interim, continue to invest heavily in what Baldwin terms, "A big DVR experience." What Baldwin also notes for the future is the idea that a lot of young people do not subscribe to multichannel pay TV, and instead rely for their video and on-demand experience almost exclusively on broadband and PCs. Baldwin sagely summarizes the current state of Microsoft thinking, as well as its view to the future, by noting, "The challenge is how to help the world capitalize on the DVR experience without having all the business models fall apart."

Microsoft

Contact Information
1 Microsoft Way, Redmond, WA 98052
Phone: 425-882-8080
http://www.Microsoft.com

Stock Symbol
NASDAQ (GM): MSFT

Key People
William H. Gates, Chairman
Steven A. Ballmer, CEO
PR contact: (206) 223-1606 and (503) 443-7070

Key Business
World's largest software company provides wide range of services including its Windows operating system, MS Office, *Xbox* game console, server and storage software, and digital music players

DVR Connection
Launched the *Ultimate TV* DVR in 2007. MS Windows-based PCs can be configured to work as DVRs. Developed the EPG/IPG for LG's LRM-519 DVR.

5.4 Others

A hodge-podge of DVR-related suppliers fills out the remainder of the DVR business models.

5.4.1   Computer-Based

As noted in Chapter 7, German-based Nero's *LiquidTV* service agreement with TiVo allows TiVo functionality on computers in the United States, Canada, and Mexico. A European deployment of the service is expected in 2009.

Several other DVR-software type services are available for computers and may be researched by using a search engine and typing in the words "DVR + personal computers".

5.4.2   Free-To-Air

Australian-based Seven Media Group, discussed in Chapter 7, "International DVR Growth," is among the first to offer its free-to-air (FTA) subscribers DVRs. The combination of FTA and DVR is a bit of a stretch for some because almost the entire FTA business model is based upon advertisements. Thus, the argument has it, if you are encouraging users to zap ads, you are encouraging them to ruin your business model.

Obviously, Seven has another plan in mind. It will undoubtedly work closely with its programmers and advertisers to see that the optimum adjustments are made, so customers can manipulate their programming, while advertisers competently deliver their messages. Many global observers will be watching the Seven DVR implementation closely. If FTA DVR business models meet with success in Asia, there are FTA systems in Europe, especially, that would benefit from the lessons learned.

5.4.3   DIY

Since the earliest days of DVRs, and before, technophiles have used their technology expertise to create their own versions of DVRs. Pre-TiVo and pre-ReplayTV stories of early developers storing content on their in-home built hard drives are the stuff of Silicon Valley folklore. The business model lies in the companies that provide software and hardware do-it-yourself DVR kits that, and their ability to sell to these hardcore DVR fanatics.

5.5   Network (Or Remote) DVRs

Network (or remote) DVRs are very likely the key to the long-term future of the DVR business. They just make that much sense and thus will quite likely become more the norm for cable and telco operators with robust two-way signal infrastructures. Thus far, only Time Warner and Cablevision Systems have ventured into these dangerous, yet remarkably rich, new technological waters. More are bound to follow.

5.5.1 Time Warner

Although it has passed the network (or remote) DVR baton onto New York neighbor, Cablevision Systems, at least temporarily, Stamford, CT-headquartered Time Warner was the first major U.S. cable operator to push the concept and development of a company-supplied remote storage center, which would take the place of hundreds of thousands (or millions) of in-home individual DVR set-top units. Yet, because it was concerned about legal and regulatory restrictions, and perhaps financial and technology limitations, Time Warner dropped its network (or remote) DVR deployment in 2003.

Today, Time Warner remains by the sidelines of Cablevision Systems' epic battle against the content providers, very likely awaiting the right time to step back in with all that it has learned and known about network (or remote) DVRs.

5.5.2 Cablevision Systems

A handful of content providers sued Long Island, NY-based Cablevision Systems in 2006 and won. This group included seven studios and networks, including ABC, CBS, NBC, Fox, Disney, Paramount, and Universal. The basis of the claim was that network (or remote) DVRs are more like VOD than they are a set-top box system. Cablevision Systems, as a service provider, has to negotiate a higher fee for a VOD license than it would for a linear programming license applied to a set-top box negotiation, and was thus set the foundation for the lawsuit. A Manhattan federal court judge issued an injunction, restricting Cablevision Systems from implementing its technologically (and otherwise) superior DVR-type service, which Cablevision calls remote storage DVR (RS-DVR).

This trial court decision was overturned by a federal appellate court in summer 2008. The RS-DVR was determined legal.

Thus, the field is set for a U.S. Supreme Court final determination or a settlement between the parties and a subsequent implementation of the new service in the years ahead (assuming the appellate court ruling is upheld by the U.S. Supreme Court).

Taking that assumption one step further, the network (or remote) DVR business model has an awful lot going for it. For one, it allows a cable or telco provider to truly begin to merge the VOD with the DVR, under one roof. It does this by bringing more of the actual product and service within the control of the multichannel system operator, not the consumer. Assuming the telco and cable system operators can make the change carefully and tactfully, most consumers will probably recognize the wisdom of the switch from in-home hard drives to hard drives elsewhere that do the same thing. Getting consumers to use and accept the network (or remote) DVR is not likely to be the core concern. This will be especially the case if the multichannel TV operators can deliver the service to consumers for free. Also, combining all network storage in one central locale will likely save substantial hardware costs for both the service operator and the consumer, as opposed to the costs of continuing to buy hardware units with costs per unit representing hundreds of dollars.

TVTechnolgy.com and fellow NAB/Focal Press author Wes Simpson, notes in his January 11, 2007, article, "What's Wrong With Network DVRs?", "With nDVR,[11] service providers can also make sure that some or all of the advertisements aren't skipped during playback. Since they are feeding the streams, they can control when your fast-forward button works. Of course, if they force too many ads on consumers, they will risk having some grumpy viewers, but if the service is very inexpensive (or dare I say free?), viewers might be willing to put up with a few ads."

Other reasons why network (or remote) DVRs resonate are because they give the operators and the content owners more control over the actual content, thus enhancing their ability to secure the content, and monetize and improve the DVR business model. Thus, for a certain kind of programming, if the ability to fast-forward ads was to be altered, what better way to do that than by way of the storage system controlled by the service provider. Or, if the stored content was to be viewed by the consumer days after its original airing, it would be the service provider who could ideally replace the old ads with more topical and current ones. Moreover, for example, if the program *House* were "DVRed" on a network (or remote) DVR system, and its ads were timed for Valentine's Day, it would make great sense for the system operator after a certain day to go in and simply replace the ads that would populate the later seen version of *House*.

Cablevision Systems concludes in a prepared statement, "This lawsuit is without merit, reflects a fundamental misunderstanding of Cablevision's remote storage DVR, and ignores the enormous benefit and well-established right of viewers to time-shift television programming. We hope and expect the court will allow our customer-friendly technological approach to move forward."

5.6 Advertisers and Agencies

As noted in Chapters 3, 4, and 6, studies by and among the networks, advertisers, and their agencies point to less-than-damning—and perhaps even fulfilling—opportunities for content creators and distributors vis-à-vis DVRs. Although common sense clearly supports the idea of lost revenues from DVR viewers not viewing ads as they used to, the current DVR model—that of making people watch the ads they fast forward through—has shown that viewers still retain marketing and branding messages. If this finding can be matured, and refined, the potential for DVRs finding peace among advertisers is greatly enhanced.

Even more surprisingly, for advertisers, the technology that makes DVRs possible is also the technology that may forever bind future advertisers to what

---

[11] The term nDVR is author Wes Simpson's acronym for a network (or remote) DVR system.

DVRs do. That technology is, of course, the ability to track what viewers watch. Assuming the proper restrictions, guidelines, and protections are in place, knowing what viewers watch and presumably like can permit great relationships between advertisers and their audiences. At the right time and place, just about any viewer is ripe for more of the same of what he or she likes. It is the place of future technology, no matter where the viewer is located or in front of what device or seeing what, to deliver that content—including commercial messages—to that viewer. That is the future of TV in America; that is the future of TV in most of the world.

5.7   Networks and Broadcast Stations

As noted in the article by Loebbecke and Radke, "Business Models and Programming Choice: Digital Video Recorders Shaping the TV Industry,"[12] networks and especially TV stations have a lot of thinking to do as it relates to the future of their businesses in a DVR world.

Indeed, if their collective legal actions in the DVR arena are the best indication of their future responses, prevailing will be difficult. The topic of DVR-advertiser balance needs remarkable study and most careful analysis, because a right or a wrong move in either direction can represent, literally, billions of dollars.

Dave Clark is Cisco's director, product strategy and management, entertainment products, which is part of Cisco's Service Provider Video Technology Group, located in Atlanta, GA. Clark describes Cisco's development and implementation of DVRs as a "really cool story." Note here that although the company engaged in most of the activity here was actually Scientific-Atlanta (S-A), because of the purchase of S-A by Cisco in early 2006, most references will be to the purchasing company and current company name, Cisco. As such, Cisco is today, along with Motorola, one of the two leading manufacturers of DVRs and related set-top units for the U.S cable

---

[12] See, *Proceedings of the Eleventh Americas Conference on Information Systems*, Omaha, NE, August 11–14, 2005, which is a good review of various business models in the new world of DVRs.

industry. Digeo is a third, up-and-coming, player in this marketplace. Pace, Panasonic, Samsung, and additional set-top manufacturers are more players in the U.S. cable marketplace.

During the early development days of DVRs and VOD, which most identify as the late 1990s and into the early part of the new century and millennium, Cisco faced many naysayers among those in the media, analyst, industry, client, and other interested communities. Specifically, they doubted the move of companies like Cisco and their cable clients into the realm of DVR, because these critics saw DVRs as a "competitive technical solution." Cisco, on the other hand, forged ahead, seeing the two, i.e., VOD and DVRs, as clearly compatible and indeed, related. Clark notes, "We took the high road, and believed that VOD and DVR were not competitive, but complimentary solutions." Perhaps as a symbol of this would-be natural affinity, at Cisco, in Atlanta, GA, during its early DVR days, the people that ran Cisco's VOD development sat physically adjacent to those that ran DVR.

Clark offers "At the time, TiVo and DISH were clearly in the lead, as far as a non-service and a service DVR provider were concerned … and there was a lot of concern in the industry about the DVR business model." Specifically, Clark points to the concern about Cisco set-top boxes already providing consumers with superior access to nonlinear content, via VOD, which could then negate the need to spend a significant level of capital expenditure (or cap ex) on a high-priced DVR device.

To answer the questions, Cisco did significant market research, which included lengthy and in-depth discussions with existing Cisco subscribers nationwide. Also working closely with cable partner Time Warner, Cisco found that, in general, subscribers in the cable arena were willing to pay a monthly premium for what a DVR could deliver them. Clark adds, "… and the Return on Investment (ROI) was a sell-in to the overall digital window, making the DVR a good business to move forward into." In other words, getting people into DVRs meant not only that churn (i.e., subscriber loss) was reduced, but once the subscriber accepted the DVR, it was much easier to get those same subscribers to buy into other digital services, such as HDTV and VOD. Clark concludes "That helped prove or disprove the fears that DVRs were just an expensive cap ex investment … it showed other intangibles that made it work quite well." Indeed, Cisco early on, like other DVR visionaries, saw the DVR as the foundation for other digital applications, such as VOD.

Further research showed that people using DVRs gradually watched more TV than they had without the DVR. Migration from mere DVR content choices to a realization that more VOD choices were also part of the

Cisco-delivered packages supported Cisco' s relatively early and aggressive moves into DVRs.

Clark boasts "Our first DVR, the *Explorer 8000* in 2002, was one of the industry's first all-digital devices, one capable of allowing consumers to both watch a live TV show and record a second show, by way of one of the industry's first dual tuner DVR offerings."

Significant additional research was done by Cisco and Time Warner, as co-developers, on the part of the DVR that can never be overlooked: the remote control. Cisco traveled often to Time Warner headquarters in Stamford, CT, intent on deciding which buttons to include, where to place them, and what each would do when pushed. Further, realizing that many of these new DVR set-top boxes would be built to last "a long time," the two partners further endeavored to create a quality product with enduring value. Clark emphasizes, "It didn't have a 90-day warranty on it, so, this DVR was built with the idea that it may have to live in multiple households over its life."

Turning to what remains today a (if not *the*) major challenge within the DVR industry, Clark laments the early process of educating and explaining to people just what it was that a DVR did and how it could so thoroughly—for the better—change the TV viewing experience. Clark explains, "Trying to explain to someone in the middle of the U.S., someone perhaps 50-years-old, was different than explaining the same thing to someone from Silicon Valley, so we got creative … we went to Tupperware-type parties to try and get the word out." Word of mouth came from exchanges such as these, and from there, like most successful consumer electronic products, the positive momentum was nearly palpable. Bill stuffers, and getting on-the-road technicians and installers to help tell the new DVR story, were additional tools. To indicate some of the challenge of getting the DVR word out, and doing it successfully, Clark notes his favorite story: the technician who describes the subscriber who kept asking, "… but where do you put the tape in, and where does it eject from?" Clark further notes that simplicity and consistency were repeated themes during the Cisco DVR launch period.

Concluding, Clark points to one additional memorable theme in the development of the Cisco DVR: that of constantly eyeing the future, no matter how successful the past or present. His example? Clark remembers the planning for HD DVRs almost before the Cisco SD DVR was released. Yet, it too, has proved remarkably worthwhile in Clark's mind. "For our first HD DVR, it was tough, being able to do picture-in-picture, and to record two HD channels, and do play-back on a third, but it was also pretty impressive, and once our subscribers saw the experience, it became even tougher for them to live without," he offers.

Cisco Systems, Inc.

Contact Information
170 West Tasman Dr., Bldg. 10, San Jose, CA 95134
Phone: 408-526-4000
http://www.cisco.com

Stock Symbol
Nasdaq: CSCO

Key People
John T. Chambers, Chairman and CEO
PR Contact: Marc Musgrove
Phone: 408 525-6320

Key Business
Cisco provides networking services and products.

DVR Connection
Develops and manufactures set-top box DVRs and DVR servers.

5.8 Summary

As Cisco's Dave Clark concludes in this chapter's final case study, a huge part of
the DVR business model has been pushing DVR up the mountain to the point
where it has become a "cannot live without" consumer electronics product and
service. Yet, as a whole, the industry certainly did not stop there. Many companies and industry subsectors also focused on items such as new developments,
financing, marketing, legal and regulatory concerns, as well as the all important
"consumer experience," to make sure the greatest success was achieved in the
mid- to long-term lives of their various business models. The three case studies
detailed in this chapter suggest varied levels of success and approaches to these
various business model concerns.

6 Customers: How to Choose a DVR?

Today's consumer is no longer asking whether they need hard drive storage for their digital content—they're asking, how much we can deliver?
—Patrick King, senior VP and GM, Consumer Electronics Business Unit,
Seagate Technology[1]

Like just about every other high-quality consumer electronics (CE) product or service, a good deal of the reason for the maintenance of quality and value of DVRs is the intra-industry competitive forces. Thus, for the consumer looking to choose a DVR for his home (or business), several types of DVRs are available, each with its own promise (and challenges). The consumer does best to attempt to make these different DVR competitors earn the business, and that is best done by the consumer doing his or her homework (and due diligence), prior to making a DVR purchase or other DVR-related commitment.

One of the first considerations a potential DVR purchaser should make is whether to rent a DVR or to invest additional sums in owning one. Beyond that, decisions turn on the types of DVRs that are available today, and differentiating between the pros and cons of the various DVRs. Lists of questions and considerations are included in this chapter for each of the three main DVR types, i.e., standalone, integrated, and remote-storage DVRs (RS-DVRs). These are intended to help the process of the consumer choosing the right DVR for the right multichannel pay TV operator he or she wishes to use and for that consumer's individual needs and desires. Other parties and entities reading this book need also to consider this material including, for example, multichannel TV operators, agencies, and their advertisers. After all, in just about every one of these worlds, it all starts and ends with the end consumer.

6.1 DVR User Demographics

Although this chapter is intended to focus on consumers, and what a consumer would want to know about obtaining a DVR, to get to that point, it probably also helps to provide information consumers might also want to know about themselves. The following information is from a mid-2007 study of more than 2000 U.S. DVR and non-DVR consumers completed by The Carmel Group.

---

[1] The Scotts Valley, CA-based company Seagate Technology (NYSE: STX) is known best for its development and manufacture of memory and storage devices, such as hard drives, which Seagate sells to CE equipment manufacturers.

These data are also intended to be of significant help to other audiences, such as advertisers, multichannel operators, agencies, broadcasters, local stations, financiers, attorneys, and others in the business of DVRs, domestically and globally. Figures 6.1 to 6.12 and Table 6.1 are used with the permission of The Carmel Group and are among several score charts and tables describing this American DVR Audience in that 2007 study.

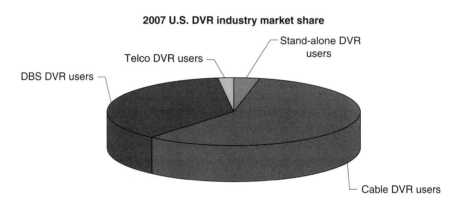

Figure 6.1 2007 U.S. DVR industry market share, split, in the order of size, among cable, satellite (DBS), telco, and standalone DVR units.

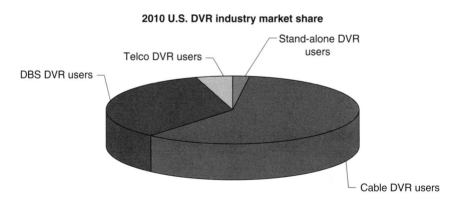

Figure 6.2 2010 projected U.S. DVR industry market share, split, in the order of size, among cable, satellite (DBS), telco, and standalone DVR units.

Table 6.1 A Profile of the "Typical" DVR User and DVR Nonuser. The Key Differentiator was the Male Gender of the DVR User Group vs. the Female of the DVR Nonuser Group

	DVR Users	DVR Nonusers
Ethnicity	Caucasian	Caucasian
Age	35–54 years	35–54 years
Location	Suburban	Suburban
Gender	Male	Female
Marital status	Married	Married
Children	No children	No children
Income	$35,000–100,000	$35,000–100,000
Level of education	College graduate	College graduate
Own or rent	Own	Own
Number of DVRs	One	None

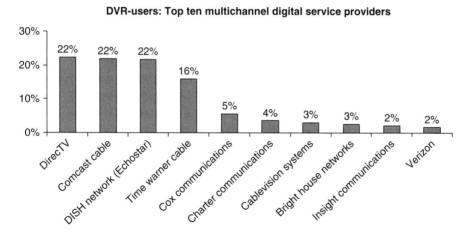

Figure 6.3 The top 10 multichannel digital services providers, among satellite (DBS), cable, and telco providers. For their size relative to giant Comcast, the satellite (DBS) providers do quite well.

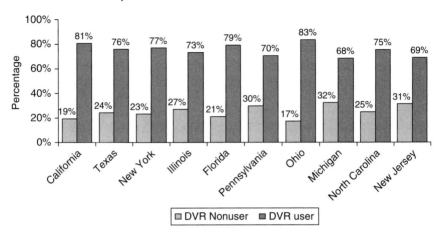

Figure 6.4 The top 10 states for DVR Users and DVR Nonusers. Surprising is not that the biggest states have strong penetration of DVRs, but that a smaller state like New Jersey has such strong interest in the DVR phenomena.

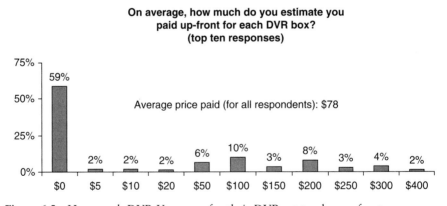

Figure 6.5 How much DVR Users pay for their DVR set-top box upfront. Interestingly, well more than half of the respondents said they paid nothing upfront for their boxes, suggesting they received them as part of a multichannel pay TV operator's promotion.

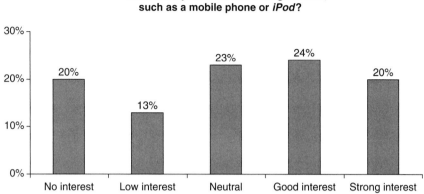

Figure 6.6 DVR Users' interest in being able to transfer content from the DVR to another device. Almost half responding to our poll exhibited "Good Interest" or better.

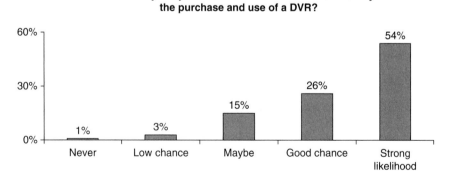

Figure 6.7 "Word of mouth" is ultimately one of the most important drivers of new CE device growth. More than half of respondents report a "strong likelihood" that they would recommend the DVR to friends and family for purchase and use.

Interesting as it relates to legal and regulatory matters, as well as sensitivity as to consumer's concern about the DVR and the operator possibly invading the DVR user's privacy, Figure 6.8 notes that only about 35% of those responding felt anything more than a moderate concern as it relates to possible invasions of privacy. Within that number, The Carmel Group notes that the higher concerns about privacy invasions came from the older respondents. With involvement in Internet services, such as FaceBook and MySpace, it is no wonder that younger DVR users are less concerned about an operator invading their privacy. This information should be of particular note to advertising agencies and their

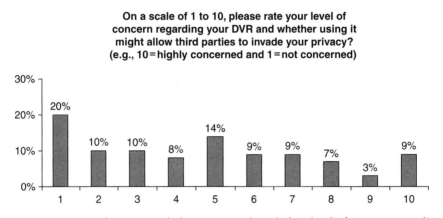

Figure 6.8 Respondents, as a whole, report a relatively low level of concern regarding privacy issues.

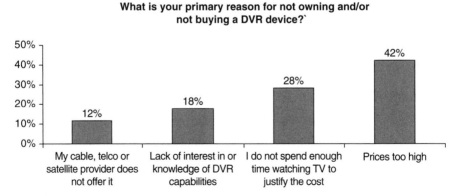

Figure 6.9 Why nonusers of DVRs are not becoming users. Not surprisingly, high cost is overall a significant concern. Also, the number of people who do not know about DVRs is further indication of the challenge of getting consumers to understand the value of a DVR in the home.

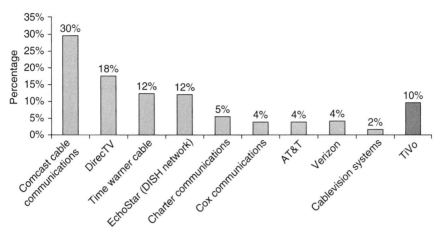

Figure 6.10 First sources of DVRs. The sources identified basically track the relative sizes of the various multichannel pay TV operators in the U.S. today, with TiVo showing a relatively strong 10%.

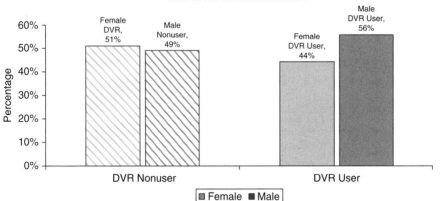

Figure 6.11 The relative gender breakout for DVR nonusers vs. DVR users. The DVR User leans relatively strongly toward a male DVR User.

advertisers, especially as it relates to using the data obtained by multichannel TV operators from viewers and their viewing habits, to turnaround and deliver to those viewers particularly relevant and helpful commercial sales and marketing information, for example.

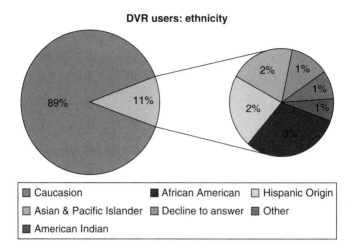

DVR users: ethnicity

Figure 6.12   Shows a fascinating breakdown of DVR User ethnicity. There are remarkable opportunities coming out of data such as these.

6.2   Rent or Buy?

A first layer of homework that is worth initially considering is that of whether, as a TV and DVR consumer, you want to own or lease the DVR equipment you obtain.

Some of this depends on one's tolerance for higher prices versus less responsibility owed to the owner of the DVR. For example, if you wish to control your expenses right upfront, you probably do not want to go out and purchase a DVR costing more than $200 at your CE retail dealer. In that case, or if you wanted to simply try the DVR out, it might be best to rent the DVR and the programming service from your multichannel pay TV operator, at least for the time being. This though, this can put you at risk for the cost of the DVR set-top box, because unless you purchase a plan to protect it, if you damage or fail to return the DVR, the cost of the box will likely be charged by the multichannel TV operator to you.

Rented from a multichannel pay TV operator, per month, a DVR typically costs $5.99. This fee covers only the rental of the integrated operator DVR set-top box. On top of this fee, operators also typically charge an additional $4.99–12.99/month for the software service. Table 6.2 shows a breakout of five different types of DVR providers. The first set of pricings is that offered by the dominant standalone DVR providers, TiVo and Digeo. The other three are those offered by typical operators among the three multichannel pay TV operators, that is, in order, satellite, cable, and telco.

On the other hand, if you want features not offered by the multichannel pay TV DVR, or you want to avoid a monthly unit rental fee charge from the multichannel pay TV operator, you may want to opt into buying your own DVR. Major companies that sell the so-called standalone DVRs include Digeo

Table 6.2 Cost and Other Comparisons of Most DVR Units on Today's Market.

DVR Provider and Model	Type of DVR	Upfront DVR Cost	Service Cost	Provider Type
Digeo	SD/HD Standalone	$799	None	Standalone
TiVo® Series2 DT	SD Standalone	$149.99	$12.95/Month	Standalone
TiVo® HD DVR	HD Standalone	$299.99	$12.95/Month	Standalone
TiVo® HD DVR Lifetime Service	HD Standalone	$299.99	$299 for the lifetime of the DVR box (transferable)	Standalone
DirecTV® and HD DVR HR20	HD Standalone	$99.97 (with rebate) or $198.97	$54.99/Month (including DirecTV and DVR service)	DBS
DirecTV® and DVR	SD Standalone	Free with service	$44.99/Month (including DirecTV and DVR service)	DBS
DISH® ViP722 DVR HD Receiver	HD Standalone	Free with service	$5.98/month	DBS
DISH® Player— DVR 625	SD Standalone	Free with service	$5.98/month	DBS
Comcast/ Motorola—DCH 3200	HD Integrated	Included in service fee	$13.95/month	Cable
Comcast/ Motorola—DCH 70	SD Integrated	Included in service fee	$8.99/month	Cable
Time Warner Cable—SA Various[1]	HD Integrated	Included in service fee	$14.15/month ($6.95 svc + $7.20 STB)	Cable
Charter Communications— SA or Motorola[1]	HD Integrated	Included in service fee	$15.00/month (HD Included)	Cable
Cox Communications— SA Various[1]	HD Integrated	Included in service fee	$17.20/month ($11.95 svc + $5.25 STB)	Cable

(Continued)

Table 6.2 *(Continued)*

DVR Provider and Model	Type of DVR	Upfront DVR Cost	Service Cost	Provider Type
Cablevision Systems—SA[1] Various	HD integrated	Included in service fee	$16.45/month ($9.95 svc + $6.50 STB)	Cable
Verizon FiOS TV	HD integrated	Included in service fee	$47.99/month (including Verizon Cable and DVR Service)	Telco
AT&T *U-Verse* TV	HD integrated	Included in service fee	$44/month (including AT&T Cable and DVR Service)	Telco

[1]SA = Scientific Atlanta.

and TiVo today. Even after a standalone set-top DVR has been purchased from anywhere pricewise ranging from close to nothing (with a multimonth subscription) to hundreds of dollars (for a multi-tuner and large hard drive DVR), the multichannel pay TV operator's monthly fee to use the software (e.g., the EPG/IPG and on-screen programming functions) typically runs another $5–12/month, or a consumer is sometimes offered a lifetime subscription covering this service. This fee for lifetime service typically runs several hundred dollars, but, in the long term, may be quite worth it. Indeed, if you are like most consumers, you will not want to live without your DVR once you have tried it, and, within a handful of years, your lifetime subscription fee will have already covered the equivalent monthly fee charged by the operator.

6.3   Types of DVRs

A key to an overall good DVR experience, usually lasting from the time the user starts using the DVR into the indefinite future, and usually an experience measured in thousands or more individual DVR user sessions, is in picking the right DVR. To choose correctly requires doing one's homework—or due diligence—and realizing that every person is different in his or her viewing preferences and thus should choose a DVR that accommodates his or her individual needs. For example, a DirecTV viewer wanting the top-of-the-line HD DVR offered by TiVo, will want to research the TiVo Web site and focus on a TiVo standalone model. This is because DirecTV no longer offers a DirecTV-TiVo-branded HD DVR. Or, a Charter Cable subscriber in St. Louis, MO, may want to choose carefully among several Motorola, Cisco (Scientific-Atlanta), or Digeo DVR offerings that are part of the standard model set-top boxes that Charter offers its subscribers. Or, in several other instances, a DVR may be available inside a new *Xbox 360 Elite* model gaming device from Microsoft; inside an *iPod*, using the "streaming networks" *iRecord* feature; inside a handheld, portable 30-GB mobile DVR from Archos; inside a *FiOS* home network system offered by Verizon; and inside a DVD set-top box, the DVR in the form of a hard drive inside that records programs. Or some exceptionally enterprising individuals may wish to build their own DVR as part of the home PC they own.

6.3.1   Standalone DVRs

Briefly defined, standalone DVRs are those that are designed to do just one thing: they deliver DVR capability to a TV monitor. This is true in the overwhelming number of DVRs that are labeled "standalone," because standalone DVR units do not contain the digital tuner or security elements that would be proprietary to the multichannel pay TV operator's system equipment. Examples would include DirecTV's tuner and DirecTV's security element, the latter of which is supplied by DirecTV's security vendor, NDS, as well as the typical cable company's QAM tuners, together with security elements provided typically by either Motorola or Cisco (Scientific-Atlanta). In both examples, neither the proprietary tuner nor the security element would be part of the standard off-the-shelf standalone DVR set-top box. And a few that would fall into this category—because they do not also provide access to multichannel pay TV channels—do other things, such as provide gaming services, and function within sophisticated corporate security systems.

Like when buying a motor vehicle these days, a consumer serves himself best by being well-informed. Thus, becoming a would-be consumer who does upfront research on the different models and features and prices of a possible standalone DVR purchase is completely apropos and strongly recommended. For most people these days, the Internet is likely the most efficient service to turn to first glean valuable information about things like consumer electronics items, including DVRs. A chat or two with a neighbor, friend, or relative who has purchased and used a DVR, or multiple DVRs, is also advisable prior to making a DVR selection.

Buying a Standalone DVR: A Due Diligence Checklist

The list below provides a good example of a set of core questions someone buying a DVR would want to have answered, probably before he or she actually presses the "purchase" button on the keyboard, or before walking into a neighborhood CE store to gather more information (and perhaps buy a DVR).

1. On a scale, would you rate yourself quite technically oriented, mildly technically oriented, or not technically oriented at all?[2]

---

[2] As a rough rule of thumb, for technophiles, the DIY DVR might be the preferred option; for mid-level technophiles, the standalone DVR might be the preferred option; and for non-techies, the integrated set-top DVR-receiver combo provided by one's multichannel pay TV operator might well be the best choice.

2. Are you a multichannel pay TV customer or do you only receive your TV via an over-the-air local TV antenna (i.e., you are a free, ad-supported, network broadcast TV viewer)?

3. If you are solely an over-the-air (i.e., free, ad supported) network broadcast TV user, will you be obtaining a analog-to-digital TV converter box in preparation for the June 12, 2009, switch from analog-to-digital signals?

4. Or, if you are an over-the-air (i.e., free, ad supported) network broadcast TV user only, will you be transitioning over to a multichannel pay TV service by June 12, 2009?[3]

5. If you do plan to transition to a multichannel pay TV service, which one will you choose, for example, cable, satellite, or telco? (See earlier discussion about this topic, the choices, and the implications.)

6. Once you subscribe to the new multichannel pay TV service provider, how do its DVR offerings compare to those of the standalone providers?

7. Does your standalone DVR unit contain a built-in slot for cable card (which will allow the standalone unit to be compatible with most, if not all, multichannel cable TV operators' systems)?[4]

8. How many more features or what special features does the standalone have that the integrated operator DVR does not? Or vice versa?

9. Because standalone DVRs usually are more expensive than integrated set-top DVRs, is the extra price for the standalone worth it to you?

10. What kinds of CE stores are available near you? Are they reputable?

11. Do you have a broadband connection?

12. Are your video viewing habits shifting from TV- to PC-based?

13. Does your PC-based video viewing accommodate the equivalent of DVR capabilities?

14. Do you have a telephone line connection (which is needed to properly install a DVR)?

15. Can the standalone DVR export video files to your computer (if the hard drive gets too full and/or if you want a portable version of your saved shows)? What is involved in that?

16. Can the standalone DVR burn a DVD of your recorded programs (if the hard drive gets too full and/or if you want a portable version of your saved shows)? What is involved in that?

17. Can the standalone DVR export video files to your VCR (if the hard drive gets too full and/or if you want a portable version of your saved shows)? What is involved in that?

18. Does the standalone DVR feature some kind of a parental control functionality?

19. Do you prefer to lease or own your DVR?

---

[3] The June 12, 2009, analog-to-digital transition forces people without digital multichannel pay TV services to choose whether to become multichannel pay TV digital subscribers in order to receive digital signals. If they do not transition to some form of digital (also including over-the-air reception via an analog-to-digital converter box), they will no longer be able to watch over-the-air free TV (after June 12, 2009).

[4] Note that this cable card slot availability is important because the standalone DVR unit's cable card slot allows you to take the unit with you from place to place as you move homes, and to reactivate the unit wherever you are, by simply acquiring a new cable card from your new multichannel pay TV cable operator, paying the monthly rental fee, and putting the proper cable card in the cable card slot.

20. If you want to own your DVR, what is the price of the DVR set-top box at retail?
21. What is the price of the DVR service? Are month-to-month only, or special longer-term, deals available?
22. What discounts are available?
23. What company is the maker or manufacturer of the hardware? Is it reputable and experienced?
24. What company is the maker of the software? Is it reputable and experienced?
25. What does the hardware do?
26. What does the software do?
27. What features does the operational or middleware software offer?
28. Specifically as it relates to the user interface (UI), how good is it?
29. How easy is it to use the on-screen programming guide, or EPG/IPG? Is it user-friendly?
30. Overall, does the standalone DVR typically involve seamless and one-step functionality to get a task accomplished, or is more work required?
31. Do the UI and EPG specifically permit searching for shows by actor, name, and/or topic?
32. Does the DVR feature functionality that notes programs a consumer likes, and then gives the consumer recommendations of other shows that are of the same genre?
33. Does the DVR system access the Internet, so that Internet video shows can be streamed and watched on the DVR-enabled TV screen?
34. Does the DVR system enable digital slide show capability?
35. Does the DVR system enable you to record programs, via use of a telephone and scheduling capability from afar?
36. Does the DVR system enable you to schedule the DVR, using the Internet from whatever distance you are away from the DVR?
37. How many tuners are available (enabling you to watch one show while recording one or more other shows at the same time)?
38. What is the size of the hard drive? How many hours of standard definition (SD) and how many hours of high definition (HD) does the hard drive allow?
39. Does the EPG/IPG display HD programs separate from SD programs?
40. Does the DVR device feature an add-on-type storage device, also known as an expander or external hard drive that will allow transfer of recorded programs from the DVR to the add-on-type storage device, when the DVR hard drive gets full?[5]
41. If there is an add-on-type storage device available, what is its cost, and what sizes or models are available?

---

[5] DVR expanders are simply external hard drives that are quite common. For example, TiVo is currently recommending and using the Western Digital WDH1S5000 model, which has a from a 500 GB up to a 1 TB (i.e., really big) storage capability, the latter of which is enough to store about 60–120 hours of HD programming, or 600 hours of SD programming. Expanders are offered by many different companies, but not usually made by the DVR providers themselves. Following is a link to http://www.amazon.com, which sells many different DVR expanders (or external hard drives): http://www.amazon.com/s/?ie=UTF8&keywords=tivo+expander&tag=googhydr-20&index=aps&hvadid=1104621461&ref=pd_sl_2scml07sar_e. Other companies making external hard drives include Apricorn and Iomega. Size-wise, DVR expanders are all generally fairly small, in the range of 3–3.5 inches in height, very thin, and they simply plug into the DVR, using an USB cord. TiVo and others also offer the Western Digital branded DVR expander for $200 on their websites. Finally, DVR expanders are ubiquitous, that is, it does not really matter what brand of DVR you have, they can be used. This may help explain why the DVR manufacturers aren't manufacturing these devices.

42. How does the standalone DVR work as part of a home network system?[6]
43. What is involved in the installation of the DVR?
44. Is expert installation available or do you have to install the DVR yourself?
45. How does the remote control device compare to others on the market?
46. Does the remote control appear to be designed with consumer friendliness in mind? Are there a lot of buttons to push or a fewer number? Do the buttons seem to make sense?

As referenced above, another part of doing one's homework would include getting valuable feedback, ideally from a good friend, a neighbor, or a family member, who has used the same device. Also, odd as it may sound, and probably not common, some people might want to know in advance what impact a DVR has on one's life, so as to *not get* a DVR. For example, most DVR users find they watch *more* TV (because the choice and control offered by a DVR means the overall viewing experience is usually of a much higher quality, making one want to do more of it in one sitting), so if watching more TV is something you are concerned about, you might want to think twice, or discuss the DVR acquisition with a spouse, or your children, or other household members. Probably much more ephemeral is grasping the idea of permitting a machine, in this case a relatively small, living room set-top box, control your life. Like the idea of watching too much TV, if the Orwellian concept of devices divining one's days and nights is offensive, products like DVRs, PDAs, and MP3 players had best be avoided.[7]

6.3.2 Integrated DVRs

As time passes, it is likely that fewer and fewer potential DVR users will come from the ranks of would-be standalone DVR purchasers. This is because the easier and almost always cheaper way to obtain a DVR is to simply sit back and react to a solicitation from your multichannel pay TV provider. And because more than 90 million of the U.S.'s nearly 115 million TV households (TVHHs) are multichannel pay TV subscribers, most people get approached regularly with a DVR offer that he or she can easily accept, simply by saying "yes" to the multichannel pay TV service provider.

This decision to accept a DVR into one's life has its own set of prior questions, as well. Many of these questions are similar to those for people considering a

---

[6] Microsoft's is a good example of a home network system. Windows *XP Media Center Edition* and Windows *Vista's Media Center* both involve computers adapted for playing music, watching movies, and pictures stored on a local hard drive or on a network drive, and watching DVD movies. Typically, media centers provide DVR functionality for watching and recording television broadcasts, as well. Most media centers also include Internet client software for checking email, surfing the web, and reading what are known as Really Simple Syndication (RSS) feeds, such as the scrolling news at the bottom of a CNN site or screen. Online, see http://www.dvrplayground. com/category/11/Windows-PC-Media-Center.

[7] See "The Age of Egocasting," by Christine Rosen, *The New Atlantis*, Fall 2004/Winter 2005, pages 51–72, http://www.TheNewAtlantis.com, for a remarkable discussion of this idea, and specifically how it relates to DVRs and MP3 players, like Apple's iPod.

standalone DVR purchase. Yet, because one's multichannel pay TV provider will almost always limit the number of DVR unit selections offered to its own customers (for competitive reasons), the number of choices among integrated DVR set-top boxes is almost always a concern. For example, if a would-be multichannel DVR subscriber is a subscriber to the EchoStar DISH Network pay TV service, the only DVR choice available through this operator is that of a DISH Network-manufactured DVR. DISH Network currently has no formal, announced relationship with Alviso, CA-headquartered TiVo, and thus, a DISH Network customer would have to make a retail or online purchase to get a non-DISH Network DVR, such as that offered by TiVo. This is another way of saying that it remains relatively rare that a multichannel pay TV operator's in-house DVR will work on another type of operator's system (e.g., a cable-supplied DVR will work on neither a satellite nor a telco multichannel pay TV operator's competing system). Nonetheless, to be clear, a standalone DVR will almost always work with any multichannel pay TV system operator's service, wherever it is located, as long as it is installed properly.

Another potentially important question is whether you choose, or have chosen, a satellite-delivered multichannel pay TV operator, or a terrestrially based and terrestrially delivered cable or telco DVR provider. The reason this choice is important is because in the satellite TV realm, a DVR is both the individual user's place to store and later playback shows and the operator's place to "push" (or send down from the satellite to store on the hard drive of the DVR) various shows, which can be later viewed in an on demand-like fashion by the satellite TV consumer using the DVR. A more detailed reason why the question of satellite or terrestrial delivery system is important is because for satellite operators trying to emulate a true VOD system (which they really cannot), the "push" of movies and other programs onto the hard drive takes up valuable storage space on the satellite TV DVR's hard drive. As such, if a consumer does not consistently remove shows from the hard drive after viewing, the DVR will then, by itself, typically automatically remove unsaved programs after the hard drive fills up, which often is a short period of time. In the end, what this really points out is that satellite TV DVR purchasers want to err on the side of a much larger hard drive, because typically that satellite TV DVR user is going to fill up the hard drive that much sooner. Also, a DVR is different from a VOD, because a DVR requires planning in advance to access programs. It also requires waiting for programs you like to be telecast, before being able to access.

Conversely, the true VOD service, offered by most large telco and cable providers, makes thousands of programs available immediately, without waiting on the part of the subscriber. More of these shows are being placed on operators' VOD hard drives daily. Those same shows can be paused, rewound, and usually fast-forwarded in the same manner as that permitted by a DVR. Also note that terrestrial DVR service offered by telco and cable companies, on the other hand, is usually tied in with a true VOD offering. This means that typically hundreds, if not thousands, of shows are stored in the operator's remotely located boxes called servers, in buildings that are usually far away from the consumer, and, again, are instantly made available, on the spot, via the phone line connection the cable or telco consumer has with the distant cable or telco storage point. A consumer simply finds the show on the EPG/IPG, pushes to "play," and via the phone line, the program is delivered from the faraway storage point to the subscriber's TV set. And because that show then is instantly available all the time to the consumer, the consumer has no real need to store that show on the hard drive of the DVR that resides in his or her home. As such, the hard drive on that in-home device is much less likely to get filled quickly by shows the consumer is less interested in permanently saving. Chapter 1 also makes a good comparison of the VOD offering versus the DVR offering. And VOD requires no waiting for the show to be scheduled for telecast. Rather, it is always available for ordering by the consumer.

Further, as time passes, it is quite possible that fewer and fewer DVRs will be installed by operators in customers' homes, because network-operated RS-DVRs and VOD services that enable the same DVR-like functionality will eliminate the need for each consumer to have his or her own DVR. But that transition is still, at best, years away, because for most consumers, they can see a true distinction between, and need for, a DVR and a VOD service. It is also years away, because (1) legal challenges to RS-DVRs remain, and (2) once those legal challenges have been overcome, additional technical concerns remain, tied in with the difficulty of building a large-scale remote-storage-based system infrastructure.

Obtaining an Integrated Operator-Supplied DVR: A Due Diligence Checklist

This list below is intended for use by the person who is a subscriber to a multichannel pay TV service. Such a person would typically include someone who subscribes to satellite TV (e.g., DirecTV or EchoStar), cable (e.g., Comcast, Time Warner, Cox, Cablevision, Charter, or many hundreds of smaller cable operators), or to a telco operator (e.g., Verizon or AT&T).

1. What type of multichannel pay TV service do you subscribe to? (See discussion above as to why this is important, or why, ideally, everyone should ask this question *before* he or she first subscribes to a new multichannel pay TV service.)
2. What is the price of the integrated DVR hardware offered by the multichannel pay TV operator?
3. Does your integrated DVR unit contain a built-in slot for a cable card (which will allow the unit to be compatible with most, if not all, multichannel cable TV operators' systems)?[8]

---

[8] Note that this is important because the integrated DVR unit's cable card slot allows you to take the unit with you from place to place as your move homes, and to reactivate it wherever you are, by simply acquiring a new cable card from your new multichannel pay TV cable operator, paying the monthly card rental fee, and putting the card into the cable card slot.

4. Can the integrated DVR only be acquired as part of a larger package or programming purchase?

5. Are there only month-to-month or possibly yearly DVR leases available, the latter possibly costing less (but requiring you to lock in for that longer term)?

6. Factoring in the long-term, multi-month programming package commitment, what is the total cost of the DVR and DVR service?

7. Who owns the DVR, once it is installed in the subscriber's home? (This is important from a consumer liability point of view).

8. If the DVR is damaged or not returned to the operator, what are the consequences?

9. Is there an equipment protection plan available to insure the integrated DVR while you use it, and how expensive is that plan?

10. What discounts are available from the multichannel pay TV operator?

11. What company is the maker or manufacturer of the integrated DVR hardware? Is it reputable and experienced?

12. What company is the maker of the integrated DVR software? Is it reputable and experienced?

13. What does the integrated DVR hardware do?

14. What does the integrated DVR software do?

15. What features does the operational or middleware software offer?

16. Specifically, as it relates to the integrated DVR user interface (UI), how good is it? How does it compare to the standalone DVR UI?

17. How easy is it to use the integrated DVR's onscreen guide, or EPG/IPG? Is it user-friendly?

18. Overall, do functions of the integrated DVR typically involve seamless and one-step functionality, or is more work required?

19. Does the integrated DVR function note the types of programs you like to watch and then present those types of programs to you in the form of program recommendations?

20. Does the integrated DVR record in HD or only in SD?

21. Does the EPG/IPG display HD programs separate from SD programs?

22. What is the size of the integrated DVR hard drive? How many hours of SD and HD programming does the DVR hard drive support?

23. Does the integrated DVR feature some kind of a parental control functionality?

24. Does the DVR system access the Internet, so that Internet shows can be streamed and watched on the DVR-enabled TV screen?

25. Does the integrated DVR system enable digital slide show capability?

26. Does the integrated DVR system enable you to record programs, via use of a telephone and scheduling capability from afar?

27. Does the integrated DVR system enable you to schedule the DVR, using the Internet from whatever distance you are away from the DVR?

28. How many tuners are available (enabling you to watch one show while recording one or more other shows at the same time)?

29. Can the integrated DVR export video files to your computer (if the hard drive gets too full and/or if you want a portable version of your saved shows)? What is involved in that?

30. Can the integrated DVR burn a DVD of your recorded programs (if the hard drive gets too full and/or if you want a portable version of your saved shows)? What is involved in that?

31.Does the integrated DVR device feature an add-on-type storage device, also known as an expander or external hard drive, one that will allow transfer of recorded programs from the DVR to the add-on storage device when the DVR hard drive gets full?[9]

32. If there is an add-on-type storage device available, what is its cost and what hard drive sizes or models are available?

33. What is involved in installation of the integrated DVR?

34. Although operators inevitably make DVR installation a part of the service, what is involved in installing the integrated DVR yourself? Is that even allowed?

35. Is the integrated DVR part of a home network system? What does that home networking functionality permit in total, and how does the integrated DVR and its operation fit into that?

36. How does the remote control device compare to others on the market?

37. Does the remote control appear to be designed with consumer friendliness in mind? Are there a lot of buttons to push, or a fewer number? Do the buttons seem to make sense?

38. How does the integrated DVR compare to the standalone DVR? Is the standalone the better option?

6.3.3   RS-DVRs

It is this author's strong conviction that remote storage DVRs (RS-DVRs) and DVR-like devices will have a significant place among television consumers and multichannel pay TV operators in the future. The August 2008 appellate court decision in New York State—which overturned a trial court decision forbidding Long Island-based Cablevision's deployment of RS-DVRs because of copyright concerns—is an indication that such technology has a place in our world. The appellate court disagreed with the lower court's and the Hollywood studio plaintiffs' position that RS-DVR systems were violations of copyrights. This case is now headed to the U.S. Supreme Court for final adjudication.

Another indication is the efficiency and control that remote-storage devices permit the operator, as well as the simplicity and efficiency that they provide the consumer. In short, the idea of a remote central server owned and managed by the multichannel pay TV operator, has some clear long-term advantages over the in-home hard drive storage offered by a standard DVR. But a single one of those is a system whereby advertisements that have grown old or stale could be automatically replaced past a certain time by the multichannel pay TV remote storage operator, such that any future viewing of that "DVRed"[10] show would present the new ad (and not the old one). Also, in this RS-DVR system, consumers could more easily be incentivized by the operator to sit through advertisements, which certainly would make the present set of TV providers—advertisers, agencies, and operators—happier about how people utilize their DVRs.

---

[9] See footnote 5 in this chapter for further discussion of DVR expanders or external hard drives.

[10] Both DVR and TiVo have been popularized in the past decade as terms, such that they are used more and more often as not only nouns, but also as verbs, to connote the act of using a DVR.

A RS-DVR service means that the operator manages what the consumer can record, and likely further restricts what the consumer can distribute to third parties. In this manner, it has the potential to be a better protector of copyrights and related proprietary rights than even the best DVR.

Obtaining a RS-DVR: A Due Diligence Checklist

This list assumes the person using this list is a subscriber to a multichannel pay TV service. It also assumes that, like Long Island's Cablevision Systems or New York's Time Warner Cable may once, that operator has worked through the dilemmas discussed in Chapter 1 and in this chapter, and now offers a RS-DVR system for the subscriber.

1. What type of multichannel pay TV service do you subscribe to? (See discussion above, as to why this is important, or why, ideally, everyone should consider the choices that comes from this question *before* he or she starts a new multichannel pay TV service.)
2. What is the price of the RS-DVR service?
3. Can the RS-DVR only be acquired as part of a larger package or programming purchase?
4. Factoring in the long-term monthly programming package commitment, what is the cost of the RS-DVR?
5. What RS-DVR discounts are available?
6. What company is the maker or manufacturer of the RS-DVR hardware? Is it reputable and experienced?
7. What company is the maker of the RS-DVR software? Is it reputable and experienced?
8. What does the RS-DVR hardware do?
9. What does the RS-DVR software do?
10. What features does the operational or middleware software offer?
11. What restrictions does the RS-DVR operator place on the use of its RS-DVR system by the consumer? For example, are there restrictions on ad-skipping?
12. Does the RS-DVR system access the Internet, so that Internet shows can be downloaded and watched on the RS-DVR-enabled TV screen?
13. Does the RS-DVR system enable digital slide show capability?
14. Does the RS-DVR system enable you to record, via use of a telephone line that signals the RS-DVR from afar?
15. Does the RS-DVR system enable you to schedule the RS-DVR, using the Internet from whatever distance you are away from the RS-DVR?
16. Using the RS-DVR system, can you watch one show while recording one or more other shows at the same time?
17. Can the RS-DVR export video files to your computer (if you want a portable version of your saved shows)? What is involved in that?
18. Can the RS-DVR burn a DVD of your recorded programs (if the hard drive gets too full and/or if you want a portable version of your saved shows)? What is involved in that?
19. Can the RS-DVR export video files to your VCR (if you want a portable version of your saved shows)? What is involved in that?

20. Specifically, as it relates to the RS-DVR user interface (UI), how good is it? How does it compare to that of the operator's integrated set-top DVR? Or to that of a standalone DVR?
21. How easy is it to use the RS-DVR's onscreen guide, or EPG/IPG? Is it user-friendly?
22. Overall, does the standalone RS-DVR typically involve seamless and one-step functionality to get a task accomplished, or is more work required?
23. Does the RS-DVR feature some kind of a parental control functionality?
24. Does the DVR record in HD or only in SD?
25. Does the EPG/IPG display HD programs separate from SD programs?
26. What is the size of the RS-DVR hard drive? How many hours of SD and HD programming does the RS-DVR hard drive support?
27. Does the RS-DVR device feature an add-on-type storage device, also known as an expander or external hard drive, one that will allow transfer of recorded programs from the RS-DVR to the side-car storage device when the DVR hard drive gets full?[11]
28. If there is an add-on-type storage device available, what is its cost and what hard drive sizes or models are available?
29. If one signs up for the RS-DVR, would one still be able to acquire an integrated DVR, and would one still want one?
30. What, if anything, is involved in installation or activation of the RS-DVR capability?
31. Is the RS-DVR part of a home network system? What does that home network permit in total, and how does the RS-DVR and its operation fit into that?
32. How does the RS-DVR remote control device compare to others on the market?
33. Does the remote control appear to be designed with consumer friendliness in mind? Are there a lot of buttons to push, or a fewer number? Do the buttons seem to make sense?

6.3.4 Other Types of DVRs

The focus of this part of the chapter is on other types of DVRs that consumers can obtain. Refer to Chapter 1 and its thorough discussion of other DVRs beyond the standard realm of standalone, integrated, and remote storage. Thus, for example, because consumers rarely are concerned with a DVR purchase as part of a security system infrastructure, that topic will not be discussed in this chapter.

Another form of DVR is that created by the more tech-savvy among us, a so-called do-it-yourself (DIY) DVR. This method of DVR access permits the builder–user to maximize the choice and options desired. For example, several tuners and a much larger hard drive can be built into a homemade DVR. Also, if you are a TiVo subscriber, or if you are looking into that option, and you want to avoid having the TiVo device track and respond to your viewing habits, a DIY DVR version is a good alternative. Further, if you wish to be able to add things

---

[11] See footnote 5 in this chapter for further discussion of DVR expanders or external hard drives.

to your DIY DVR, such as a larger hard drive, or an additional tuner (so that you can record additional show(s) simultaneously), then the DIY model is for you.

Note, however, that the custom-built DVR can be expensive. An example is a possible fee to use operational software, which is usually the case with operational software from companies such as Microsoft. Linux, another operational software provider, is renowned for its free software. Specific DVR DIY software programs include those from companies calling themselves MythTV, SageTV, Freevo, and GB-PVR.[12] Minimal requirements when building a from-the-ground-up DIY DVR are a TV capture card and DVR software (from companies like those mentioned above).

Finally, a home-constructed DVR offers itself without recurring monthly subscription fees, or the cost of buying the device at retail, or renting the device from another party. Two online Web sites offer further views of the DIY DVR process: one is called "DVRplayground," and is accessed at http://www.dvrplayground.com/category/11/Windows-PC-Media-Center; the other is titled "Lifehacker: Tech Tricks, Tips and Downloads for Getting Things Done." The latter contains an excellent article written by Adam Pash, which can be accessed online at http://lifehacker.com/software/dvr/hack-attack-build-your-own-dvr-165963.php.

Arbitron Inc. (NYSE: ARB) is a media and marketing research firm, serving the media (i.e., radio, television, cable, online radio, and out-of-home products and services), as well as advertisers and advertising agencies in the United States. Arbitron's core businesses are measuring network and local-market radio audiences across the United States; surveying the retail, media, and product patterns of local-market consumers; and providing application software used for analyzing media audience and marketing information data. Part of the company's recent focus has been on the development of what Arbitron terms its "Portable People Meter," which is new technology used for the research of media and marketing.

Through its Scarborough Research joint venture with The Nielsen Company, Arbitron provides additional media and marketing research services to the broadcast television, newspaper, and online industries. Arbitron's marketing and business units are supported by a research and technology

---

[12] The websites for these companies are typically accessed by going to a search engine service online, such as Yahoo! MSN, or Google, and typing in the name of the company.

organization located in Columbia, MD. Its executive offices are located in New York City.

Since 2004, Arbitron has been measuring the rate of consumer adoption of DVR technology in the form of TiVo, as well as DVR services provided by cable companies and satellite TV companies. The data attributed to Arbitron are collected through random digital (telephone) dialing (RDD) sample recruitment; it is projectable to the entire United States population aged 12 or older.

As it relates specifically to this book and to the topic of DVRs in the United States today, below are a handful of the fascinating statistics and trends Arbitron has collected and observed during the past several years since 2004.

As a whole, these Arbitron data indicate the following key areas:

- Growth of U.S. DVR users, especially following the cable industry's mass foray into DVRs during 2004–2005
- A broad range of interest in DVRs among varied age groups; the upward income demographic skew
- A broad spread of DVRs inside the four U.S. geographical regions; an equal spread of reasons for using a DVR (e.g., time-shifting vs. ad-skipping)
- A firm indication of future DVR growth prospects

More specifically, Arbitron 2004 to current DVR-related data indicate the following:

- In 2004, Arbitron asked a random sample of Americans, aged 12 years or older, "Do you currently own a TiVo?" 2.2% of Americans said "yes."
- In 2005, Arbitron expanded the DVR ownership question to include non-TiVo branded DVR services.[13] The new question became, "Do you currently own a Personal or Digital Video recorder, such as a TiVo?" From 2.2% a year earlier, 6.4% of Americans aged 12 or older said "yes."
- One year later, Arbitron began tracking the usage of specific types of DVR set-top boxes and services and the data shows that 2006 was the year during which DVR use in America grew substantially. The bullets below summarize these data.
  - Do you currently own/use a TiVo-branded DVR?
    - 2006: 7.7% said "yes"
    - 2007: 9.1% said "yes"
    - 2008: 9.8% said "yes"
  - Do you currently own/use a DVR supplied by a local cable company?
    - 2006: 9.2% said "yes"
    - 2007: 12.9% said "yes"
    - 2008: 16.4% said "yes"

---

[13] Author's note: This expansion was intended to account for the fact that in that time frame, the U.S. cable TV operators had decided to addend their in-house VOD offerings, adding new in-house DVR offerings, in the form of new, individual set-top DVR units manufactured almost exclusivity by either Cisco (which purchased Scientific-Atlanta in 2006) or by Motorola.

- Do you currently own/use a non-TiVo branded DVR from a satellite TV company?
  - 2006: 8.2% said "yes"
  - 2007: 10.6% said "yes"
  - 2008: 11.9% said "yes"
- A summary of these three bulleted sets of data points above finds that during 2006, 17.9% of Americans aged 12 or older stated they owned/used some type or make of DVR. By 2007, that number had grown to 24.9%; and by 2008, that growth had risen to 27.9%.
- Between 2006 and 2007, use of DVRs by Americans, aged 12 and older, increased by 39%. Between 2007 and 2008, the DVR use increase among the same age group was still a healthy, but more modest, 12%.
- Upon analysis of DVR owners/users in 2008, Arbitron found some interesting, and sometimes counterintuitive, characteristics had emerged. For example, contrary to popular perceptions about many new CE products, DVR usage was not the exclusive domain of the younger generation. Granted, DVR usage was somewhat higher among teens and young adults, but not by that much.
  - 12–17 years old: 33%
  - 18–24 years old: 28%
  - 25–34 years old: 29%
  - 35–44 years old: 29%
  - 45–54 years old: 29%
  - 55–64 years old: 25%
  - older than 65 years: 22%
- DVR adoption is also geographically diverse. Ownership/use is less in the Midwest, but not by much.
  - Northeast: 29% own/use a DVR
  - South: 29% own/use a DVR
  - Midwest: 24% own/use a DVR
  - West: 30% own/use a DVR
- When it comes to income levels and DVR use/ownership, there are some clear-cut differences
  - Under $25,000: 20% own/use DVRs
  - $25,000–50,000: 25% own/use DVRs
  - $50,000–75,000: 29% own/use DVRs
  - $75,000–100,000: 32% own/use DVRs
  - $100,000 or more: 48% own/use DVRs

- DVR usage profoundly affects TV viewing among its users. Aside from changes in actual viewership of particular programs, DVRs allow for partial or nearly complete commercial avoidance. Arbitron was curious to see which functionality was most important to users—the ability to watch programs through time shifting that they might not otherwise get to watch, *or* the ability to fast forward through commercials. In 2008, Arbitron fielded this question among DVR owners aged 12 or older, who record programming: "Which one reason is more important to you in choosing to record television programming?" What Arbitron found was that 45% feel time-shifting is the most significant feature of the DVR; nearly half (i.e., 49%), see commercial avoidance as the

most attractive characteristic of the DVR; and nearly one quarter (i.e., 24%), could not choose between the two, and thus said both functions are equally important. The results have significant implications for both TV programmers and the advertisers who support these shows.
  • Ability to watch shows when it fits your schedule: 44.9%
  • Ability to skip or fast forward through commercials: 49.4%
  • Both (volunteered): 23.5%
  • Finally, Arbitron looked at the future of DVR ownership. Over the past 3 years, Arbitron has fielded the following question among DVR nonusers. "In the next 12 months, do you plan to purchase or use a DVR, such as a TiVo or one supplied by a local cable or satellite TV provider?" While actual growth was not as aggressive as the anticipative trends (which is to be expected), the steady increase in interest, year-to-year, shows that *DVRs are not a fad, and the TV industry needs to line up its business models with this new paradigm* (emphasis added).
  • 2006: 9.3% of DVR nonusers plan in the next 12 months to obtain a DVR
  • 2007: 9.6% of DVR nonusers plan in the next 12 months to obtain a DVR
  • 2008: 10.4% of DVR nonusers plan in the next 12 months to obtain a DVR

Arbitron, Inc.

Contact Information
142 W. 57th St., New York, NY 10019
http://www.Arbitron.com

Stock Symbol
NYSE: ARB

Key People
Stephen B. Morris, President and CEO
PR Contact: Gary Holmes
Phone: 646-654-7990

Key Business
Provider of radio station audience ratings in the United States. Also provides market research for cable TV, Internet, and outdoor advertising

DVR Connection
Has conducted several studies relating to cable TV and satellite viewer behavior and DVRs

6.4 Summary

A good deal of time, effort, and analysis are behind much of the consumer-related and consumer-directed information contained in this chapter. That can be seen easily by looking at the handful of consumer survey information, in the form of the charts and a table that begin the chapter. They combine to present a fascinating look at the American consumer and DVRs. Yet, beyond that view of the consumer, the remainder of the chapter is aimed at assistance for the consumer, largely in the form of questions a DVR consumer should want to know about as part of his or her education process. Further, for consumers and wider audiences reading this chapter, the case study of Arbitron and accompanying Arbitron DVR information are of particular interest.

7 International DVR Growth

Internationally, DVR expansion is all about the price of the service (for the operator and the consumer), and the presence of digital competition in a specific region.
—Dr. Steven Wuang, President, Broadband Division, Unihan Corporation

Fairly typical of technology growth in areas of the world other than North America is a rather consistent focus on two major developmental areas, Europe and Asia. In the case of these two large geographical regions, many individual countries display examples of companies within them that have deployed DVRs. Moreover, within North America, yet still within the relative definition of "international," also lies Canada.

Further, in the case of DVRs, some appropriate coverage is also provided to South America. In the case of this Spanish- and Portuguese-speaking continent, however, two now merged former rivals, the companies Sky Latin America and DirecTV Latin America, are today responsible for almost 100% of the DVR deployment there.

Worth also noting is the fact that the country entries below do not represent an exhaustive review of the pertinent DVR literature and developments in these four major geographical regions, but rather a relevant snap shot of significant global DVR growth, circa 2009–2010.

In addition, from a "size-of-potential-market relative to potential for growth" point of view, established DVR vendors would be wise to focus their energies on future international growth, if for no other reason than because of the sheer numbers of TV Households (TVHHs) globally that do not have DVRs today (and therefore could have a DVR—or more—tomorrow). The estimated current base of global DVR deployment is between 50 million and 60 million units, which is about 4–5% of the current global base of just over one billion TVHHs.

7.1 Canada

Like many other areas of the world, especially the United States, DVRs in Canada are driven by two major groups of telecom providers: the large cable operators and the two main satellite TV providers, Star Choice and ExpressVu. Accepting the wisdom of the industry quote featured at the beginning of this chapter, Canada has been and continues to be a hotbed of DVR growth because of the presence of significant digital multichannel pay TV platform competition and the ability of service providers and their customers to pay the price of DVR set-top boxes.

In addition, Canadian consumers are given the option to purchase software that can be downloaded onto one's personal computer (PC), thus permitting DVR capability without having to buy a cable- or satellite-supplied or stand-alone DVR set-top unit. DVRs can also be obtained by way of the so-called Canadian "gray market," as well as via purchases of devices such as TiVo's standalone boxes, made outside of Canada by U.S.-based TiVo. The "gray market" in this instance means the purchase of a DISH Network or DirecTV set-top DVR unit in the United States (accompanied by a registration of an owner address in the United States), but actual use of the unit is within Canada, which is a violation of Canadian laws. This "gray market" in Canada remains a prevalent problem for Canadian telecom authorities.

The lead Canadian cable multichannel pay TV providers are Toronto, Ontario-based Rogers Communications and Calgary, Alberta-headquartered Shaw (http://www.shawcable.ca). Shaw is also a satellite TV company, thus delivering signals both terrestrially via cable wires and by satellite for its direct broadcast satellite (DBS) service, called Star Choice. Rogers Cable (http://www.rogerscable.ca), on the other hand, is the largest TV provider in the nation of approximately 32 million residents, [1] but, unlike Shaw, Rogers' video focus is on cable.

The other major satellite TV provider in the Canadian marketplace is Bell ExpressVu, which is largely owned and controlled by the large Canadian telco, Bell Canada. ExpressVu's DVR lineup can be accessed by visiting the online site of http://www.expressvu.ca (which, fittingly, will bring the searcher to the Bell Web site). The U.S.'s number two satellite TV provider, size-wise, EchoStar, supplies its product line of DVR set-top boxes to ExpressVu's Canadian customers. Canadian telco video provider Bell Canada's DVR offerings can be reviewed at http://www.bellcanada.ca (in conjunction with its subsidiary, ExpressVu's, DVR offerings).

7.2 Asia

Several countries in Asia today offer their populations solid opportunities in the realm of DVRs. Yet, regardless of what those markets represent to the DVR industry today, undoubtedly, the real story for DVR in Asia is the *future*, especially as it relates to the Asian population base and its many hundreds of millions of TVHHs. According to company officials in the Asia region, current DVR deployment in Asia hovers around three million, meaning the potential for growth in the region is measured by numbers most consumer electronics and TV executives can only dream about. Focused in this chapter, in order, are Australia, South Korea, Taiwan, China, Japan, and India, because of their

---

[1] The current country figures in this chapter relating to population, as well as Households (HHs) and TVHHs, are taken from the 2008 edition of "Pocket World in Figures," published by *The Economist*.

present DVR deployment, their population base, or their telecom development potential. Additional countries in the region include the following:

- Cambodia (14 million inhabitants[2])
- Indonesia (with 22 million people and 59 million HHs)
- Malaysia (25 million people and 5.6 million HHs)
- Myanmar (50 million people)
- North Korea (22.5 million people)
- New Zealand (4 million inhabitants and 1.5 million HHs)
- the Philippines (with 83 million people and 17 million HHs)
- Singapore (4 million people and 1 million HHs)
- Thailand (64 million people and 17 million HHs)
- Vietnam (84 million inhabitants and 25 million HHs)

7.3 Australia

Although one of the smaller Pan Asian nations population-wise, the former British colony "down under" represents one of the region's highest per capita quality of living levels and thus is a prime spot to launch DVR businesses.

San Francisco, CA-based OpenTV and Alviso, CA-based TiVo (located some 60 miles to the south of OpenTV, in the San Francisco Bay Area) both have a bull's-eye on the world's largest island nation and its roughly 20 million inhabitants. Both of these United States DVR industry pioneers are aggressively competing to deliver DVR functionality to all Australians.

OpenTV software has been deployed by most of the world's vertical multichannel pay TV providers, including those such as Foxtel and Austar in Australia. As such, OpenTV is in a position to observe and comment upon several global trends. One such global trend affecting OpenTV partners, especially in Europe, is that of a standard model, entry-level, set-top box that necessarily includes a DVR. Once that model of "standard DVR" becomes the norm, those service providers providing the set-top DVRs will instead compete on the basis of bigger and bigger hard drives, costing the consumer less money, together with numerous tuners that allow multiple playback and simultaneous recording features.

A second feature is that of "DVR stickiness," whereby once a consumer is hooked into the world of DVR—by a specific provider—that consumer then does not leave the service. Part of the reason for that loyalty is that the consumer's personal content resides on the specific provider's DVR, and if service is terminated, the content is lost to the subscriber forever.

Further, especially in places such as Australia and Europe, and elsewhere globally, new service provider models call for a DVR set-top box to be provided to a new subscriber, with the DVR service provided "free" for the first 3 months, after which the DVR shifts to a pay service. The take-up rate for the pay DVR service

---

[2] In some instances, country data showing the number of HHs was not available from the preferred datasource, *The Economist*.

beyond the first 3 free months is "quite high," notes an OpenTV spokesperson. A fourth global trend observed is that of DVR providers paying the costs themselves of deploying DVR functionality, as opposed to earlier models that required substantial investments on the part of consumers. One example in this direction is the increased availability of Universal Serial Bus (USB) ports on set-tops without DVRs, and the accompanying "side car" recording devices that allow transfer of content from the "standard" set-top box, i.e., one without a DVR, onto the side car device. In this world, the provider cares less and less about the cost to add a DVR because the sidecar device and it storage is so cheap.

TiVo's Australian venture began officially in July 2008, when it announced its venture with Australia's Seven Media Group. In a press release calling itself "one of Australia's leading integrated media companies," Seven describes itself as a national, satellite-delivered, advertising supported "free-to-air"[3] provider in Australia. The press release also claimed that "70 per cent of Australians ... chose free over pay television" [meaning seven of 10 Australians, or roughly 14 million, take free satellite-delivered free-to-air (FTA) TV, as opposed to the remaining six million, who either receive their TV signals via pay services (such as cable or satellite TV), receive it via over-the-air terrestrial broadcast TV, or do not watch TV at all].

The TiVo DVR product in Australia gets sold to the country's approximately 7 million TVHHs, through the 190-store Harvey Norman-owned home retail consumer electronics and entertainment complexes, called Harvey Norman and Domayne.

In an apparent break from monthly service charge models offered by TiVo in the United States, the same Australian press release noted, "Customers will not be tied to an ongoing subscription plan and as new features become available TiVo high definition (HD) automatically updates using the home broadband connection." This no-monthly payment charges model was likely a requirement of doing business with the Seven organization, inasmuch as the Seven FTA system is already a free, ad-supported business model, and adding a TiVo (or any other) service with a monthly service, would contradict the nature of that service. It also likely would have created an undue burden on Seven and its customers. Instead, the cost of the TiVo in the Seven system is charged up-front, as is described subtly in the last few sentences of the July 1, 2008, Seven-TiVo press release: "Having a TiVo HD DVR means no monthly fees for pay television. The TiVo HD DVR will be available in retail stores from 29 July for a cost of Aus. $699.... TiVo, TV Your Way—without the monthly cost."

Furthermore, emphasizing future broadband Internet content delivery options that are planned, the release states, "Via the broadband connection, consumers can access new features and functions on their TiVo unit as they are introduced. For example, in addition to TV-specific features—the TiVo HD DVR will soon support viewing family photos on the television (optional upgrade), as well as

[3] "Free-to-air," in this instance, means the TV service is delivered, via a satellite, to a broad national footprint of users who need only a satellite dish and a set-top box to receive advertiser-supported free television.

watching favorite YouTube clips. Video content from the Internet is also on the horizon, by hiring a movie and downloading it through the home's broadband connection directly to a TiVo HD DVR for viewing."

Other DVR competitors in The Land Down Under include multichannel pay TV providers, Foxtel and Austar. Satellite- and cable-delivered pay TV provider Foxtel, with more than 1.5 million subscribers, began offering DVRs in Australia in February 2005; satellite-delivered pay TV provider Austar's DVR deployment began in 2007. Austar lists slightly more than 700,000 subscribers, as of the commencement of Q4 2008.

In July 2008, Foxtel enlisted News Corp.-owned NDS to build its next generation of DVR set-top boxes, in this case a four-tuner HD DVR model and newly-designed EPG/IPG. The new HD DVR model, labeled a Foxtel *iQ2*, is both standard definition (SD) and HD compatible; its multiple tuners allow viewer access to two shows simultaneously, as well as concurrent access to live TV and on-demand content. Foxtel's July 30, 2008, press release claimed that within a "few weeks" since its launch in June 2008, the *iQ2* had more than 20,000 Foxtel customers upgrade to HD services and the *iQ2* HD DVR. Foxtel's 2005 DVR launch made it the first in Australia to deploy DVRs for its subscribers. The *iQ2* HD DVR features a 320 Gigabyte hard drive, allowing approximately 30 hours of HD storage or 90 hours of SD.[4] Foxtel is owned by Telstra Corporation Limited (50%), The News Corporation Limited (25%), and Consolidated Media Holdings Limited (25%).

Austar closely followed rival Foxtel's HD DVR release, by announcing, in September 2008, its selection of French-owned Thomson to develop and supply a four-tuner HD DVR platform, along with extensive systems' integration services. No date, however, was mentioned for the launch of the new HD DVRs. The new box is set to mirror Austar's current MyStar branded DVR set-top box, which features both dual satellite and dual terrestrial tuners, as well as the experience of watching and simultaneously recording both Austar-delivered satellite content and local FTA services.

Concluding its September 22, 2008 press release, Austar further described itself, "Austar is a leading provider of subscription television services in regional and rural Australia, with more than 700,000 customers enjoying principally satellite digital television services. Internet and mobile telephony services complete Austar's product offering. Austar is also a significant provider of programming in the Australian television market through its 50% owned joint venture, XYZnetworks, which owns and/or distributes Nickelodeon, Nick Jr, Discovery Channel, Channel [V], Channel [V]2, MAX, Arena, The LifeStyle Channel, LifeStyle Food, Country Music Channel, and The Weather Channel. Liberty Global Inc., the largest international broadband cable operator in terms of subscribers, holds an indirect controlling stake in Austar."

---

[4] The number of hours recorded on a HD DVR will depend on the mix between HD and SD, as well as on the mix between channel genres. Typically, for example, high-action rate sports takes up much more space than a movie.

7.4   South Korea

A June 2008 headline in an online publication called Global Services, reads, "Wireless Portable DVRs in South Korea Support Bluetooth and Wi-Fi." Although the devices featured in this article skew more toward commercial- and enterprise-level security DVR deployments, the article itself is a good example of the cutting edge technological superiority of this small Asian peninsula country. Indeed, many say that South Korea preceded the United States by at least a couple of years, when it comes to the early deployment of DVRs (at least for security purposes). South Korea's population base is 48 million; its TVHHs base is more than 16 million, out of a total of 17.4 million HHs.

Other online sites for more data about security-based DVRs in South Korea include the following:

*   http://www.security.globalsources.com/gsol/I/Standalone-DVR/a/9000000086061.htm
*   http://www.security.globalsources.com/gsol/I/Mobile-DVR/a/9000000095147.htm (Mobile DVR manufacturers)
*   http://www.chinasourcingreports.com/csr/Security-Products/CCTV-Digital-Video-Recorders/p/CSRCVR/Executive-Summary.htm
*   http://www.asmag.com/asm/common/article_detail.aspx?module=5&c=3&id=184 (a first rate article with profiles depicting South Korean manufacturers and exporters)

7.5   Taiwan

Apparently because of its status as one of Asia's leading nations for cable deployment—at a penetration rate of over 80% of TVHHs—and because of its status as one of the leading nations in Asia for broadband deployment, the country of Taiwan was first selected by industry pioneer, TiVo, to roll out its first Asian DVRs, during the late 2005 time frame. Taiwan has a population of 23 million inhabitants, and roughly 6.3 million TVHHs, one of the highest TV penetration rates in Asia.

In mid-2006, TiVo sought to grow its TiVo standalone unit sales in Taiwan by offering the Taiwanese a second model TiVo DVR, with less storage, but also with a significantly lower price. Together with licensee TGC Taiwan, Inc., TiVo's second set-top box offered consumers 80 gigabytes (GB) of storage, vs. the 160 GB in its first box. The newer box retails for NT$12,900 (US$396.40). There is no subscription fee for the first year, and an annual subscription fee of NT$1500 (US$46) starts in the second year. A shop manager at a Tatung Co. store on Nanking East Road near Taipei said that customers had been slow to respond to TiVo. Tatung, along with Synnex Technology International Corporation, and PC Home Online, are the channel distributors for TiVo in Taiwan. A 2006 article about TiVo in Taiwan, from the *Taipei Times* newspaper, notes, "There is a lot of explaining to do for general customers regarding what TiVo is all about. But the machine is popular among those who have lived in the U.S. before, and who know its special features," said the manager of the store at Tatung Co., who refused to be named. The store had sold only two TiVo units in the past 6 months, he said. (See http:// www.taipeitimes.com/News/biz/archives/2006/06/13/2003313358.)

7.6 China

Like its neighbor, Korea, China also offers a substantial footprint on the side of the DVR industry related to security devices. The Web site for a company called DEC, at http://www.decindustry.com/, provides an example of one of literally hundreds of Chinese concerns dedicated to providing primarily hardware for those wishing to purchase security-related DVR systems. A quality article from China Sourcing Reports, labeled "Sourcing Report: CCTV Digital Video Recorders," can be accessed online at http://www.chinasourcingreports.com/csr/Security-Products/CCTV-Digital-Video-Recorders/p/CSRCVR/Executive-Summary.htm.

Another prime example of DVR development and growth in China comes from a Forbes.com article in late 2007, focused on a Chinese company, called BlueStar SecuTech, Inc., which stated it has signed five new contracts worth about 7.5 million renminbi (RMB) with China Construction Bank, Huaxia Bank, China Everbright Bank, Bank of China, and An Heng Testing company. The provider of digital video surveillance solutions to corporate clients in China said it will provide DVRs to replace those in the 400 ATMs (automated teller machines) of the Beijing branch of China Construction Bank. Banks in China are required under government legislation to replace all DVRs that are more than 5 years old. BlueStar said it has been the sole provider of DVR products since 2003 to the Beijing branch of China Construction Bank, the country's third largest bank. This Forbes.com article can be accessed online at http:// www.forbes.com/afxnewslimited/feeds/afx/2007/11/26/afx4372346.html.

As is true primarily in the Asia countries of South Korea, Taiwan, and China, this security-related DVR development and growth is important for Asia (and the world), because it provides a strong manufacturing base to grow DVRs well beyond the somewhat limited commercial and enterprise sectors and deeply into the almost unlimited residential DVR sector. Development of TVHH DVR penetration in nearby locales, such as Australia, provides great fodder and lessons for growth in the other 15+ Pan Asian countries.

7.7 Japan

For U.S. DVR aficionados, the first link to Japan and DVRs is probably a connection to ReplayTV, and its acquisition in 2001, by Japanese-based SonicBlue. This progressed to a purchase of SonicBlue out of bankruptcy, in mid-2003, by the Japanese holding company, D & M Holdings, which then, in late 2007, sold its remaining DVR software portfolio to the U.S. satellite TV duopolist,

DirecTV. Indeed, going to http://www.replaytv.com/, today leads a searcher directly a Web site page completely controlled by the DirecTV Web site.

The SonicBlue situation "is a sad story, but an isolated incident that doesn't reflect the overall health of the DVR industry," said Carmel Group analyst Sean Badding in 2003, acknowledging that SonicBlue officials might have—like many in the industry—overestimated the pace of growth of the DVR market-place, when it came to its investment in the company and subsequent results.

Because of its high standard of living, relative sophistication technologically, and large and quite competitive pay TV marketplace, Japan is yet another prime market for the further rollout and aggressive deployment of DVRs.

Currently, estimates suggest that DVRs in Japan have, like in the United States, begun to replace old-style VCRs, when it is time to change set-top boxes. A 2005 study by Dentsu notes that 15% of Japan's TVHHs had DVRs. (See, http://www.dentsu.com/marketing/DVRs.pdf). The same study goes to great lengths, however, to point out the differences between the two markets of the United States and the United Kingdom, on the one hand, and Japan, on the other. The Japanese Electronics and Information Technology Industry Association estimated in the same study that, by 2009, Japan's base of DVRs would rest at close to 32 million DVR units. This growth comes from a year-end 2008 estimate by The Carmel Group of nearly 3 million currently deployed DVR units in Japan. Japan's population base is 128 million; its TVHHs base is 45 million, from a HHs base of 48 million.

7.8   India

Following the theme of this chapter, that of the potential of international DVR growth, one would be remiss to leave out India. With 1.1 billion inhabitants—a number that, by 2020, is expected to surpass that of China, the world's largest country, which today has roughly 1.3 billion inhabitants and more than 200 million HHs—India is prime for much telecom development, certainly including multichannel pay TV, and thus DVRs. Indeed, even if India simply adopts the FTA DVR model, as Seven is doing in Australia, the growth poten-tial is huge. The Carmel Group estimates India will host 10 million DVR users by the end of year 2016.

As but a single example of the DVR potential in India, Hathway, one of India's leading providers of digital cable services, has chosen NDS' *XTV* brand for a planned 2008–2009 launch of the country's first cable industry DVR.

7.9   Europe

Although it is still rather embryonic, Europe is actually the world's second larg-est center for DVR growth, following the United States. The core reason for this success is Rupert Murdoch, and his company, News Corp.'s, focus on the development of DVRs during the past half decade or so. Specifically, in the United Kingdom, Murdoch's controlling ownership of multichannel pay TV operator, BSkyB, has meant BSkyB has become the predominant provider of DVRs in Europe and certainly among the top 7–10 providers globally. Through his control of Sky Italia, Murdoch has also pushed DVRs deeply into Italian TV society.

Other countries focused on in this section, primarily because of (1) their population base, (2) competitive telecom landscape, and (3) competitive growth potential, include France and Germany. Although not specifically mentioned in this chapter, the European countries of Spain, Poland, and Italy are also expected to promote significant DVR growth, if for no other reason than their relative sizes, population-wise and TVHHs-wise, and the relative sophistication of their telecom infrastructures.

7.10   England

Without question, the main DVR force for the 60 million inhabitants in the United Kingdom today is News Corp.-controlled BSkyB and its *Sky Plus*-branded DVR product. According to U.K. TV expert, Chris Forrester, and his *Rapid TV News* service, an estimated more than 3.5 million BSkyB customers subscribe to the *Sky Plus* DVR service; of those, approximately one-third are thought to also be HD subscribers. An October 31, 2008, press release from BSkyB, reports that as of the close of third quarter 2008, BSkyB's total subscriber growth exceeded 9 million, from among 26 million HHs, and the *Sky Plus* DVR product added 421,000 customers in the quarter, meaning that service was subscribed to by more than 4 million TVHHs. Also, as it relates to other digital products and their growth, BSkyB states record *Sky Plus* HD growth during the quarter, with 93,000 signing up for the service during the three-month period, taking the *Sky Plus* HD total to 591,000 TVHHs.

As for other digital services, *Sky Broadband* added 164,000 customers during the quarter, taking that count to 1.792 million TVHHs. The *Sky Talk* voice offering netted BSkyB 120,000, for a final tally of to 1.361 million TVHHs. These datapoints add convincing weight to the argument that implementation of digital DVR strategies not only bring in new subscribers, but also keep existing subscribers from churning out (or leaving the service) and help to drive subscribers toward subscription to other advanced digital services. Equally importantly for most multichannel pay TV operators is the increase in the Average Revenue Per Unit (ARPU). In the case of BSkyB, the October 31, 2008, reporting listed a year-over-year increase of 19 pounds, totaling 430 pounds of ARPU for the year.

Nonetheless, because U.K. cable is such a diminished product subscriber-wise (at least relative to 9+ million BSkyB), this means that one less equally competitive force is unavailable in the United Kingdom to drive the deployment of DVRs. This alone significantly differentiates almost all of Europe from the United States. Further, less TV content is typically available in the United Kingdom from the core cable and satellite TV providers, than would be the case in the United States. This could further dampen longer term prospects for DVR growth in the United Kingdom. The lack of cable also suggests that video download and similar Internet video services might have more traction in the United Kingdom than similar services might have in the United States.

Other DVR offerings in the island nations of Ireland, Scotland, and England are provided by the FTA satellite TV provider, Freeview. Named in a fashion similar to rival BSkyB's *Sky Plus* DVR service, *Freeview Plus* offers DVRs manufactured by makers such as Sony, Toshiba, Samsung, Panasonic, Humax, Daewoo, Hitachi, Sharp, and Thomson, as well as lesser known makers such as Wharfedale, TVonics, Goodmans, Thomon, Sagem, and Topfield. In Ireland, since 2007, video service provider UPC is offering a Thomson-branded 160 Gigabyte DVR *MediaBox* that competes with those of its satellite and digital terrestrial competitors.

Interestingly, a DVR-type service that would be the equivalent of the peer-to-peer BitTorrent music and other file-sharing technology was introduced in 2007–2008. The U.K.-based service, called *TVCatchup*, would have permitted one user's DVR to record from another user's DVR via the Internet. With up to 10 gigabits of online storage, the CatchupTV service would allow one who did not program his or her own machine to record a program at its regular broadcast time to still have the option to record it from another user for viewing within 24 hours. TVCatchup was supported by ads and purported to be fully legal, but some broadcasters objected to it on copyright grounds. As a result, TVCatchup suspended operations, giving the following explanation on its Web site:

"Dear Member

In recent days, TVCatchup has become aware of the Broadcaster's (BBC, ITV, Channel 4, Five) increasing concerns over the free personal recording functionality that this website offers (sic).

On 15th February, our hosting was terminated without warning and we presume this was at the request of such Broadcasters.

Given that this will no doubt happen again, TVCatchup has therefore voluntarily suspended its services whilst the concerns of the Broadcasters are addressed.

We apologize to all for this temporary interruption to service.

This page will provide a service update as matters progress.

TVCatchup.com

16th February 2008"

7.11 France

For many years, France and the United Kingdom have been the leaders when it comes to offering their inhabitants cutting-edge TV and advanced services in Europe. For the French population of 60.5 million, and its 25 million HHs,

DVRs come in several forms. Today, in France, DVR deployment is estimated in the low single digit millions; however, it is expected to grow to be among the European leaders, in the double digit millions, within the next 5–7 years. Interestingly, the term in French for the term DVR is translated as *magnétoscope numérique.*

One dominant French DVR is the NDS- and Canal Plus-supplied middleware and side-car hard drive used by roughly 250,000 Canal Plus HD customers, among a total of more than 10 million satellite-delivered Canal Plus multichannel pay TV service subscribers. This latest offering, as of August 2008, is a side-car type device that attaches to an existing Canal Plus HD set-top box, thus permitting the viewer to utilize DVR functionality (which was not designed or built into the original HD set-top box), without having to purchase an entirely new HD DVR set-top box. Specifically, Canal Plus subscribers purchase or lease the new side-car set-top box (which is really little more than an external hard drive storage device) and simply connect it to their HD set-top box via the USB port, whereupon the software middleware (which has already been downloaded by Canal Plus to the HD set-top box) detects the addition of the new external hard drive and formats the hard drive on the original set-top for use as a DVR. The new system also allows subscribers to use more than one hard drive if they wish; thus, there is literally no limit to the amount of shows a customer can store.

Other storage device vendors eyeing France include Seagate, Western Digital, and Pioneer. Consumers in France may also purchase standalone DVR devices from well-known CE manufacturers, such as Humax. Under the Sony umbrella, a new service for the *PlayStation 3* offered additional DVR functionality to be quickly added for customers in France, as well as in the United Kingdom, Italy, Germany, and Spain during 2008. This permits customers of Sony's *PS3* to use the device as a media center instead of just a gaming device.

On another platform, that of the France Telecom (FT) Internet Service Provider (ISP) Digital Subscriber Line (DSL) video offering, termed Wannado, DVR options are in the process of being offered to customers (see http://www.free.fr).

7.12   Germany

One could say that Germany is a "leader" when it comes to DVR deployments, but that would not be true in the normal sense. Rather, a German-based company, called Nero, is leading TiVo into the world of DVR TV on laptop computers and PCs. It is the first time a TiVo DVR service has been fully integrated into a PC. There is no first year $12.95/month TiVo fee for the new service, called *LiquidTV TiVo* (and by Nero), although it is not available for Apple computer owners. Renewal will cost $99/year. Mimicking what OpenTV has noticed (see the section on Australia), Nero and TiVo are counting on the popularity of the TiVo interface and brand to overcome the $99 renewal hurdle. The service was first featured in the United States, Canada, and Mexico during late 2008 and later in Nero's home country during 2009. Prior to Nero, Britain was the only country in Europe where TiVo had subscribers. Notes *USA Today*'s Edward C. Baig, in a review of the new service dated October 8, 2008, "As with other software-based DVRs such as SnapStream Media's *Beyond TV* program, you can watch, schedule, record and pause live TV on your PC.... But Nero includes the familiar TiVo interface and electronic programming guide, plus many other TiVo features. These include suggestions on what to watch based on your viewing habits, the *Season Pass* feature for automatically recording favorite series, parental controls and the 'WishList' feature which helps you find programs based on an actor's name or other criteria."

The *LiquidTV* package of $199 retail includes a remote control, but one could chose to control everything on screen via the computer's keys and on screen tool bars. For an additional $99, the user can download the Nero *LiquidTV* recording software. Also, a user has to supply his or her own compatible TV tuner. Although accessible via the computer, the *LiquidTV* service does not automatically offer links to *Amazon Video on Demand* and YouTube. Further, if a user has a "real" TiVo device in his or her home, the Nero *LiquidTV* software is capable of transferring shows via one's home network to the PC. In addition, recordings can be exported to an *iPod* or a Sony *PSP* or burnt on a DVD.

Nero is also important because it highlights the global trend to want to watch, and thus control, one's video experience, not just from a television, but also from other devices in the home media chain, for example, a PC or laptop. Germany and Japan are indicative of this trend, if for nothing else, measured by the number of new computers that are being shipped in those countries with TV tuners built in. What is also worth noting is that a lot of satellite and cable companies are building and using their Internet protocol-based television (IPTV) infrastructure to further the appropriate viewing on TV on PCs and laptops. These trends, in turn, point to another platform (and set of locales) for the deployment of a DVR experience.

Elsewhere in Germany, DVR deployment is minimal (at least compared to the United Kingdom), also, again, reflecting the DVR growth potential in this country of 82 million, and nearly 40 million HHs, with more than 97 color TVs per 100 HHs, according to *The Economist*. Many expect a solid future market for TV sets with DVRs built into them at the factory to be popular in German TVHHs.

7.13   South America

A summary of DVRs in South America is essentially a summary of one service provider that is, throughout the subcontinent, offering DVRs, and that is DirecTV Latin America. With core operations in the most populated countries of Brazil and Mexico, DirecTV Latin America faces little or no competition within most countries in the region, as it relates to the deployment of DVRs. Some of this is also tied to the relative lack of multichannel pay TV competition within South America and the relatively low earning and expenditure power of the typical South American inhabitant. For example, cable has had a relatively slow growth cycle in South America, indicated in part by the fact that Argentina remains the only country in the region where cable has created a relatively solid footprint. Because of this situation, the focus within this South America subsection of this "International DVR Growth" chapter shall be on those two "growth" countries, i.e., Brazil and Mexico, and the DirecTV systems within each.

7.14 Brazil

The South American country of Brazil is unique in a couple of respects, as it relates to this book about DVRs.

First, it is the largest country in South America population- and area-wise, with a population estimated at approximately 190 million inhabitants and a landmass of 8.5 million square kilometers (which compares to the United States, including Alaska and Hawaii, at 9.4 million square kilometers). Both these figures rank Brazil among the top 10 in the world today. It is also the largest country in the region as it relates to TVHHs, with roughly 110 million.

The second area of Brazilian uniqueness as it relates to DVRs is that it is the only country in the region of Latin America that, as its main language, speaks Portuguese. Thus, whatever a regional sub-continent satellite service provider, like DirecTV Latin America, does in the entire region, it *must* include the Portuguese-speaking people of Brazil. This also means that for many items under the DirecTV Latin America umbrella, efforts and expenditures must not only be made to accommodate hundreds of millions of Spanish-speaking customers, but also the same number of Portuguese-speaking customers. Furthermore, other than at the coast, it is very much a rural country, which means that even before the introduction of DirecTV Latin America and the Murdoch-owned Sky Latin America, there were many millions of satellite dishes set up to receive the country's seven over-the-air channels retransmitted via satellite.

One of the "accommodations" aimed at gaining and maintaining millions of new DirecTV Latin America subscribers, in place for many customers since 2003, has been DVRs. Like Murdoch-controlled entities elsewhere in the world, the then Murdoch-owned and -controlled Sky Latin America opted to compete with rival DirecTV Latin America in the form of a DVR offering from sister company NDS. NDS deployed DVRs in Latin America in the form of the NDS *XTV*-brand DVR, which had earlier also been introduced for Foxtel in Australia, BSkyB in the United Kingdom, and for DirecTV in the United States. The specific

DirecTV service provider in Brazil is named DirecTV Brazil. Like its sister to the north in Mexico, the first iteration of DirecTV Brazil was formally established on December 15, 1996. The new company was a joint venture between BSkyB, News Corp., Liberty Media, and Organizacoes Globo.

NDS' first DVR for Sky Latin America in Brazil offered two tuners and 70 hours of standard definition recording time. Since late 2003, when this first DVR launched, not only have DirecTV Brazil and Sky Brazil merged into one satellite TV company, but like elsewhere in the world, several additional generations of newer DVR models have been introduced.

Once a competitor—perhaps another Brazilian satellite TV provider—recognizes the potential for DVR growth in Brazil, expect it to aggressively begin using DVRs for what they are best at doing: getting new subscribers, keeping existing subscribers happy (and spending more ARPU), and driving the competition crazy.

7.15 Mexico

DirecTV Mexico is the dominant DVR provider in this Spanish-speaking country of 107 million and nearly 25 million HHs. It, too, offers its subscribers DVRs under the *Sky Plus* label used in the United Kingdom and elsewhere. The Mexican company was founded in mid-1996, a joint venture between British Sky Broadcasting (BSkyB), News Corp., Liberty Media, and Grupo Televisa. It was formally launched on December 15, 1996.

Joshua Danovitz, General Manager for TiVo's International deployments, is in charge of the Alviso, CA-based DVR company's small, yet burgeoning, number of global DVR forays into an international market that represents a potential 1+ billion TV households, almost all but about 4–5% of which are without DVR functionality today.

Moving into this global realm has meant TiVo and Danovitz have had some fascinating introductions to executives at some of the world's major cable multiple system operators. This is because of what Danovitz describes as the worldwide popularity of the TiVo brand and TiVo product. Indeed, international media has been good to the U.S. DVR pioneer, actually labeling the act of using a DVR as "to TiVo" a show. This "popularization" of the TiVo brand name inevitably reminds people whenever they use it of an important commercial entity behind the service of DVRs.[5]

At the outset, a phenomena that Danovitz suggests shows the uniqueness of Asia and Europe, is the existence of a very large base, relatively speaking, of FTA and Digital Video Broadcasting-Terrestrial (DVB-T) platforms. DVB-T is a terrestrially delivered digital signal that is advertiser supported and thus "free" to its users, without having to pay a monthly user fee. FTA is referred to as a satellite-delivered and terrestrial-delivered advertiser-supported programming service that is also without monthly subscriber fees, its business model instead depending on the advertising model that is the foundation of free-over-the-air television in the United States and many other countries. Trying to sell DVRs into DVB-T and FTA systems, being perceived as harming or completely negating advertising, branding, and messaging, is a challenge. Nonetheless, TiVo has met with significant success in this arena, having entered into a summer 2008 launch with FTA Australian service, Seven. In addition, the DVB-T example comes from the United Kingdom, where over 10 million HHs use the Freeview-branded service. The core British service also offers 35 video channels, as well as 30 audio channels. FTA is quite popular as a service in the rest of Europe. Yet another new platform, that of IPTV, offered primarily by telephone and cable companies globally, offers another set of challenging new platforms for companies trying to grow DVRs globally.

Danovitz, rather than seeing these new platforms as a challenge, instead prefers to focus on each new one as an opportunity, for TiVo and its brethren. Nonetheless, cost and the ability to offer competitive programming, especially premium content, are core issues facing the DVR industry when attempting to introduce themselves into these new ad-supported platforms.

The bottom line, Danovitz contends, is that "These different companies, on different platforms, doing much the same thing, have to compete and deliver more than TV." He sees his job at TiVo as " ... getting the operator

[5] Important to note also is that for copyright and intellectual property reasons, TiVo resists people using "TiVo" to describe the act rather than the product and service developed and manufactured specifically by TiVo.

a good experience that it can then pass on to a satisfied customer." Citing a new DVR in a customer's living room, Danovitz does not just see the DVR as pause, rewind, storage, and fast forward, but rather to also have the TiVo be capable of connecting with a broadband source and permitting remote and mobile scheduling. He sees great opportunity in the global transition from analog to digital. Returning to the United Kingdom, Danovitz notes BSkyB and Virgin Media, and their apparent "lock" on consumers there, as he opines, "Yet others could argue they both are about to get surpassed, because of the analog-to-digital transition and the DVR experience."

Looking then at Asia, Danovitz summarizes, "It's too big an area to give a synopsis in one fell swoop. Japan, China, India, and the others, they're each one so different."

Using the subcontinent of India as an example, he labels the country "hyper interesting" because it is likely the largest opportunity and most challenging of all in Asia. To begin with, the Indian government has recently issued five separate licenses to five separate satellite companies. Yet, the scenario is ripe for consolidation in many people's minds, because the survival of five companies is so unlikely, especially in light of the relatively low ARPU paid by consumers in India for television-related consumption. Danovitz points out that even if a company were able to acquire the top 20% of the country's wealthier users, it would still be tough to make a new video project work in India. Other challenges include the lack of infrastructure and concerns about the availability of broadband services in many parts of the country. Cultural challenges are also present as with any group of people, an example of which is the fact that, many people in India cycle through cell phones at the rate of 2 or 3 a year. To further exhibit the point, Danovitz notes, "People gather at their homes in a different way, and when they do, they invite multiple layers of family to their home. That is a cultural dynamic that influences many parts of telecom growth, but, on the other hand, the growth of proper and necessary infrastructure is very slow."

Danovitz points out that China presents yet another set of challenges and opportunities. He believes, "China is really interesting, because the telecom and DVR opportunity there is really about how IPTV changes the Chinese landscape (especially involving the telephone companies), and cable, probably a little more about cable." China is home to a huge number of cable companies, yet only a small number are deploying digital services and infrastructure such as fiber, yet those that do might have as many as 15 million subscribers. Moreover, while adding advanced services, such as HDTV and DVRs, might be attractive, these cable and telco companies are under great pressure from customers and the government to ramp up their broadband offerings. Because of these concerns, TiVo has not yet entered into agreements with Chinese cable or telco companies, even though a few examples of "generic" DVRs are beginning to surface within the Chinese marketplace. Danovitz summarizes about the DVR opportunities in China, "China will have a quick route to DVR maturity, once it starts, but the challenge is still very much a common one: ARPUs are still very low. Yet, on the other hand, when you take that ARPU, and you times it with 1.3 billion potential users, that's its own solution." Perhaps as one of the better testaments to TiVo's interest in countries like China, Danovitz also served on the board of a TiVo licensee focused on Asia with an initial launch in Taiwan, helping it grow its multichannel and advanced services business.

Wrapping up his abbreviated global review in the island nation of Japan, Danovitz notes it has already gone through its own analog-to-digital transition. Further, because of existing competitors, such as Jupiter on the cable side and SkyPerfect on the satellite side, the market in Japan is already rather heated as it relates to DVR deployment. Yet, in both instances, Danovitz believes, technical and engineering challenges have made DVR growth in Japan less than what it might otherwise have been. Telcos in Japan might take risks with advanced services such as DVRs, as they, too, position to compete against cable and satellite video providers.

Joshua Danovitz summarizes TiVo's global DVR growth possibilities, "DVR growth is much more dynamic, especially in Europe and Asia, and very different from the U.S. We will learn a lot, see a lot of opportunities, and a lot of challenges, as well."

Tivo

Contact Information
2160 Gold Street, Alviso, CA 95002
Phone: 408-519-9100
http://www.tivo.com

Stock Symbol
NASDAQ (GM): TIVO

Key People
Thomas S. Rogers, CEO, President and Director
PR Contact: Krista Wierzbicki, 408-519-9100

Key Business
Pioneered the DVR, and brought DVR to mass market based on a subscription service

DVR Connection
Sells TiVo branded DVRs, as well as third-party TiVo-enabled DVRs sold through retailers

7.16   Summary

DVRs for billions of people, rather than DVRs for mere millions, is a remarkable leap of faith. Yet, it is perhaps the best statement leading into Chapter 8, "Future of DVRs," i.e., that experts can even soberly believe that such a growth cycle is possible. That said, it is not only possible, but likely. The only real question is whether we are talking 10 years or 20 years; either way, the DVR soon becomes a standard part of every new set-top box, cable, telco, or satellite, and that is what not only drives an industry, but creates a commodity. In short, DVRs are on their way to becoming an international CE commodity.

8 The Future of DVRs

The traditional television business model is doomed. It's just a matter of time before TV goes through a radical business transformation. TV is no longer an isolated, special business; it's one distribution channel for video in an interconnected, digitally converged world.
  —Kevin Werbach, Assistant Professor, Legal Studies and Business Ethics, Wharton School of Business, University of Pennsylvania

The two sides have to talk now, because the DVR threatens both networks and advertisers, if they don't.
  —Brad Adgate, Vice President, research, Horizon Media

This incredible technology that we have developed should be used to raise up and educate our numbers, not reduce them to test subjects in a misguided Pavlovian experiment.
  —Julian Klappenbach, Software Architect, Visual Technologies, from the August 27, 2004 article, "Advertising: Adapting The Business Model"

Rarely in the past seven to eight decades, has there been a new CE device that has drawn the kind of consumer cache and interest that the DVR has. This development is quite comparable to the transition from black and white TV to color TV, which transpired in the late 1950s and early 1960s. That, too, was a change that quickly took people from something they could live without, to something they could not live without. Today, despite the concerns of marginal marketing, consumers suffering from digital overload, and restrictive DVR pricing, the concept of the DVR and what it does for consumers prevails. Indeed, the satisfied demand for what DVRs offer will lead, in the next 10–15 years, is to a point where DVRs (or their equivalent as it relates to content storage and manipulation) become very nearly ubiquitous in large parts of North America, Asia, and Europe.

8.1 Questions of Form

At the same time, set-top box-type, individual, home unit DVRs will be under pressure on numerous fronts, including from multichannel pay TV operator-supplied RS-DVR and VOD systems. This is because the core functions that RS-DVR and VOD offer (or will offer) to consumers will eventually substitute for just about everything that a consumer can get from his or her own, in-home, individual, set-top unit DVR. Also, because they involve storage for thousands or more at a single, often faraway, central location, RS-DVRs are a lot less cumbersome and less labor-intensive for the multichannel operator and consumer than having to acquire, set up, and maintain an additional individual set-top box unit, thus adding additional expense, hassle, and clutter within the consumer's living room, den, or bedroom.

Moreover, as noted in Chapters 1 and 6, the future of DVRs also lies in other CE devices. This is because the concept of DVRs and video storage on a hard drive, flash drive, or other storage device, is easily transportable to just about any CE device. Indeed, as an example, it is not too far off that many, if not most, car manufacturers will likely create vehicles in their factories that not only offer video to passengers, but also offer DVRs (or their equivalent) to go along with that in-vehicle video content. This is a logical extension of satellite radio operator SiriusXM's portable satellite radios, many of which contain the equivalent of a DVR (call it a digital audio recorder, for lack of a better term). Furthermore, DVRs will very likely progress significantly along with the burgeoning mobile information and entertainment market, making the DVR concept almost ubiquitous in that future arena, as well. It is not too tough to imagine every person's individual mobile unit having an individual DVR-like capability for every type of digital content that comes into (or goes out of) that device.

As noted in the quotes at the beginning of Chapter 1 and this Chapter (especially that of Digeo's CEO, Greg Gudorf), however, new *layers* of DVR capability inevitably will become the next generation of development for the product and service called the DVR. Thus, for instance, video begins to get stored not only from a cable, telco, and satellite source but also from an IPTV source. Indeed, the DVR device needs only a connection to the proper source; it will become more oblivious as to what and where that source is and what it records. Future DVR users get better and better at adeptly arranging and organizing all their media inside the DVR, and in using the search and critical electronic program guide or EPG/IPG functions to quickly locate vast stores of their own and others' content. This content includes almost every imaginable form of self-made content and content made by others, in still, video, audio, data, and in just about any format that can, as a digital file, be reduced to ones and zeros.

Recommendations of forthcoming content become more frequent and more understandable by just about everyone (i.e., they are no longer limited mostly to just the young and the tech geeks or early adopters). And finally, the DVR gets so that everybody using it innately understands that one of its best features is its ability to be controlled from afar by its user, either via a cell or landline telephone command, or via a communication infrastructure such as the Internet.

Yet realistically, this new technology route could go badly for the continued deployment of individual, in-home DVRs and their progeny. That is, the potential of VOD and RS-DVR systems combined to do everything for a consumer that his or her individual in-home DVR unit does is great. In short, if everything is available all the time, why do you need a storage center?

The other side of this possible future is the idea that for your own self-created content, you might prefer to keep it closer to home than keep it with your multichannel pay TV operator on its RS-DVR system (the one that the operator owns and controls). That may well end up being the sole and main future reason for owning and using an individual, in-home DVR, that is, to more completely own and control one's own content, be it still pictures, videos, audios, or really any form of digitally stored content or media.

8.1.1   Legal, Technology, and Other Concerns

Further, hanging like a dark cloud over all of the optimistic or quasi-optimistic DVR future are some core concerns about legal matters and use matters, which could do much to derail the fast train that is the DVR. How do multichannel pay TV operators manage the challenges of consumers wishing to stretch the limits of "fair use"? How adept and agile will advertising agencies and their advertiser clients be at tapping into the rich subscriber user data, and then using these data to present advertising in such a way as to make subscribing consumers want to see those ads? Will networks and other content distributors teach future generations of advertisers and their agencies how to properly advertise in a DVR or DVR-like TV world? Will they be able to get those clients to continue to pay for those ads (despite the influences of DVRs)? Will the 30-second advertising "spot" go the way of the dinosaur? Will another time form replace it? Will consumers accept incursions into their viewing privacy, in the form of data collected about them, which are then relayed to eager salespeople? Can consumers be incentivized to watch ads in return for their ability to view longer form shows shown without ads? How companies and society deal with those matters will have much to do with when and where—and how successfully—we deploy our future DVRs (and/or DVR-related devices).

8.1.2   DVR Marketing and Vision

Beyond technology, marketing in a DVR world is yet another view of the future which needs attention. As noted further in this chapter, the idea of DVRs and DVR-like capabilities pervading the future of TV, are not overstated. Nonetheless, the idea that DVRs necessarily spell the end for advertisements (because people zap ads and thus get nothing from those ads) is proving incorrect. Indeed, in the "DVRed TV World of Tomorrow"—where DVR use in North America and globally grows significantly in the 2009–2015 timeframe—creative commercial and agency types do such a good job of making commercials, that those commercials actually resonate with (and have value for) consumers, even in the fast-forward speed that runs six times normal speed.

Carrying that "resonate" concept one step further, using creativity together with amazing technology, the future of DVRs ties directly in with the future of commercial messages. Thus, a viewer's interest in a certain product, service, or type of product/service—likely motivated by a particularly creative advertising vehicle—causes the consumer to stop and request more ads and/or information about the product/service. Or, in a related sense, that consumer interest causes the data-gathering capabilities of a DVR to deliver him/her more ads and/or information about the products or service, which the consumer can choose instantly to accept or reject. In this world, if operated correctly, the consumer finds relevance, assistance, and solace in his or her connection with the DVR and the functionality behind it. Yet, in the end, one thing is certain in the DVR World of TV's Tomorrow: The genie is out of the bottle, and the balance of power and control has clearly shifted from the network and other distributors of video and other content, to the actual user of that content; indeed, this is a shift that is likely to remain permanent for a long time to come (if not forever).

Perhaps one of the best visions of DVRs tomorrow is from a high-level TiVo executive, Jim Denney, who strongly supports the notion of linear, live, real-time preprogrammed linear channels, well into the future. "The future of DVRs will be a combination of content coming from a wide variety of sources. This will include traditional 'linear' TV and on-demand, indeed all kinds of professionally produced content and personal content. Thus, the user should not care about the source of the content, just how it relates to them and how easy it is to find it." In that vein, TiVo states it is always looking to incorporate new content from new sources into the DVR experience. Thus, a new product and service like YouTube gets welcomed into tomorrow's DVR fulcrum.

This chapter concludes with a look at "The DVR of the Future," according to one respected observer, with some recommendations for further reading on the subject of the future of the DVR industry, and with professional analyst projections as to the future estimated growth of traditional individual in-home DVRs.

8.1.3   DVRs vs. Various New Developments/Competitors

The key competitive players identified below present a solid representation of where DVRs may change course in the years ahead. Among them, the handful of key issues facing each of them separately, as well as a few issues facing some more than others, are also given light.

Remote DVRs Trump In-Home DVRs?

RS-DVRs are clearly the wave of the future, despite what one trial judge decided, in 2007, in a New York state federal court. Having overcome a core copyright argument, the appellate court in that RS-DVR case overturned the trial court and, in mid-2008, ruled in favor of the RS-DVR originator in that case, i.e., Cablevision Systems. This now leaves the decision open to further interpretation, by the U.S. Supreme Court. It is this reviewer's strong opinion that the appellate court decision is most likely to remain intact. Indeed, rather than making content more vulnerable to copyright infringement, the development and implementation of a wide-scale RS-DVR system arguably better restricts how individual users use and reuse all TV-type content. This is because the system operator, in this case Cablevision Systems, has the ultimate say over how and when the content is used by the consumer in the RS-DVR system. The system operator owns and controls the storage of the content and thus controls the content itself. Thus, if the system operator decides to restrict how quickly a consumer can fast forward through an advertisement, or if the operator decides to say that certain ads can never be fast forwarded through, then that is something the operator is capable of doing (especially because it owns and controls the hardware and software that makes those changes). Another example would be the operator's ability to replace advertisements in a show that has not yet been viewed, so as to make those ads current with the time frame within which the show is watched.

Further, because a multichannel pay TV operator like Cablevision Systems already has a relatively strong relationship with various content providers, ad agencies, and ad clients, those multiple entities will likely have a much better rapport via the implementation of an RS-DVR system than they would have had with a more traditional individual, in-home DVR set-top box arrangement. Moreover, customers of the multichannel pay TV operator are more likely to prefer a system that gives them instant access not only to tens of thousands of VOD shows, but also to storage in the hundreds of hours (or more?) that does not involve another cumbersome and costly set-top box in one's living room, along with added wires and monthly fees to rent the box (or the fees involved in buying the box, if that is the case). The one caveat, however, for multichannel pay TV operators implementing RS-DVR systems is that they must be very mindful of not trying too hard to control the actual subscriber-user of the RS-DVR system, or to offend him or her by unduly and inappropriately abusing their trust or their privacy. This can be a fine line in today's world.

For the future, the RS-DVR system allows the multichannel pay TV operator to build the RS-DVR software and hardware on a large scale. Typically, this involves at least hundreds of thousands of system subscribers (if not millions), and implementing the RS-DVR system on a mass scale, involving many types of added features another type of multichannel individual unit, in-home DVR provider would never attempt. Thus, for example, deploying storage solutions for hundreds of thousands or millions of single system subscriber-users suggests that the multichannel pay TV operator would be much more likely to drive down the cost of storage/user, than would a corresponding standalone DVR provider, or even an integrated DVR provider. Not having to mass produce, distribute, track, and maintain hundreds of thousands or millions of set-top boxes has huge advantages for cable and telco operators, and perhaps one day for satellite operators, as well. Having all or most of the system's DVR storage capacity in one or a handful of key locales has logistical and cost advantages that are also quite evident. Further, as the key business players in the DVR world combine to better collect and better utilize key subscriber-user data that emanate from DVR use by that customer, the RS-DVR is likely to provide better, cheaper, and more accessible data than hundreds of thousands of in-home individual set-top DVRs (be they standalone or integrated units).

VOD Trumps In-Home DVRs?

In recent years, more observers are pointing to a would-be ally of the DVR and saying that it will become the true "Darth Vader of Tomorrow's DVR Industry." This evil in the guise of a friend would be various forms of cable- and telco-delivered VOD. Because the capabilities of video and audio on-demand services are improving so quickly and so substantially and because they are being embraced by not only huge and powerful cable companies but by equally (or more) powerful telephone providers (such as Verizon and AT&T), it is quite possible that these true on-demand versions of content delivery and storage may make DVRs unnecessary and redundant, and thus less valuable.

Nonetheless, in systems with less robust bandwidth capabilities, such as those of the current AT&T operation in much of the United States today, the dominance of VOD over DVRs will be much slower to develop. That is because, in those AT&T fiber-to-the-node (vs. fiber-to-the-home Verizon systems), the inability to carry the higher-bit rate functionality will mean that DVRs will have to fill the gap, if those systems are to remain competitive against robust cable systems, for example. On the other hand, in Verizon systems, or in the higher-bit rate cable systems nationally, the functionality of VOD will quickly absorb most of that functionality for which an individual in-home DVR is known and desired.

With extremely high-bit rate and high-bandwidth instant on-demand delivery, there is less need to store content for later use. Instead, with a highly functioning VOD system, one just orders a program and it is there. And it is there over and over again the majority of times, for free. Watching the same program, instantly, on-demand, the next day becomes the norm, rather than the exception. The program is stored by the system operator far away, it is always available, endlessly, and can be paused, rewound, and replayed, at will—just like the functions of the individual, in-home DVR. When VOD systems also allow real-time pausing, rewinding, and replay of *live* content, the nearly full takeover of DVR functionality by VOD services will be complete. Reasonable estimates of when this "VOD Trumps DVR" cycle completes are in 5–15 years, dependent upon the technological superiority of the local cable or telco system. The development of certain legal issues, such as whether a RS-DVR-type system violates copyright and intellectual property rights, will also affect the speed with which the VOD overtakes some or all elements of the DVR.

On the other side of this debate are those that see two other possible outcomes. First would be the one that is mostly likely, where DVR features are combined more with the features of VOD, but DVRs stay around for many decades, especially in the smaller and less technologically robust of the nation's and the world's cable and telco systems. Also, DVRs are likely to be a part of satellite TV systems for a very long time, as well. This is because "true VOD" is challenged in the satellite TV realm. VOD in satellite today is actually centered around the DVR, in that programs are sent by the satellite operator and cached ahead of time on the DVR's hard drive, for playback later on. Chapter 6 further discusses this separation between what the satellite industry calls VOD, and what the cable and telco operators offer as true VOD. More recently, satellite multichannel pay TV operator DirecTV has unveiled a rather robust Internet-delivered programming service it calls VOD, and EchoStar's DISH Network has a somewhat less robust Internet-delivered VOD service, as well.

Video Downloads vs. DVRs?

Another area where a huge degree of change is in the air involves the realm of video downloads. Coming through the Internet, the quality of these video images has improved markedly in recent years and is likely to continue to do so. In a mere handful of years, Internet-delivered video is expected to rival or excel the quality and volume of cable-, telco-, and satellite-delivered video.

As noted earlier, the concept of a DVR-like device storing any and all available video and other digital content is so attractive that it will inevitably be built into devices that move or are stationary, in home, on the road, or at the office. As such, devices that capture Internet-delivered digital content, like PCs, laptops, PDAs, MP3 players, and other still-to-be-unveiled devices that capture content, will do what DVRs do, but they will do that for and within those devices only. Moreover, as more viewing time transitions (and gets substituted) from basic TV to these new devices, the time a traditional in-home, individual DVR gets used becomes less and less. As such, these new uses and devices further threaten the future for the traditional DVR industry.

Video Downloads and Streaming in a DVR World

A *video download*, like streaming video, is one of two methods of viewing Internet-delivered media (e.g., video, audio, and animations) onto a personal computer, laptop, or portable mobile device.

According to http://www.mediacollege.com/video/streaming/overview .html, downloading involves saving an entire file on a computer (usually in a temporary folder), which is then opened and viewed. This has some advantages (such as quicker access to different parts of the file), but has one big disadvantage: one has to wait for the whole file to download before any of it can be viewed. If the file is quite small, this may not be too much of an inconvenience, but for large files and long presentations, the wait can be very frustrating and counterproductive. The easiest way to provide downloadable video files is to use a simple hyperlink to the file. A slightly more advanced method is to embed the file in a Web page, using special HTML code. Delivering video files this way is known as HTTP streaming or HTTP delivery. HTTP means Hyper Text Transfer Protocol and is the same protocol used to deliver Web pages. For this reason, it is easy to set up and use on almost any Web site, without requiring additional software or special hosting plans. Note, however, that this is not technically "true" video streaming—the best it can do is a passable imitation.

Streaming media, on the other hand, works a bit differently—the end user can start watching the file almost as soon as it begins downloading. In effect, the file is sent to the user in a (more or less) constant stream, and the user watches it as it arrives. The obvious advantage with this method is that no waiting is involved. Streaming media has additional advantages, such as being able to broadcast live events (sometimes referred to as a "Webcast" or a "Netcast"). True streaming video must be delivered from a specialized streaming server.

Progressive download is a hybrid method of viewing media via the Internet. In this method, the video clip is downloaded, but begins playing as soon as a portion of the file has been received. According to http://www.mediacollege.com, this method simulates true streaming, but does not quite have all the advantages.

Online Video Streaming vs. DVRs?

In the same manner as video downloads, streaming video offers an alternative to the functionality of a typical DVR. As content viewing and the related acts of storage and other forms of content manipulation become more common on devices other than traditional DVRs attached to traditional TVs, people will expect to have and use what DVRs offer on these other devices and with other technologies, as well. Indeed, because what a basic DVR does is so attractive, that implementation elsewhere is only natural and to be expected.

Thus, like the transition away from landlines in the telephone world, which were replaced by wireless cell phones, so, too, will consumers, especially early adapters, transition away from two separate monitors, instead opting for a single one. In many cases, instead of it being a standard-type TV monitor, that device will instead be a PC monitor, and the form of content manipulation will be different than that of a traditional DVR or even RS-DVR. The previous section in this chapter describes the basic differences between DVR functionality and the functionality of Internet-delivered media.

8.2   Various Entities and the Impact of DVRs

One of the better ways to predict the future of DVRs is to assess that future as it relates to the key players on the DVR game board. These include, of course, the consumer, as well as those that attempt to maneuver in and around that consumer to create their business models, i.e., the ad agencies, broadcasters, cable and telco operators, satellite operators, Internet operators, and finally, those that actually drive the most of the rest toward success or failure, that is, the advertisers who pay for the shows and seek to present their products or services.

8.2.1 The Consumer

For a consumer, the idea of a DVR is analogous to the idea of going from a car's hassle-prone stick shift, to an effortless automatic transmission. The automatic one just works better, and only the rare consumer would ever choose the former over the latter. However, the idea is actually much more than this. The idea of a DVR is that of a device that so alters what machinery can do to enhance an experience, that there are few analogies that do it justice. That is why it is fairly easy to predict the concept of DVRs becoming more the norm, than the exception, as it relates to the future of TV and TV-related information and entertainment-related content presentation.

It sounds all too cliché, but remains the truth: the real beneficiary when it comes to the best future of DVRs and DVR-type products and services will be the individual consumer. As the future expands, each will have added choices for DVRs and what DVRs do. Not only will there be, as noted further in this chapter, more and varied devices, but the cost will decline, and the accessibility of the forms and models will increase.

In the future, as noted in Chapters 1 and 6, DVRs or their functions will come in the form of in-home individual DVRs, RS-DVRs, and do-it-yourself (DIY) home-built DVRs. In addition, everywhere digital content is distributed, and those distributing it will probably either implement or consider implementing a DVR-type capability. In sum, predicting the ubiquity of DVRs (and DVR-like functionality) is becoming less and less risky, as the notion of the DVR and what it does captures each new consumer.

8.2.2 At Retail

CE dealers nationwide welcome the introduction of DVRs and their expansion into the universal mindset of almost all TV consumers. This is because the standalone version of DVRs offers CE retailers opportunities to enhance their bottom lines and get consumers to like and thus watch more TV. Even if the CE retailer cannot get a consumer to buy the standalone DVR, the DVR experience in any form causes consumers to watch more TV. Increased TV viewing frequently then leads to the desire to obtain a better screen, which typically leads to the purchase of an expensive or relatively expensive large HDTV set. Thus, be it a standalone DVR purchase or a large-screen HDTV that is triggered by a multichannel pay TV integrated set-top DVR, the CE retailer wins. Yet another relevant example is that of home theatre components, which get sold in greater quantity as more people enjoy their content more.

Even under the RS-DVR model, consumers predictably will like their TV viewing more with the choice and control that the RS-DVR gives them. As such, in the majority of cases, that enhanced TV viewing and enjoyment inevitably leads in a similar mode to the desire to see the best pictures and video possible, typically in the form of a new HDTV monitor from the local retail CE dealer.

Moreover, as new devices are developed and the natural move becomes to add in a DVR-like function, CE retailers will sell these, as well.

8.2.3 In Education

DVRs and DVR-like functionality will be a necessary part of most high-tech future educational software, across all means and modes. This is because what a DVR does is closely tied to what a good education does: it enhances the ability to absorb and learn.[1] Similar to the ability when reading a book or an article to stop and reread a confusing or otherwise not clear section, the ability to stop and replay and maybe even replay again (until one "gets it") is really the core idea behind most education. The DVR can match the same function.

Thus, in college and university laboratories, as more of the learning base shifts to teaching via video and similar content, students will seek to download or somehow store that content for review later. As such, the ability of educational institutions and their educators to provide viable recording and storage options, for each and every student, may well dictate a good deal of their future success.

8.2.4 In Security

DVRs in security applications are often termed closed circuit TV (CCTV). They have more frequently begun replacing old-style VCRs in many locales, because they offer more flexibility and more features to their owners and users. Detection and documentation thus become that much more professional. According to Wikipedia, for example, "A DVR CCTV system provides a multitude of advanced functions over VCR technology, including video searches by event, time, date, and camera. There is also much more control over quality and frame rate, allowing disk space usage to be optimized, and the DVR can also be set to overwrite the oldest security footage should the disk become full. In some DVR security systems, remote access to security footage using a PC can also be achieved by connecting the DVR to a local area network (LAN) or the Internet." On a more technical level, security DVRs may be categorized as being either PC-based or what is termed "embedded." A PC-based DVR's architecture includes a basic PC, with a video capture card that is designed to capture video images. An embedded type DVR, on the other hand, is specifically designed as a DVR, with its operating system and application software contained in firmware or read-only memory (ROM).[2]

8.2.5 Advertisers and DVRs

In the DVR realm, other than the consumer, perhaps no other entity has so much to lose, and yet potentially so much to gain, as the advertisers of video on TV.

---

[1] See "DVRs Make Me (and My Family) Smarter," http://carmelgroup.com/publications/document/tivo_makes_me_and_my_family_smarter/.

[2] See http://en.wikipedia.org/wiki/Digital_video_recorder.

From the late 1990s, when DVRs first came onto the TV game field, to a time a decade later, DVRs remain a real concern for advertisers and their progeny. That is most obviously because DVRs do a great job of permitting users to "zap"[3] advertisements. This author knows of no consumer survey that has not indicated at least a better than 50% rating when it comes to how many users use their DVRs to skip ads. Indeed, several studies have stated that skipping commercials is the primary reason as many as 70% or more people obtained and use their DVRs.[4] Nonetheless, creations of ads that are relevant, to consumers and ads that convey a message, even though delivered in a fast forward mode, are two keys to the future of commercials in the TV and related environments. Importantly, with billions of dollars in U.S. TV ad spending on the line annually, giving agencies and advertisers a reason to keep paying to produce and deliver commercials is an important motivation for cablecasters, satcasters, telcocasters, and broadcasters, to say nothing of new Internet and mobile distributors of content.

Placement and Logo Time

Yet more surveys and research are also indicating that despite the fact that many, if not most, DVR users are "zapping" or skipping ads on a consistent—and persistent—basis, those user consumers are also receiving ad messages while the zapping occurs. Two methods of enhancing that process are currently being focused on. First is the placement of an ad within a group of advertisements, called a "pod," and the other is the placement and timing of brand logos within a given advertisement. Both these methods are seen as effective when it comes to getting brands into the view and consciences of consumers, despite the speed in which they occur on the screen. Thus, for example, placement of an ad at the beginning or the very end of the pod are thought to be particularly effective by some, because these placements are less likely to be zapped by consumers going into or coming out of ad groupings.

One of the reasons this "ad message absorption during program zapping" is so important is because the measurement and TV rating entities can actually measure shows that are stored for later viewing, and then, are actually viewed, later. Such a measurement not only indicates that DVRs mean people using them watch more TV, but also that people watching time-delayed shows are still absorbing ad messages. As such, measurement agencies' measurement of

[3] "Zap" in this sense connotes being able to push a button and subsequently fast forward at one or more speeds through advertisements, thereby avoiding at least the video details and all of the audio from those ads.

[4] A 2007 study of 2200 Internet respondents by The Carmel Group, found that at least nine out of ten respondents use their DVRs to skip ads for shows previously recorded at least half of the time; and a remarkable 77% skip ads at least three quarters of the time; and four out of ten skipped ads on these programs 100% of the time. For more information about this in-depth study (and more recent versions), go to http://www.carmelgroup.com. Note also the discussion of and inclusion of several charts from that consumer study by The Carmel Group, included in Chapter 6.

ads during recorded shows can also become a measurement by which networks, agencies, and their advertisers negotiate ad costs. Thus, the stage is set for a great debate over whether "DVRed" shows should count toward advertising dollar costs, ratings, and payments. And if the premise of "ad message absorption during program zapping" is valid, then it opens the door to many other strategic and tactical technological and TV production methods and devices that will adjust, but probably retain, advertising and advertising messages.

One particularly important part of most TV screens in the future, where commercials are far from hitting their stride, are the parts of a typical on-screen EPG/IPG. Because so much of the future of TV is centered around this "killer application,"[5] where so much TV will start and end in the future, finding a novel, creative way to present commercial messages on this canvas will go a long way toward spelling the success of commercials in a DVR world.

Other Ad Alternatives Addressing the Impact of DVRs

In the future, alternatives to the ill effects of DVRs will include many nuances, creations, devices, and designs.

One example has already been implemented, in its earliest stages. As early as 2005–2006, the Ford Motor Company began working with the *American Idol* and Fox TV producers to include the cutdown lineup of *American Idol* finalists in a Ford commercial that is presented in such a way that it looks like a part of the *American Idol* show. That way, the thought has it, people would be less likely to DVR their way through that type of "contestant-enhanced advertisement." The viewing results support this development.

Product placement is another alternative to the negatives of DVR commercial zapping, yet product placement creates issues for agencies because they typically are not compensated by distributors for placing ads. Closely related to this method is one offered by virtual advertisement companies such as Princeton Video, whereby the sign behind the dugout during a baseball game is digitally altered to change the advertisement digitally, although for the live viewer, the position of the sign on the field remains static.

Other methods include using other lengths of commercials to deliver certain brand and other messages. Thus, instead of the tried and true 30-second spot, a 5-second or 2-minute spot might be tried. Worth noting is the fact that most DVR users find a 5-second advertisement too short to bother fast forwarding.

Another method deployed is to leave the logo of the advertiser centered prominently on the screen, in the form of a brand logo, for 3 or more seconds. This is said to make it much more likely that the logo will be portrayed and seen by the viewer during the fast forward mode, thus validating the all-important (and paid for) ad impression (despite the zapping of the actual commercial). Notes NBCU's Dr. Janet Gallent, vice president, Consumer Insights and Innovation

---

[5] The term "killer application" in reference to the on-screen EPG/IPG, is attributable to the first one to use it, former Sirius Satellite Radio CEO and chairman of the board, Joe Clayton.

Research, and principal investigator of a March 2009 joint NBCU-Strategic Insights and Innovations study, entitled, "DVR 2: Understanding Advertising Communication in Fast Forward Mode," "This study of DVR users and DVR nonusers strongly recommends new methods that advertisers and ad agencies must use to deal with the argument that DVRs are the death of advertisements, which is clearly not the case. As broadcasters, we are trying to control our destiny in this new DVR world and concurrently optimize advertisers' continued use of our medium." Additional methods the study suggests include the following:

- Display the logo and/or brand throughout the ad
- Limit the number of ad scene changes
- Production-wise, maintain an "even, somewhat fast-pace" through the ad
- Do not rely on audio (e.g., instead use on-screen words as visual clues)
- Provide distinct color contrasts between background and the text and/or logo to enhance legibility.

In addition, self-described "Internet marketing driver" Glenn Gabe, also recommends that, "Combining your high-end TV commercials with a robust Internet microsite, and then utilize (sic) paid search, organize search, email marketing, social media, blogging, display advertising, etc., to drive people there is a smart way to go." This merging of the best from the TV world and the best from the Internet world of advertising has become not only a recent trend but almost a "must do" for most in today's advertising leaders (and many followers).

Another method suggested in a Frank Ahrens August 20, 2006, *The Washington Post* article, entitled "Pausing the Panic," has standalone and network DVR operators, such as TiVo, selling DVR customer data to the networks and advertisers. Meanwhile, other methods of encouraging DVR users to watch their commercials are being created, whereby those that do patiently (and presumably) attentively view all of a given commercial, are then provided special content that non-DVR and non-ad viewers are not given. Thus, for example, DVR users would be given a special opportunity to play in a special game with clues embedded in the ads, but they may only do so if they watch all of the preceding ad.

Yet perhaps the truest Holy Grail of advertising in a world of DVRs is that of advertising presented in such a relevant and personal way that the subject of the ad gladly gives up his or her personal time and data to get more information. In the future, the beginning of this process will include advertisements targeted not just by demographic or regional characteristics, but by zip code, then household, based upon, in the apt words of *Wired* magazines' Frank Rose, "... what the individual people there watch and want."[6]

Table 8.1 shows the various advertising alternatives offered, together with a description of the pros and cons for each.

---

[6] See, Rose, Frank, *Wired* magazine, October 2003, issue 11.10, "The Fast-Forward, On-Demand, Network-Smashing Future of Television," at www.wired.com/wired/archive/aa.10/tv_pr.html.

Table 8.1 Future Advertiser Answers and Alternatives to the DVR

Future Advertiser Answers and Alternatives to the DVR			
Answer/Alternative	Description	Upside	Downside
Ad Placements	Occurs when a product is inserted into the show, such as a Coke being drunk by an actor during a "Friday Night Lights" show	If a piece of content is perceived to be part of a show, the message is less likely to be zapped	Agencies typically get paid for traditional ads; tougher to pay them for (and thus incentivize them) to do placements
POD Placement	The place within a group of ads shown between regular programming can determine if the ad is fast forwarded or not, for example, studies show the popularity of placing at the beginning and end of a set of ads in a typical pod	Viewers are less likely to "zap" ads going into or out of ad groupings	Cost may be higher in the future for "valued" pod placements
Different Length Ads	Although the 30-second spot is the paradigm of broadcasting, it is now under pressure also from ads of 5 seconds to 3 minutes	The door gets opened to new (longer and shorter) forms of advertising	Doing things differently is often stressful, more difficult, and costs more, at least in the beginning
DVR-Friendly Ads	Involves ads that employ methods of production that enhance the possiblity of getting the ad message and/or brand message across, e.g., holding brand on-screen longer and placed in the middle of the screen	Permit distributors, like broadcasters, to continue to charge for ads, even if they are "zapped" by DVR users.	Doing things differently is often stressful, more difficult, and costs more, at least in the beginning

(Continued)

Answer/Alternative	Description	Upside	Downside
Targeting/ Personalization	Using data acquired from viewers' use of their DVRs, advertisers send personalized ads to viewers containing information about products they actually want to learn about	Can target specialized ad messages to specific demographics, based on viewing preferences	Increased cost to tailor specific ads to increasingly specific consumer-demographics
Ad Search and Previews	Combining TV ads with Internet "microsite" to encourage paid search, organized search, email marketing, social media, blogging, and display advertising	Allows viewer additional media and access points from which he/she can get information about products he/she is actually interested; increases choice.	Increased competition among advertisers. Increased production costs related to higher quality
Viewer Response to Ads	Occurs when viewers are offered a choice of ads to watch, for example, a la carte style ads where they can learn more about the product being advertised	Viewers watch ads about products they want to learn about	Increased cost to create ad-specific special content
Ads that Work in Fast Forward Mode	Using timing sequences that allow ads to show essential information even when viewed in fast-forward; less reliance on audio and more on visual clues	Increase the visual effectiveness of "zapped" ads	Limits number of screen changes or other options for ads viewed at normal-speed

HILL HOLLIDAY

Today, a top question among advertising agency Hill Holliday[7] is how it—and its advertising clients—will reach viewers who use DVRs.

With studies from researchers, eMarketer and The Carmel Group, projecting that between 33% and more than 50% of U.S. homes will have a DVR by 2010, Hill Holliday and the rest of the advertising/communications industries are fully aware that they need to rise to the challenge of viewers fast forwarding through commercials and brand messages.

There are many ways to ensure that a brand is exposed to its intended audience, as explained by those who buy commercial time for Hill Holliday's roster of clients. Hill Holliday's Stacey Shepatin, director of national broadcast, and Guy Rancourt, Hill Holliday's associate media director, provide insight by way of the following Q & A session. They present these views on behalf of Hill Holliday.

How do you "beat" DVR?

Stacey Shepatin: There are various options, from limiting commercial interruptions, to ad-buying tactics, to brand integration. First and foremost, people want to see a good story, so a compelling commercial, with captivating creative work, will often stop people from fast forwarding. We know, from TiVo's second-by-second data, viewers will more often by-pass the fast forwarding, and watch a commercial that is recognizable, entertaining, and iconic.

Beyond good creative work, another prime method is "brand integration." This method has worked well for many of our clients. Brand integration means getting a product or a brand name into the content of a program. Depending on the way it is done, it is also referred to as "product

---

[7] Hill Holliday, owned by the Interpublic Group of Companies and headquartered in Boston, MA, with offices in New York, NY, Miami, FL, and Greenville, SC, describes itself as one of the top communication agencies in the nation. Founded in 1968, Hill Holliday positions itself as having won every major award for advertising excellence and effectiveness. Among its clients are leading national and regional brands, including Anheuser-Busch, AOL, Bank of America, Chili's Grill and Bar, Cleveland Clinic, Covidien, CVS/pharmacy, Dunkin' Donuts, Harvard Pilgrim Health Care, Liberty Mutual, The Massachusetts State Lottery, Novartis, Partners HealthCare, Procter & Gamble, the Rockport Company, TJX Companies, and Verizon Wireless. Hill Holliday is found on the Web at http://www.hhcc.com.

placement," "product integration," and "branded entertainment." There is a wide range. It can be as simple as having a product on the set in view, or it can be deeper—having the brand play a part, maybe even be a character, in the plotline. It's a delicate balance, and must be done well to maintain the integrity of the production, and not overwhelm the viewer.

Guy Rancourt: For example, we arranged a brand integration for Dunkin' Donuts, the world's largest coffee and baked-goods chain, on "Big Brother," a reality show on CBS. Part of the show involved the show's competitors earning rewards, and on one week, they received a treat of Dunkin's products. Integrations on an unscripted program like this can bring about unintended bonuses. The contestants were thrilled about getting treats from our client; one even commented about naming a child after Dunkin's Coolatta and gushed that receiving Dunkin' Donuts that week was a major boost to morale.

Moreover, we are always developing new ways of integrating our clients' messages. One endeavor involved the show "The Factory," on Spike TV. It featured the lives of four "regular Joes," who work in a factory together. The audience is composed of a young, male demographic, that Dunkin' Donuts is seeking. Hill Holliday developed an integration, using segments that were filmed on a set, similar to that of "The Factory," with the characters interacting with Dunkin's products.

To the viewer at home, the segment looked like another part of the episode. It was seamless. To make its appearance more seamless, the piece aired at the end of a program portion, but before the commercial pod[8] began. So, overall, viewers at home were less apt to fast forward past these specialized segments, since what they were watching looked like it was part of the program. Dunkin' used six different content segments in "The Factory." We made these integrations subtle, so they literally would not turn off viewers.[9]

How do you go about deciding how and where to integrate a brand name/product?

Stacey Shepatin: Hill Holliday's approach is to understand our clients' positioning, the challenges they are facing, and to identify the target

---

[8] A "commercial pod" is another way of saying a group of commercials bunched together between the segments of a typical TV program.

[9] Author's note: As explained in the earlier part of this chapter, during 2008 segments of Fox's *American Idol*, the U.S. car company, Ford, worked with the show's producers and contestants, integrating the latter into story segments involving interactions with Ford vehicles. The Ford segments were made to look like an integral part of the *American Idol* show (rather than a separate ad). This is yet another typical example of clever and creative ad agencies and their advertiser clients finding ways to make the best out of a "DVR World" environment. In this world, rather than seeing the DVR as an enemy, advertisers instead fashion the DVR, the VOD, and what these products and services do, as allies in the game of placing ad messages appropriately in front of viewers.

consumer. What shows are these consumers watching? When are they sitting in front of the television? What type of programming draws them in? Once we get these answers, we then gravitate toward the type of programming that resonates with our client's customers.

For example, our client, CVS/Pharmacy, which operates more than 6300 pharmacies nationwide, wanted to make an emotional connection with viewers, while finding a program that aligned with its message that CVS is there to help those who care for others. Through research, Hill Holliday determined that one of the best ways to demonstrate this commitment was by forging a partnership with ABC's "Extreme Makeover Home Edition," because of that show's audience and content. The show chronicles a needy group, or a family, receiving a newly renovated home. The client communicated its message by making a prominent donation to the featured family in several episodes. Each donation reflected the client's understanding of that particular family's struggle, caring for their loved ones. They would do this by providing, for example, significant medical procedures and treatment for four brothers and sisters who had the same rare disease. CVS saw an instant response via its connection with the show, and it is building on that platform.

If the right programming for our client doesn't exist, we will help create it. In the case of Hill Holliday client Liberty Mutual—the sixth-largest property and casualty insurer in the United States—we wanted to partner with a network to create programming based on the notion of responsibility (i.e., doing what is right, over doing what is easy). This stems from Liberty Mutual's TV campaign with the tagline, "Responsibility. What's your policy?" We constructed a deal with NBC to help create a television movie event, entitled "Kings," using a plot that aligned with the company's message of doing the right thing. The pilot and the first episodes of a television series, based on "Kings," are in development, with the series set to debut in 2009. Liberty Mutual is collaborating with the network and will be the presenting sponsor of the pilot.

How do you measure the success of something like brand integration?

Stacey Shepatin: Analytics and metrics for brand integrations are still evolving. There is no standardized method right now. We have been able to track some indicators that integrations are making a difference, such as surveys and, of course, the overall success of the client's sales. After integrations on the show "Miracle Workers," CVS was measured by IAG as the top-performing brand integration of the year, based on a positive change in brand perception. In another case, Dunkin' was listed as a top 10 superbrand in the "fast food" category by *Brandweek*, which reported the chain boosted sales by 7% in 2007.

What are the ways advertising agencies work around the DVR, ideas that involve using actual commercials? Does this involve the buying tactics you referred to earlier?

Guy Rancourt: Yes it does. Media buyers can use several tactics. First, we can benefit from an isolated pod, which is a very short commercial break, just 30 or 60 seconds long. This takes advantage of the viewer who takes a bit of time to realize he needs to fast forward. An isolated pod also capitalizes on the opportunity that a viewer is simply too lazy to skip through such a short break. Isolated pods are not usually available on the broadcast networks; they are more often on cable-type networks, such as Turner, F/X, and Spike.

There are also certain kinds of programming that are, to some extent, DVR-proof. These typically include live sports events and news programs. Viewers tend to watch these shows live, because watching them later will make them dated and irrelevant. Another type of show that viewers tend not to record is that of a syndicated series, like *Seinfeld* or the *Simpsons*. People do not feel compelled to watch these shows later, since they are regularly available.

Stacey Shepatin: One major cutting edge method coming into play is called a "podbuster." In essence, this involves creating a series or a story among the commercial breaks that draws viewers in, so they do not want to fast forward past the ads. Viewers get caught up in the story. Hill Holliday is applying this concept for one of our top retail clients.

Guy Rancourt: Finally, a debate is growing regarding the pod position of an ad—that is, where in the commercial break the ad sits. Because of DVRs, the coveted positions are now both the first position and the last position in a commercial break. Those commercials usually are seen by DVR users who are slow to fast forward or who do not want to miss any part of the program that airs after the break. Presently, the networks determine which commercial runs in which spot during a break, and they typically give all advertisers even rotations. There is a growing perception that a more creative commercial will compel the network to place it in one of these two optimal spots, because viewers will likely stick around for the commercials, providing the program with higher ratings. On the flip side, the less sexy and less appealing commercials may be relegated to middle positions.

Have DVRs made an impact in other ways?

Guy Rancourt: Yes. Another way Hill Holliday and other advertising agencies are responding to the DVR dilemma is by being able to offer more accurate measurements of viewership. For example, in early 2007, Nielsen rolled out new services that allow us to measure just the commercial time within a program. Previously, deals were negotiated with rating estimates based on the entire program duration—commercial time and program time, averaged together. Now, however, with this offering of commercial ratings guarantees, we get a more exact indication of how many people watch our commercials and are therefore exposed to our clients' messages. We look for the average of all commercial minutes within a program. Nielsen can measure these commercial ratings for a program during the live broadcast, or include 1, 3, or 7 days of DVR playback. Nielsen counts only those viewers who watched the commercials during playback. The industry standard has been called "Commercial Ratings Plus 3 Days," or C3, as it is now commonly known.

What's Hill Holliday's view of the future of DVRs, from the advertising agency's perspective?

Stacey Shepatin: The DVR is one of many new technologies that force us to look more closely at how we get our messages across to consumers. With consumers in control of their viewing habits, advertisers need to be savvier. Advertisers need to find ways to have their messages actually *sought out* by buyers.

Message avoidance is not just a television issue. It is an issue facing all media (e.g., print, online, radio, and out-of-home display advertising), so it is incumbent on advertisers and agencies to find more creative, compelling ways to reach their target audiences.

Surprisingly, research from eMarketer shows that a significant portion of people still view commercials when they watch recorded programs, particularly when they watch soon after the original broadcast. This proves that consumers are willing to watch advertisements, especially when they carry strong, relevant messages. Hill Holliday and the advertising/communications industries overall continue to innovate and create these messages. We are always adapting and preparing ourselves for the next technological hurdle we must overcome.

Hill Holliday

Contact Information
53 State St., Boston, MA 02109
Phone: 617-366-4000
http://www.hhcc.com

Stock Symbol
A subsidiary of the Interpublic Group

Key People
Michael Sheehan, CEO; Stacey Shepatin, director of national broadcast; Guy Rancourt, associate media director

> **Key Business**
> Advertising agency
>
> **DVR Connection**
> Advertising agency that studies the impact of DVRs on its clients.

8.2.6 Broadcasters and DVRs

The transition U.S. broadcasters made from analog to digital transmissions of signals on June 12, 2009, places them in a unique situation. All of a sudden on that date, a large swath of digital spectrum was handed over to these more than 200 sets of local broadcasters, which is the digital spectrum that automatically allows most DVRs to operate. That is because, like their titles, DVRs are digital, and the transmission of digital signals by broadcasters, as well as the receipt of enough digital spectrum to allow broadcasters to offer consumers other broadcast services, means significant new opportunities for broadcasters during and after the first quarter of 2009.

Also worth mentioning is the idea that billions of dollars in ads are possibly being sacrificed annually to avid DVR users in tomorrow's DVR-TV world. As such, understanding of the previous section of this chapter, describing methods broadcasters, advertisers, and agencies can undertake to maximize the commercial and visual effectiveness of even "zapped" ads, is critical. According to industry pundit, Gary Arlen, writing September 22, 2004, for the publication, *TVTechnology*, "With so much rhetoric and venom swirling around the DVR-advertising conundrum, it is stunning to see so little attention is focused on new ad skills that will be needed to present information in the combined VOD/DVR environment." Disturbingly, years later, this sage observation is still on target.

Possible scenarios are developing among particularly imaginative broadcasters, advertisers, and their agencies, whereby television viewers would be offered a choice of which commercials they want to watch. Broadcasters and their partners would present a pool of advertising from which, a la carte style, the consumer would choose. Indeed, perhaps even one or more "advertising channels" would be presented by various multichannel pay TV operators, in conjunction with advertisers and agencies. According to Visual Technologies architect Julian Klappenbach, "The choice would not only benefit all by allowing the consumer to get information about products in which they have a real interest. It would also help raise the quality of advertising, as competition would drive up standards." Consumer education under this model has the potential to rise to heretofore unmatched levels.

As it relates specifically to broadcasters and DVRs, Rob Hubbard, head of the broadcasting side of decades-old St. Paul, MN-headquartered Hubbard Broadcasting, adds, "My DVR thoughts? First and foremost, the DVRs are misunderstood by us as broadcasters. Some think they destroy broadcast TV, others think they enhance it, but the net reality is probably neutral, especially for the impact on hit programs." Hubbard champions the quality of the core content, that is, the program itself, as a guide to what happens to advertisements, especially for middle Americans using a DVR. And like others interviewed for this chapter, Hubbard believes the real future for DVRs is that they compete readily with other devices, technologies, and more often than not, the pie grows. In that vein, competing things, like VOD, Internet-delivered video, and other technologies, survive—and maybe thrive—as well. In addition, broadcasting, like DVRs, also remains popular despite competition, if for no other reason than that it does what it does for mass audiences better than any other medium. Morgan Murphy Media president, Elizabeth Murphy Burns, adds, "The important emphasis on what Rob Hubbard said is on that word 'neutral,' together with the idea of anywhere, anytime, and anyplace, and in that context, I believe that DVRs remain a benign influence."

Yet, at the network and local levels, working with advertisers and their agencies to develop new DVR-based creativity and effectiveness with consumers, is probably critical to the future success of broadcasters. This theme is recognized, detailed, and supported in this chapter's "Advertisers and DVRs."

8.2.7   Manufacturers and DVRs

CE manufacturers might have been the key players in tomorrow's DVR industry, had things gone differently among the early creators of DVRs. Thus, for example, if DVRs were not recognized early on by people like DirecTV's former CEO, Eddy Hartenstein, and by EchoStar's chairman and CEO, Charlie Ergen, for their ability to affordably reign in subscriber churn and drive the growth of new subscribers, the business might well have gone to the CE manufacturers instead.

Indeed, focused on the potential for strong sales at CE retail, a few early CE pioneers like Sony, Phillips, Panasonic, and Pioneer, did, in fact, make their own leap into the in-house manufacture of DVRs and other wedded devices, such as DVR-DVR combinations. Yet because the multichannel pay TV industry—especially the cable operators, who followed the satellite operators big time into DVRs—took such control over the manufacture and distribution of DVRs, their competition proved too great for the majority of CE retail manufacturers. Indeed, the two sole CE manufacturers who were able to thrive in the new cable-dominated world of DVRs were (and are today still), Motorola and Cisco (formerly Scientific Atlanta).

Although the competition from the multichannel pay TV makers (and their CE affiliates, like Motorola and Cisco) remains quite formidable, future CE manufacturers at retail are expected to continue to try to produce CE devices in the future, that will feature DVR or DVR-like functionality. A perfect model for this growth, and one that is predicted by many, is that of a DVR function being built at factory into most future television sets, as well as many other in-home and portable CE devices.

8.2.8   Cable and Telco Operators and DVRs

Cable and telco operators involved with DVRs have a couple of key things in common. For one, they both have robust, two-way lines into the homes they serve. For another, they both can use these lines to deliver true, two-way services, such as VOD and telephone service. Then, this leads both of them to deliver bundles of services using their own lines into the home, for example, telco, video, and Internet broadband. They also are the only two multichannel providers that can successfully merge and integrate true two-way VOD services with DVR services.

Cable

Ironically, leaders of the U.S. cable industry once perceived DVRs to be a product and service that they wished to avoid. That was because VODs were seen as the single focus of advanced digital services, and DVRs were seen as hard to manage from a copyright and intellectual property point of view. This view has obviously changed, whereby today there are more DVRs deployed by cable multichannel pay TV operators than by satellite multichannel pay TV operators or by standalone DVR users combined.

Simultaneously, cable multichannel pay TV operators such as Cablevision Systems and Time Warner Cable (located next to one another, respectively, in New York's Long Island and in New York City) have forged new territory developing a next generation of DVRs, in the form of what is termed RS-DVRs. This concept here is one whereby the multichannel pay TV cable or telco operator builds and maintains a terrestrial infrastructure which includes buildings far from the customer's home, wherein servers with storage built into them handle the functions of the typical in-home, individual DVR today.

Although the ability to conduct this RS-DVR implementation remains tied up in legal questions and thus is not quite ready for full and aggressive development, final legal approvals are expected during the next couple of years.

Once that legal blessing arrives, cable and telco multichannel pay TV operators will slowly begin eliminating the costs (and hassles) to themselves and their customers of purchasing and deploying in-home individual DVR set-top boxes. Instead, the future of DVR functionality will be handled and controlled by the multichannel pay TV operator, via an RS-DVR system. In that mode, all of the individual consumer's DVR storage will be kept in a server owned by the operator and housed in a building likely far away from the consumer's home.

Later in the RS-DVR lifecycle, it starts becoming more and more tied in with the multichannel pay TV operator's VOD system, whereby ultimately the two become seen as one functionality under one product and service name.

The only exception to this scenario appears to be one that involves a small handful of consumers who resist system control of their content. Almost like a science fiction movie of the future, this small group will continue to insist upon owning and controlling their own content within the physical confines of their own home or other property.

Telco

Frankly, the telco build-out picture does not appear to be all that different today than that of the cable multichannel pay TV operators. Over the years, the telcos have, in fact, become more like cable operators, and the cable operators more like telcos. Thus, today, and into the future, their core offerings will overlap. Both cable and telcos will offer digital phone, Internet and, of course, TV.

In addition, both cable and telco operators will spar over dominance in the advanced services areas, which include things like HDTV, DVRs, VOD, home networks, and interactive TV (iTV). These areas are so important to these cable and telco multichannel pay TV operators because they keep churn down and help to enhance subscriber growth and subscriber spending on monthly services [also known as average revenue per unit (ARPU)]. And let there be no doubt: these areas are also important to other multichannel pay TV operators, such as satellite TV providers, EchoStar, and DirecTV. Moreover, just around the corner, other Internet and mobile-based operators will start to deploy advanced services like HDTV, DVRs, VOD, home networks, and iTV, so that they too can begin competing with these traditional multichannel pay TV operators for a bigger slice of consumers' future telecom entertainment and information dollars.

Perhaps the best example today of a telco multichannel pay TV operator moving smartly and aggressively into the new world of DVRs is Verizon. As the case study in Chapter 1 recognizes, Verizon has progressed down the new DVR road to the point where it no longer offers SD versions of its DVRs, but rather only HD DVRs.

Satellite Operators and DVRs

A look at DirecTV's Web site, at http://www.directv.com, under the consecutive headings of both (1) "services" and "digital video recording," as well as (2) "TV Schedule" and "DirecTV On Demand," shows all that the satellite-centered multichannel pay TV operator is offering its customers in the realm of what DirecTV terms "on-demand content." Going online to the DISH Network Web site, at http://www.dishnetwork.com, under the consecutive headings of both (1) "learn" followed by "dishDVR," and (2) "entertain" followed by "DISH on Demand," brings a customer to DISH Network's version of DVRs and its "on-demand" services.

What is important to note, however, is that, for the time being, the satellite-centered infrastructure of these two multichannel pay TV operators does not permit them to offer consumers what some who are knowledgeable in the business call "true VOD," or "true on-demand" service. Thus, because of the ahead-of-time planning required to receive certain programming via content downloaded to the hard drive of a DVR via satellite (versus the instant availability of every program chosen via landline-delivered cable and telco content delivered from a head-end server), and because of the fewer number of programs available via satellite, satellite multichannel pay TV service customers cannot just pull up an EPG/IPG, push a button, and have that same level of service available instantly via satellite. So, what is a diminished version of "true VOD" and "true on-demand" in some people's minds occurs primarily because of the high costs and physical limitations of having a viable, always on, two-way satellite channel back and forth with, to, and from the consumer.

On the other hand, a strong counter argument to that of the "pure VOD" claimants is that most consumers do not suspect the difference between satellite-delivered and cable- or telco-delivered VOD, because both satellite and cable–telco versions of DVR/VOD do essentially and similarly what consumers want from a VOD service (be it DVR- or server-based). Moreover, many argue that the delay or lag time that accompanies DISH Network's and DirecTV's satellite-delivered VOD services often also accompanies cable- and telco-delivered VOD.

In the case of DirecTV, since the summer of 2008, it has offered its satellite service customers who have concurrent Internet capability the opportunity to also download movies, TV shows, and other content via the Internet. DirecTV has also gone to great lengths to improve its DVR- and VOD-related EPG/IPG, such that it allows content programmers to update their own "on-demand home channels" that they offer to their consumers so that those consumers can simply and efficiently navigate through thousands of programming offerings.

Although not as robust as DirecTV's, DISH Network too has implemented a "VOD" or "on-demand" service via Internet, and how long it takes before that Internet service rivals DirecTV's remains an open question as of this publication. Conversely, since August 2008, DISH Network has pushed its own technical boundaries by being the first in the multichannel pay TV industry to offer its consumers the high-definition programming in 1080p and MPEG-4, which together present the highest and best HD resolution currently available.

In sum, it is fair to say that DirecTV and DISH Network have addressed a part of the limitations of their satellite infrastructure by implementing the Internet-delivered VOD service (to supplement the satellite-delivered VOD). This was done in large measure to address the pent-up demand of its customers seeking something akin to the "true VOD" that is currently offered by DirecTV's cable and telco video service rivals.

Worth also highlighting for the future of DVRs is the EchoStar and DISH Network group of companies' foray into the world of Sling Media, the set-top portable media device maker that EchoStar purchased in 2007. Under its subsidiary, EchoStar Corporation (NASDAQ: SATS), the Colorado-based telecom entities are attempting to tie the Sling technology and DVRs in with live and recorded content for what EchoStar calls its "whole home mobile TV everywhere solution."

Nonetheless, even without "true VOD," as they have since the earliest days in 1998–1999 of DVRs, the EchoStar and DISH Network group of companies, and DirecTV, are expected to continue to pay great emphasis to the basic elements of DVRs. In addition, they should be expected to be constantly looking to find novel implementations of DVR and DVR-related technology. This permits them to stay up with, and maybe even ahead of, their cable, mobile, and telco rivals in their race for more and happier customers (i.e., customers that are higher paying and also less likely to churn to other services).

DirecTV was among the first multichannel pay TV operators to offer DVRs to its customers, having pioneered multichannel pay TV DVR deployments—along with EchoStar and its DISH Network—in the 1999–2000 timeframe, under the aegis of its then senior vice president, Larry Chapman. In those early days, DirecTV entered into a cooperative agreement with one of two then independent DVR developers, the Alviso, CA-headquartered TiVo company. That DirecTV–TiVo relationship has seen its share of ebbs and flows, especially following the purchase in January 2004 of a controlling interest in DirecTV by Rupert Murdoch's News Corp. Upon achieving control of DirecTV, the TiVo-DirecTV set-top box DVRs were promptly marked for next-generation replacement in the form of the DirecTV-branded set-top DVRs, built by News Corp.'s subsidiary, the technology, and hardware supply company, NDS. Murdoch and News Corp. having departed the DirecTV relationship in mid-2008, DirecTV soon after signed a new agreement with TiVo to begin development of a TiVo/DirecTV HD DVR device; DirecTV also currently has an advertising agreement with TiVo, while continuing to support more than a million existing TiVo DirecTV subscribers.

These days, the NDS-set of boxes and deployments are controlled internally at DirecTV by its senior vice president Romulo Pontual. Pontual began his telecom career in the early 1980s, working for the Brazilian telecom, Embratel, and moving, in 1988, to Luxembourg to work for Societe Europeene des Satellites (SES Astra) until 1996. In that year, Pontual transitioned to News Corp., and its short-lived U.S. subsidiary, ASkyB, where he focused on content delivery, such as ethnic local channels. His direction through the years has included direct-to-home (DTH) services in New Zealand, Italy, the United Kingdom, and Latin America, as well as the design of set-top boxes. Pontual came to DirecTV in 2004.

Asked to identify his focus while at DirecTV during the past 4–5 years, Pontual immediately highlighted his concern for the delivery of first-rate content. "I have constantly tried to marry the road map of tech with the best content experience … this has meant acquiring things such as solid content, superior packages, good video quality, and offering interactive TV services, a good user interface, and a first rate standard remote control." As an example of the due diligence completed under his watch, Pontual notes his DirecTV team reviewed no less than 15 UIs that were available to DirecTV and NDS at the time of their early DVR development. Toward the goal of consumer user friendliness, Pontual also made it a priority to provide all of DirecTV's NDS-supplied set-top DVR boxes with the same interface and same remote control unit, which are interchangeable throughout the DirecTV system.

Pontual concedes, "In the day-to-day in any organization, it can sometimes be difficult to migrate to what seems to be obvious. It's not often easy to find a road map to get you there on time. But because we concentrated on converged hardware and software capabilities, that did a lot to advance our system and lower costs."

Pontual also highlights another of the big DirecTV challenges, which was to try to get the next generation of set-top boxes ready for, and transitioned to new MPEG-4 and HD technology standards especially with 36 million prior generation MPEG-2 set-top boxes—which has now grown to 42 million total DirecTV set-top boxes market wide. And along the way, Pontual notes that DirecTV had to make the transitions to new and better boxes and technology in such a way that "the bottom line works."

Asked about the 2004–2008 downsizing of the original joint venture with its early partner, TiVo, Pontual offers an explanation. He states that rather than being forced by News Corp. to accept an NDS-dominated relationship, DirecTV's thinking was more along the strategic lines of instead moving to a new hardware vendor, because DirecTV wanted to depart a situation where it would always have to share revenues and decisions with a rather independent third party. "We wanted to drive our own destiny," Pontual explains. He adds, "It was not about optimizing the profitability of TiVo, but rather that of our customers."

Turning to the important question of DirecTV and DVRs in the future, Pontual echoes his peers among top-level DVR executives, noting, "The TV experience we want people to have entails good content, and allowing people to experience the entertainment whenever they want ... the service we want to provide our subscribers allows them to view what they want, anytime they want." More specifically, DirecTV and Pontual are quickly embracing the concept of the whole-home DVR solution, meaning content controlled by the DVR in one room is available in every other TV set within the same household.

Supporting that concept is the fact that, according to DirecTV, nearly 50% of its current subscriber base take some form of advanced service[10] from the multichannel pay TV operator. Further, DirecTV has made

---

[10] "Advanced service" in this instance includes DVR, HDTV, HD/DVR, interactive TV, and VOD.

sure its new MPEG-4 set-top boxes are universally capable of becoming networkable via simple satellite downloads sent from DirecTV's network handful of operations centers.

Toward that next ultimate goal of the truly networked home, capable of many things, DirecTV began the goal, 2 years ago, of having all of what is today nearly 20 million subscribers begin regularly accessing this new generation of "intelligent set-tops." These devices connect to the home network and integrate all the devices in any given home. These features include the following:

- Internet through the home router
- Which creates connections, via DirecTV's new VOD service begun in July 2008, to Internet-delivered TV content
- Interactive type content on PCs, such as, photos, delivered to other devices, such as large-screen TVs in different rooms
- Video in the TV room that comes from or is delivered to a different room

Hand-in-hand with these features is an additional DirecTV priority, that of spending the time and effort on technology and related concerns, such that whatever it is that is offered, actually works, works consistently, and is never something the customer has to worry about being available.

Indeed, in his own home, Pontual offers the example of his family's vacation pictures being downloaded to his family's DVR, then being consistently accessible in every room in the home, for access at any time on any screen. This is the type of functionality that Pontual aims to offer and have delivered to the majority of people in tomorrow's TV markets.

Pontual concludes, "As DirecTV goes ahead, it has to have that connectivity, and to work that well. It needs to provide a service level that is itself the next revolution in the connected home."

DirecTV

Contact Information
2230 E. Imperial Hwy, El Segundo, CA 90245
Phone: (310) 364-6000
http://www.directv.com

Stock Symbol
NASDAQ: DTV

Key People
John Malone, Chairman
Chase Carey, President and CEO
PR Contact: Jade Eksted
Phone: (310) 964-3429

Key Business
Direct broadcast satellite television provider in the United States. Operates Sky Latin America, including Sky Brasil and DirecTV Latin America; all of these systems include DVR products and services.

DVR Connection
One of two of the earliest pioneers to offer its customers DVRs.

8.2.9   Internet Operators and DVRs

Some of the larger and well-known technology companies, such as Google, Apple, and Yahoo!, are also said to be looking into the core capabilities of DVRs as they relate to these companies' control and manipulation of digital content. Many observers see the future including a "hybrid" solution, wherein a computer's hard drive will be used not only to record content, but to also serve to store downloaded content. Hard drives connected to monitors in the form of computers will morph into hard drives being connected to TV sets and similar devices, making the TVs and computers of the future very similar devices. As such, not only does the number of these devices in each home increase, but these Internet service providers gain market share, as well.

Another area of potential growth is that of DVRs connected to the Internet for security purposes. In this case, the Internet is the link from the viewer to the DVR, wherever the former (and the latter) are located.

Video Downloads

Video downloads involve Web sites that offer full-length versions of popular movies, cartoons, TV shows, and other content, typically for free. They are also typically ad-supported, involving ads featured at the beginning of content, ads on the sides of the home page, and otherwise embedded in both the Web site and the video being shown. Although the quality of the video can vary significantly dependent upon various technical features (e.g., the bandwidth offered by one's Internet service), the basic concept is fairly simple and fairly functional.

Unlike a DVR, however, the content is downloaded once a button is pressed, and thus, the viewer has to wait for the content to come into the computer before activating certain features, such as the fast forward mechanism. Also, of course, unlike most DVRs, video downloads are made to computers, and thus, there is no remote control. Instead, the fast forward, pause, and rewind functions are controlled via the computer mouse device.

Nonetheless, albeit it currently small—especially relative to DVDs, which still dominate the movie landscape—the slice of the movie video pie will grow, especially among younger users and ones that rely more on smaller and mobile devices (other than TV monitors) to view their video content.

According to a researcher, the NPD Group, "41% of dollars budgeted for movies and video went to DVD purchases, 11% went to buying TV shows on DVD, 29% to DVD rentals, and 18% on movie tickets. The caboose for this entertainment train, meanwhile, is the digital format, which only attracted 0.05% of consumer spending." Because DVDs are firmly entrenched in the U.S. entertainment scheme, people have been using them for years and are comfortable with that format. On the other hand, video downloads are a new idea for most people; it was only as recently as mid-2008 that digital versions of new releases came out on the same day as DVDs.

Nonetheless, the studios, CE, and technology sides of the telecom entertainment and information market get it. Apple, Amazon, and NetFlix are each promoting the digital delivery via downloads to computers, while big CE manufacturers such as Sony and Panasonic are building Internet connections directly into their TVs, to permit users to receive early every form of digital content.

Does this mean competition for those embedded in the traditional DVR industry? You bet.

Online Streaming Video

Another form of potential competition to traditional DVR forms and models comes from what is termed streaming video. This and video downloads, a similar form of Internet-delivered media, are discussed at greater length earlier in this chapter.

8.2.10 Others and DVRs[11]

At the 2008 International Broadcasters Conference in Amsterdam (IBC), Swedish company Edgeware displayed its recent DVR-related development, which was a server designed for a multichannel operator's central node (or operations center).

---

[11] Further reading about the "future of DVRs," can be accessed easily by typing in the words "the future of DVRs" into any search engine. Other resources include (1) Wilbur, Kenneth C., Ph.D. Student, "Modeling the Effects of Advertisement-Avoidance Technology on Advertisement-Supported Media," Copyright 2004, University of Virginia; (2) Wilbur, Kenneth C., kwilbur@marshall.usc.edu, "How the Digital Video Recorder Changes Traditional Television Advertising," Copyright 2007, University of Southern California; (3) Lowrey, Tina M., Shrum L.J., and McCarty, John A., "The Future of Television Advertising," Copyright 2004; (4) Loebbecke, Claudia, Radtke, Stefan, and Huyskens, Claudio, "Innovative Media Technologies: Digital Video Recorders Changing the Ad-TV Business Model," Proceedings of the 12th Americas Conference on Information Systems, Mexico, August 4, 2006; (5) Beebe, J., "Institutional Structure and Program Choices in Television Markets," *Quarterly Journal of Economics*, v. 91-1, 1977, pages. 15–37; (6) Chorianopoulos, K. and Spinellis, D, "Coping With TiVo: Opportunities of the Networked Digital Video Recorder," Telematics and Informatics, 2006, http://www.itv.eltrun.aueb.gr/about/editors/chorianpoulos; (7) Fortunato, J. and Windels, D., "Adoption of Digital Video Recorders and Advertising: Treats of Opportunities," *Journal of Interactive Advertising*, 2005, v. 6-1, pages. 137–148; (8) Harvey, M. and Rother, J., "Video Cassette Recorders: Their Impact on Viewers and Advertisers," 1986, v. 25-6, pages.

Within this server, Edgeware reports, its flash memory has the capability of collecting and storing huge sums of content from hundreds or thousands of channels, simultaneously. Aimed at an IPTV audience of cable and telco multichannel operators, the new service, in the words of its CEO Joachim Roos, "… enables a unique possibility for service providers to easily integrate on-demand functionality within existing or new networks—minimizing CAPEX, OPEX and time to market." According to the company's Web site, at http://www .edgeware.tv/, the service supports Video On-Demand, TV On-Demand, Time Shift TV, Pause Live TV, Catch Up TV, nPVR and Ad Insertion. Continuing, Edgeware states, "By combining solid-state flash memory and hardware accelerated streaming, [our] Orbit 2x [product] offers a radically different approach to server design, translating technology to unmatched customer value." Edgeware concludes by noting its system solutions have been chosen by leading service providers, ranging from hospitality to Tier One operators.

It is precisely these type of advance technology solutions that promise to propel the concept of DVRs deeper and deeper into the infrastructure that makes up multichannel TV, especially that of cable and telco companies.

Sony's Nick Colsey, its in-house DVR guru, notes, "The future of DVRs is the network DVR, without question. The hard disc gets bigger, but not necessarily all that much cheaper, which means it can be accessed by more people. In the end, the DVR world begins using the power of the network, a basic broadband connection, and cheap storage in the node or cable-telco operations center. Every set-top and every TV eventually has access to that operations center, where the intelligence and storage reside."

Yet perhaps the best way to talk about the future of DVRs, especially relative to competitive devices or technologies, is to return to the source that started this book. Digeo's CEO Greg Gudorf does not see the future of DVRs in a simple black vs. white, or that "we go one way and they go the other way." Rather, like many who have studied CE and technology for decades, Gudorf sees the pie growing, and both DVRs and their so-called competition finding a place in the hearts, souls, minds, and pocketbooks of next-generation users. Gudorf noted examples of this "the pie gets bigger" phenomena in AM-FM radio vs. LPs and CDs, and in large video libraries like Blockbuster vs. CDs and other in-home portable media. In the end, rather than have one new technology completely replace another, consumers find a place in their lives for both. Gudorf summarizes and concludes, "In the end, the consumer doesn't care where it comes from, they just want it affordably and they want it now. We always underestimate how long it takes to bring any new technology to life, and we typically overestimate how quickly the prior technology will succumb." Amen.

19–27; (9) Loebbecke, C., "Digital Video Recorder-Driven Impacts on the Video Content Services Industry," June 14–16, 2004, Proceedings of the 12th European Conference on Information Systems (ECIS), Turku, Finland; (10) Picker, R., "The Digital Video Recorder: Unbounding Advertising and Content," The University of Chicago Law Review, 2004, v. 71-1, pages. 205–222; and (11) Evain, J., "PVR (Personal Video Recorder), DVD and Mass Storage Devices: A Promise or a Threat for Broadcasters?", September 19–20, 2005, EBU, Geneva, Switzerland.

8.3   The DVR of the Future

Returning—for the sake of simplicity and clarity—to the concept of the individual in-home units, the self-described "entrepreneur and Internet journalist" Chris Tew posted a "DVR of the Future" feature in early 2007 (http://www.webtvwire.com/the-dvr-of-the-future). Tew envisioned the future of multiple in-home set-tops converged into one, single, super box, which he titles "The Ultimate DVR." Tew sees this transition occurring "… maybe within 3–5 years." The list below comprises an edited version of Tew's compilation of the core features contained within "The Ultimate DVR."

The Ultimate DVR features[12] the following:

- Record and schedule TV and Internet recordings
- Smart recording, where the DVR chooses the best shows to watch, based on what you watch, for example, the actor you like
- An all-in-one recordable HD DVD and Blu-ray drive
- Fast forward and rewind live TV
- Ability to receive to over-the-air and IPTV broadcasts
- Ability to play all media, from any PC, in the house, over a home network
- A built-in browser for Internet surfing
- A built-in podcast/vodcast aggregator, so you can subscribe to online radio and TV shows
- The ability to send live TV, recorded TV, and video from anywhere on your network, over the Internet, so you can watch TV anywhere (similar to the functionality of EchoStar's Slingbox)
- A built-in smart TV guide that highlights shows of interest to you and also connects you to related Internet video
- An instant recommendation feature, that tells you the best thing to watch right now (e.g., a recording, a live TV show, an on-demand show, or a vodcast), also allowing you to specify a specific genre
- A unified search, which searches media on your home network, recorded shows, TV schedule, online video, and vodcasts
- A VOD service, where you can rent and buy movies online, direct, from your multichannel pay TV provider, and save them to your DVR
- The ability to upload your videos and recordings to a Web site, and share with other people who use that DVR
- Integration with popular portable media players (PMPs), so you can take video on the move
- The ability to control any PC on your home network and view that PC as if you are using it
- A built-in games console for playing games, so you can play games online and buy and download games online, through your TV
- A hefty hard drive, including the ability to use Network Attached Storage, or hard drives on other PCs, if needed

---

[12] Chris Tew, WebTVWire: The Business of Internet TV and Video, March 31, 2007. Posted in MediaExtenders, News, TV Gadgets, and Equipment. Property of Chris Yew. All rights reserved. Used with permission.

Yew adds, "Can you think of anything else to add?"

Worth repeating at this point is the information featured in Chapter 1 offered mainly in the form of the Figure 1.6 projection chart that shows the estimated growth of DVRs across all segments of standalone and multichannel pay TV operators in the United States, through 2010. This is the point, not more than a couple of years from now, when DVR penetration pushes into 50% of all U.S. TVHHs.

8.4 Summary

In summary, the future of DVRs is strong. The future of DVRs is also fraught with questions. This is because of new forms of hardware and software that are doing differently what the core pioneer DVRs of the late 1990s once did, yet the newer versions are doing the same basic DVR functionality more cheaply or more elegantly, or with more quality and enhancement, for less money. Thus, just like the road to improvement of just about any popular device, in the home, in the car, or in the office, this too, will be the future of DVRs.

Appendix A

Glossary

The terms in this glossary are intended to cover most aspects of this new technology called digital video recorders (DVRs). Yet, the reader will note that many are actually terms embedded in the older, and larger, television industry, because DVRs remain such an integral part of that bigger picture.

Access Card It is a credit card-sized plastic card supplied to a valid subscriber by a multichannel TV company, such as a pay TV direct broadcast satellite (DBS), cable, or telephone company. The access card, when properly activated by the company and the user, is placed in a small, narrow slot in the back or the front of the set-top box and is used by the consumer to legitimately access the content supplied by the pay TV provider. The core intent of the access card is to make the pay TV content only available to and only accessible by the legitimate multichannel pay TV subscriber. The same functionality would be important for any multichannel pay TV provider deploying a set-top box, whether the set-top box included a hard drive and a DVR, or not.

Bandwidth It is a telecommunications term referring to the ability of a signal transmission device to carry a given quantity of signal through its transmission infrastructure. Thus, typically, the bandwidth of a cable operator will be different from that of a satellite/DBS provider. Bandwidth is a much sought after resource, and very few multichannel operators or other suppliers of content within the telecommunications realm are ever heard to say they have enough, or even rarer still, too much, bandwidth.

Business Model With regard to DVRs, the term business model refers to the manner in which the costs associated with the DVR product or service are met, or, ideally, exceeded by the revenue for the organization and doings.

Cable It is the term used to describe the part of the multichannel pay TV industry that delivers its signals via landlines and typically provides consumers with a "triple play" of telecom services, that is, video, voice, and Internet broadband.

Chip It is the term used in the computer industry to define a piece of silicon placed on a wafer, permitting computer functions to be processed and delivered to the screen as content. Every DVR contains a set of chips that perform the processing functions.

Churn It is a TV industry term indicating the subscribers who terminate their multichannel service for any given reason.

Content Content is the term used in the TV business, which as an industry also sometimes uses the term "software," to define the programming that actually reaches a viewer in either an ad-supporter-free TV world or in a pay TV subscriber market. Content can typically refer to data in the form of really simple syndication feeds, photos, PowerPoint images, video, and audio content.

Cost Per Thousand (CPM) Because the letter M is the roman numeral for 1000, CPM represents the standard unit of costing used in advertising to compare the display rates of mass media advertisement. CPM is used in the pricing of display locations for advertisements, usually increasing or decreasing with the quality of the audience and scarcity of display opportunity.

Customization In the context of DVRs, customization means what a DVR—and thus an operator—is capable of doing to learn the viewing and content preferences of its viewers. This then serves two distinct purposes: one is to offer the customer similar content in the way of recommendations and the other is to provide information about the viewer for advertisers and agencies so that the two can use that data and provide more relevant and useful information for that specific viewer. (See also, the term "personalization," below, which captures the same basic concept.)

Digital Subscriber Line (DSL) It is a group of technologies that provides digital transmission of data via the infrastructure of a local telephone network. As compared to analog infrastructures, DSL substantially increases the capacity of common telephone lines to transmit content to homes and businesses.

Digital Video Recorder Better known by its acronym DVR, it is a device that is comprised of a hard drive and, in older models, a chip that transfers analog content to digital content, both of which are core elements that allow a television viewer to manipulate the content on the screen. This control by the viewer permits live content to be recorded, paused, rewound, and played thereafter at any time, as long as the content remains stored (or recorded) on the device's hard drive. A DVR also permits a viewer to select a program choice from a grid (also called an electronic program guide (EPG)), press the record function, and then have the machine store the content for later viewing. Typically, a DVR comes in the form of a set-top box, which is purchased by a consumer for placement in the home, or is offered by a multichannel operator for placement in the home. In the former case, the set-top is called a standalone DVR because it only serves as a DVR. In the latter case, the set-top is called an integrated DVR because it serves the functions of DVR and receiver–decoder for access to the multichannel operator's scrambled signal. The primary advantage of DVR technology is that it allows for much longer recording times over traditional VCR or other recording technologies and enhanced control over the programming content by the user. Some multichannel operators are also engaging the concept of DVR functionality placed at a storage device at a central location, which may be miles away from the viewer's home. DVRs have, in the past, also been called personal video recorders (PVRs), although the term PVR has become archaic, and thus has been replaced in most circles by the term DVR.

Direct Broadcast Satellite (DBS) The term and acronym referring to satellites launched and positioned 22,300 miles above the equator, in geostationary orbit, which then serve as relay points from uplinks on earth to downlinks back on earth. In the case of DBS multichannel pay TV operators, like DirecTV and EchoStar in the United States, the uplink is a core transmission center controlled by that operator; the downlink is typically a consumer user's home satellite dish, usually mounted on the outside of the consumer's home, which collects the signal from the DBS satellite and delivers it to the receiver–decoder, which processes the signal and then delivers it to the TV screen.

Electronic Program Guide (EPG) An EPG also known as interactive program guide (IPG). An EPG/IPG is an on-screen guide to scheduled broadcast television programs, typically with functions allowing a viewer to navigate, select, and discover content by time, title, channel, genre, etc., by use of the remote control.

Encoder It is a device used to convert a signal or data into a code. The code may serve any number of purposes, such as compressing information for transmission or storage, encrypting or adding redundancies to the input code, or translating from one code to another. In terms of DVRs, this is done by means of a programmed algorithm, whereas most analog encoding is done with analog circuitry.

Fiber To The Home (FTTH) It is the fiber optic cable used to replace the standard copper wire used for telecommunications. FTTH is desirable because it can carry high-speed broadband services integrating voice, data, and video, and runs directly to the junction box at the home or building. FTTH is also sometimes termed fiber to the premises (FTTP).

Fiber To The Node (FTTN) FTTN, also called fiber to the neighborhood, is similar to fiber to the home, in that its fiber optic cables that are capable of delivering high-speed bandwidth are connected to a cabinet that is capable of serving several homes or small businesses (i.e., a neighborhood). Customers connect to this cabinet using traditional copper coaxial wires.

Free-To-Air (FTA) FTA signifies a multichannel TV service provider that offers TV via a business model that relies on advertiser-supported TV channels, instead of consumer subscriptions. This model is quite popular in Europe, and Australia has also recently adopted a new form of FTA (See, chapter 7, "International DVR Growth").

Free TV It refers to the channels that one is able to receive via the analog signal, without cable or a digital receiver. It is also referred to as "ad-supported," "broadcast," or "over-the-air" television.

Hard Drive The flat, round disk inside of a DVR device onto which the digital ones and zeros of digital content are recorded. In the late 1990s, which were the early days of consumer DVRs for U.S.-based consumers, a hard dive costing $230 would typically store 14 hours, or 14 gigabytes, of standard definition (SD) content; almost 10 years later, the typical cost of the same size hard drive is $50. Indeed, the cost of storage, for example, in the case of DVR hard drives, continues to decline.

High-Definition TV (HDTV) It is the term used among television industry personnel and lay people today to define a level of digital TV transmission that exceeds that of SDTV. HD today has several levels of pixel transmission quality that satisfy the requirement to be termed HDTV.

Integrated DVR Set-Top Box The "built into" or "integrated" STB means the DVR functionality is combined with the cable or satellite STB functions into one STB. This is the wave of the future and the reason most new DVR STBs will be provided by cable, telco, and satellite multichannel operators.

Integrated Receiver–Decoder Set-Top Box (IRD) It is the metal box that typically sits on top of or beside the TV screen or monitor inside a consumer's home. There are typically two main types of DVR set-top boxes: one is the standalone set-top box, which functions only as a DVR, and the other is an integrated receiver–decoder box, which functions as both a DVR and the box that permits access to scrambled (or encrypted) signals offered by a multichannel content provider (such as a cable, or satellite, or telco video provider). The set-top box holds many parts, chief among which are important chips and a memory storage device called a hard drive, onto which ones and zeros of digital content are stored for later use. These boxes also provide two-way communications with the operator to enable premium services such as VOD.

Interactive Program Guide (IPG) It is a grid-like chart displaying programming information, such as the names, times, and descriptions of programs telecast, yet these days, typically only found on multichannel pay TV operators' systems. An IPG, also known as an EPG or Electronic Screen Guide (ESG), is an on-screen guide used to display broadcast television programming. It allows viewers to navigate content by channel, title, time, genre, or other means via a remote control, keyboard, or other device. An EPG/IPG also allows viewers to search by subject, view program reviews, and apply parental controls.

Interactive TV (ITV or iTV) It is the interaction of television viewers with television content as it is being viewed. Ranging from "low interactivity," that is, changing volume or channels or cameras, to "moderate interactivity," that is, video on demand (VOD), to "high interactivity," that is, a viewer can influence the actual content as they view it. Interactive TV is generally referred to in regards to "high interactivity" television.

Internet Protocol Television (IPTV) It is the television content that is received by end users or consumers via the Internet, instead of through traditional broadcast delivery mediums such as cable and satellite. For noncommercial consumers, IPTV is generally offered in a bundled format known as a "triple play," which combines IPTV, Internet access, and voice over Internet protocol (VOIP), which is actually Internet-based telephony.

Media Center A computer-based system that has been specifically adapted for playing music, as well as watching video and pictures stored locally or on a network. Also, when a TV tuner card is installed in the unit that represents the media center, watching or recording live video content is permitted.

Moving Pictures Experts Group (MPEG) A joint working group of the International Standards Organization (ISO) and the International Electrotechnical Commission (IEC) that is responsible for setting international video and audio encoding standards.

MPEG-2 An encoding standard for video content and programming with broadcast TV quality, typically used for DVD, digital TV, or motion video.

MPEG-4 An expanded original MPEG standard to support 3-D content, video/audio "objects," and other multimedia representation and distribution. MPEG-4 is based on Apple's *QuickTime* file format, and offers a number of compression options.

On-demand It refers to the capability of viewers to watch content at the push of a button and at their convenience rather then the scheduled broadcast.

Pay TV It refers to subscription-based television services, usually provided by both analog and digital cable and satellite, but also increasingly by digital terrestrial methods.

Personalization This is a term meaning to tailor a consumer product, electronic or written medium to a user, based on personal details or characteristics they provide. With respect to DVR, this includes using data related to specific viewer preferences to make recommendations or offer a more custom product offering. (See also, term above, "customization.")

Picture-in-Picture Delineates a software feature of a DVR or other device that permits a viewer to observe a condensed version of a video (and audio) signal displayed as a smaller part of a larger video (and audio) on-screen display.

Remote Storage DVR (RS-DVR) Also referred to as network DVR (nDVR), this storage is done exclusively by the multichannel TV operator in its facility instead of by the consumer in the home. Litigation between content holders and system operators has impeded the early growth of this service; however, most in the industry believe its future is bright.

Return On Investment (ROI) ROI is the primary monetary measurement for financial analysis of any investment. ROI, often called rate of return, or simply "return" is the ratio of money gained or lost on an investment in relation to the amount of money spent or invested.

Satellite A satellite in a telecommunications context refers to a transmission device that is stationed in space for communications purposes, and receives communications from a terrestrial "uplink" station, then sending the same communication back to the earth for receipt via an antenna. Antennas linked to a receiver that has been specified to acquire the satellite's communication are able to restructure that signal, typically for both secured and unsecured uses.

Satellite Broadband Distribution "Satellite broadband distribution" refers to a means of content distribution via a high-speed satellite Internet connection that does not require a terrestrial signal (such as a mobile signal, a phone line, or a hard-wired cable connection). Satellite broadband connects a computer to a satellite via a satellite modem linked to a traditional satellite dish.

Satellite Footprint "Satellite footprint" refers to an area of the earth that a satellite signal is able to access at any point in time.

Set-Top Box A set-top box (STB) or set-top unit (STU) is a device that connects to a television and an external source of signal, turning the signal into content, which is then displayed on the television screen.

Standalone DVR STB The term "standalone" means the box is not intended to serve another purpose, such as that of a cable or satellite STB, but only delivers that DVR provider's service, software and hardware to the consumer. (But see, "Integrated DVR

Set-Top Box," above). The standalone represents the dying side of the DVR industry, inasmuch as most people will get the DVRs from their multichannel provider, especially as DVR companies, like TiVo and Digeo, do more deals with more multichannel providers, such as DirecTV and Comcast.

Standard Definition (SD) It is the term used to define digital transmission of a signal in a lower quality definition than what is typically termed HDTV.

Standard Digital (SD) Also known as standard definition TV, SD is the U.S. digital television standard format created in 1998 that refers to the 525- and 625-line TV formats.

Storage Like computer storage, it allows users to save, store, and retrieve data/content at their convenience. In the case of DVRs, users are able to store programming data/content onto local or remote storage for later use.

Streaming Video It is the distribution or delivery of uninterrupted video via a telecommunications network, typically the Internet or an intranet that does not require downloading by the end user. Streaming requires an end-user medium, such as a personal computer, to buffer a few seconds of video data before being displayed on the screen so that the medium can stay ahead of itself throughout the stream. The word "stream" refers to the delivery method and not the display or transmission devices. Streaming video will be used more on digital signage systems.

Time-shifting The industry term that captures the concepts of viewing in the future, viewing at will and viewing only what is desired, is called "time-shifting."

TV Household (TVHH) It is the telecom industry phrase used to define a household, typically inhabited by more than one person, that contains an operational TV set.

User Interface (UI) User interface (or human computer interface) is the aggregate of means by which people—the users—interact with the system—a particular machine, device, computer program, or other complex tool.

Video Cassette Recorder (VCR) It is a type of video tape recorder that uses removable videotape cassettes containing magnetic tape to record audio and video from a television broadcast, so that it can be played back later.

Video On Demand (VOD) VOD refers to a system that enables the user to select and watch video content, on demand, instantly, from another locale, on a television set or web browser, via a network, as a part of an interactive television system. VOD allows users to select and watch/listen to video or audio content on demand by either streaming the content through a set-top box allowing viewing in real time or downloading the content to a device such as a PC, DVR, PVR, or portable media player. Examples of VOD include pay-per-view services offered by cable and satellite operators as well as DVR services, which allow users to download programming content for storage and viewing at a later date.

Appendix B
Companies Driving Global DVR

Company	Headquarters	Web site	Company's Description of Key Business	DVR Connection
Anixter	Glenview, IL	http://www.anixster.com	Anixter Inc. is the world's leading supplier of supply chain services and products used to connect voice, video, data, and security systems.	Supplies electronic wiring and cable used in DVRs.
AOLTV	Scranton, PA	http://television.aol.com	Provides consumer device for web access by using television for display instead of a monitor and also TV shows online.	Early investor in DVR technology.
Apple (Apple TV)	Cupertino, CA	http://www.apple.com/appletv	Apple TV lets the customers to rent movies direct from TV and also enables them to view YouTube videos, TV shows, and photos. Device also allows you to listen to podcasts, music.	Provides *Apple TV* devize with built-in DVR capabilities. Apple TV comes with up to 160 GB, for storing content.
AT&T	Dallas, TX	http://www.att.com	Provider of both local and long distance telephone services, DSL Internet access, and wireless service in the United States with 71.4 million wireless customers and more than 150 million total customers; deploys DVRs to its video customers.	Provides AT&T *U-Verse* television receiver with DVR capabilities.
Axis Communi-cations (1)	Lund, Sweden	http://www.axis.com	Axis provides IP-based network video solutions that include network cameras and video encoders for remote monitoring and security surveillance.	Axis provides video recorder solutions as well as video management software with recording capabilities in the surveillance/security camera recording industry). Provides network video products.

Company	Location	URL	Description	Notes
Avtrex	Santa Clara, CA	http://www.avtrex.com	Avtrex provides software to leading consumer electronics manufacturers for managing and recording digital TV and presenting digital photos and music.	Provides DVR software.
Bosch Security Systems (1)	Ottobrunn, Germany	http://www.boschsecuritysystems.com	Product portfolio comprised of CCTV, IP network video solutions, access control, intrusion detection and control, Fire Alarm, Security Management.	Bosch also fits into the security camera sector. Provides network video products.
Cablevision Systems	Bethpage, NY	http://www.cablevision.com	Cablevision Systems Corporation is one of the nation's leading telecommunications and entertainment companies and the fifth largest cable provider in the United States.	Cablevision deploys DVRs to its video customers.
Charter Communication	St. Louis, MS	http://www.charter.com	Offers advanced communication services, including video, high-speed Internet, and telephone. Individually or combined in a bundle, these services provide their customers with tremendous value in the form of entertainment, information, and their electronic connections to the world.	Deploys DVRs to its video customers.
Cisco	San Jose, CA	http://www.cisco.com	Key businesses include designing and selling networking and communications technology and services under five brands, namely Cisco, Linksys, WebEx, IronPort, and Scientific Atlanta; builds DVRs for its video customers.	Cisco's subsidiary, Scientific Atlanta, manufactures and deploys digital set-top boxes with DVR capabilities to a number of major cable providers.

(Continued)

Company	Headquarters	Web site	Company's Description of Key Business	DVR Connection
Comcast	Philadelphia, PA	http://www.comcast.com	Provider of cable TV, broadband Internet, and phone.	Deploys DVRs to its video customers.
Concurrent	Essex, UK	http://www.concurrenttechnologies.com	Offers design and development of high performance single board computer products.	I could not find too much on these providers.
Cox	Atlanta, GA	http://www.cox.com	Providing digital cable television and telecommunication services in the United States.	Deploys DVRs to its video customers.
Dedicated Micros (1)	Chantilly, VA	http://www.dedicatedmicros.com	Dedicated Micros makes themselves as the most experienced security product manufacturer in the industry. They offer a full line of security surveillance products, including digital video recorders, remote viewing software, virtual matrix solutions, enterprise-class management tools, analytics, and analog and IP cameras.	Dedicated Micros, designs and manufactures DVRs for use with video surveillance equipment.
Digeo	Kirkland, WA	http://www.digeo.com	Digeo provides lucrative, cost-effective and content-rich media solutions to customers nationwide.	—
Digimerge	Carrollton, TX	http://www.digimerge.com	Digimerge Technologies Inc. offers a family of products focused on the emerging trend for integration of digital video surveillance and the PC with its associated web-based applications and solutions.	Designs and manufactures DVRs for use with video surveillance equipment.

DirecTV	El Segundo, CA	http://www.directv.com	Direct broadcast satellite television provider in United States operates Sky Latin America, Sky Brasil and DirecTV Latin America.	DirecTV deploys DVRs to its satellite TV subscribers.
Dish Network	Meridian, CO	http://www.dishnetwork .com	Direct broadcast satellite service that provides satellite television, audio programming, and interactive television services in the United States.	Dish Network deploys DVRs to its satellite TV subscribers.
Disney	Burbank, CA	http://disney.go.com	Disney is one of the largest media and entertainment corporations in the world and has become one of the biggest Hollywood studios, as well as the owner and licensor of eleven theme parks and several television networks including ABC and ESPN.	Disney is one of many broadcasters that may opt to get more involved with the DVR world, especially once the analog-to-digital transition occurs on February 17, 2009.
Echostar Communi- cations	Englewood, CO	http://www.echostar.com	Set-top boxes hardware provider for direct broadcast satellite and other multichannel service providers.	Provides set-top boxes with DVR capabilities to direct broadcast satellite providers.
EverFocus (1)	Taipei, Taiwan	http://www.everfocus .com	A leading video surveillance company with a goal that for every product that we manufacture it be easily installed with minimal maintenance. CCD cameras, digital video recorders, electronic access control panels and readers, video processors, and other CCTV and access control peripherals.	EverFocus designs and manufactures DVRs for video surveillance equipment.

(Continued)

Company	Headquarters	Web site	Company's Description of Key Business	DVR Connection
GE	Fairfield, CT	http://www.ge.com	NBC Universal is a leading media and entertainment company in the development, production, and marketing of entertainment, news, and information worldwide.	GE/NBCU is one of many broadcasters that may opt to get more involved with the DVR world, especially once the analog-to-digital transition occurs on February 17, 2009.
Hauppauge	Hauppauge, NY	http://www.Hauppauge.com	The company is a worldwide leader in developing and manufacturing PC-based TV tuners and data broadcast receiver products. Hauppauge's products allow PC users to watch television on their PC screens, videoconference and create both still video images and digital TV recordings.	Designs, manufactures, and sells DVRs for use with Satellite and Cable platforms. Product range includes HD DVRs and also DVRs designed for use with analog TV.
Hewlett-Packard	Palo Alto, CA	http://www.hp.com	HP specializes in developing and manufacturing computing, storage, and networking hardware, software and services. Major product lines include personal computing devices, enterprise servers and storage devices, and printers and other imaging products.	HP has a long history of involvement with memory-related devices and services.
Honeywell	Morristown, NJ	http://www.honeywell.com	Honeywell is a diversified technology and manufacturing leader of auto-mobile products and services; control technologies for buildings, homes, and industries; automotive products; power generation systems; specialty chemicals; fibers; plastics and advanced materials.	Honeywell designs and manufactures DVRs use with for video surveillance equipment.

Humax	South Korea	http://www.humaxdigital.com	As the leader in the most state-of-the-art set-top box technology, Humax can respond faster and more accurately than its competitors in the ever-changing global market.	Designs and manufactures set-top boxes with DVR capabilities.
IBM	Armonk, New York	http://www.ibm.com	Manufacturers of computer hardware and software, and offers infrastructure services, hosting services, and consulting services in areas ranging from mainframe computers to nanotechnology.	Like HP, IBM had storage products but none that seemed to relate to DVRs.
Insight Communications	New York, NY	http://www.InsightsCommunications.com	Insight Communications is the tenth largest cable operator in the United States offering bundled, analog and digital video, broadband Internet, and voice telephone services.	Deploys DVRs to its video customers.
Intel	Santa Clara, CA	http://www.intel.com	Intel is the world's largest semiconductor company and the inventor of the x86 series of microprocessors, the processors found in most personal computers.	Intel-designed processors are used in DVRs. Intel also designs software and hardware for use in DVRs as well as with digital surveillance systems.
Interact TV	Westminster, CO	http://www.interact-tv.com	Products blend digital media, broadband, and home networking, then bring it to the end-user through a television interface creating a more relaxed and orderly environment.	Not applicable

(Continued)

Company	Headquarters	Web site	Company's Description of Key Business	DVR Connection
Intransa (1)	San Jose, CA	http://www.intransa.com	Intransa shared can leverage your existing cameras, DVRs, software and cabling infrastructure using the power of IP.	Provides IP video surveillance solutions for DVRs. Intransa also offers video storage solutions for digital entertainment distribution through IPTV and video on demand (VOD), digital storage for medical imaging, and consolidating storage. Intransa also delivers IP storage solution upgrades for existing DVRs.
LG Electronics	Seoul, South Korea	http://www.lge.com	Primarily focuses in electronics and information and communication products: digital display and media, digital appliance, and telecommunication equipment.	Designs and manufactures DVRs for use with cable and satellite platforms.
Microsoft	Redmond, WA	http://www.microsoft.com	World's largest software company provides wide range of services, which includes its Windows operating system, MS Office, Xbox game console, server and storage software and digital music players.	Provides a digital media player with DVR capabilities (64 MB of flash memory). Also provides Xbox game console with storage capabilities.
Motorola	Schaumburg, IL	http://www.motorola.com	Manufacturer of wireless telephone handsets, cable and satellite TV set-top box hardware, wireless network infrastructure equipment HDTVs.	Manufactures and designs digital set-top boxes with DVR capabilities.

Nero	Karlsbad, Germany	http://www.nero.com	Nero AG develops and distributes the world's leading digital media solutions for consumers and professionals.	Creates software that allows interface with Tivo and to watch TV on a PC. Automatically records all selected media on the PC hard drive.
Nextel	Reston, VA	http://www.nextel.com	Allows customers to use their mobile phones to remotely record television shows.	Allows customers to use mobile phones to remotely record television shows.
Panasonic Security Systems (1)	Secaucus, NJ	http://www.panasonic.com/security	Panasonic Security Systems is a leader in both professional video surveillance and digital signage solutions.	Panasonic designs and manufactures DVRs used with for video surveillance equipment.
Pelco (1)	Clovis, CA	http://www.pelco.com	Pelco is a world leader in the design, development, and manufacture of video and security systems and equipment ideal for any industry.	Pelco offers an extensive line of DVRs for video surveillance uses.
Phillips	Amsterdam, Netherlands	http://www.philips.com	A global leader in healthcare, lighting, and consumer lifestyle, delivering people-centric, innovative products, services and has established its presence in about 60 countries.	Philips designs and manufactures set-top boxes with DVR capabilities for satellite platforms (not sure about cable platforms).
Pioneer Electronics	Long Beach, CA	http://www.pioneerelectronics.com	Specializes in digital entertainment products and is well known for technology advancements in the consumer electronics industry.	Pioneer designs and manufactures DVRs for use with satellite and cable platforms.
ReplayTV	Santa Clara, CA	http://www.replaytv.com	Manufacturers of consumer video device, which allows users to capture television programming to internal hard disk storage for later viewing.	Designs and manufactures DVR device for DirecTV (I think exclusively).

(Continued)

Company	Headquarters	Web site	Company's Description of Key Business	DVR Connection
Rogers Communication	Toronto, Ontario	http://www.rogers.com	Rogers Communications Inc. is a leading provider of wireless, cable TV, hi-speed Internet, and home phone services to consumers and businesses in Canada	Deploys set-top boxes with DVR capabilities to its video customers.
Samsung	Seoul, South Korea	http://www.samsung.com	A world leader manufacturing pioneering products and technology in the semiconductors, telecommunication devices, and home appliances fields, which will make Samsung Electronics a most competitive total solution provider in digital convergence.	Designs and manufactures set-top boxes with DVR capabilities for use with cable and satellite platforms.
Scientific Atlanta (Cisco)	Lawrenceville, GA	http://www .scientificatlanta.com	Scientific Atlanta (Cisco) offers a wide range of innovative products and solutions, including switched digital video and IPTV, designed for service providers in mind.	Scientific Atlanta (Cisco) manufactures and deploys digital set-top boxes with DVR capabilities to a number of major cable providers.
Seagate	Scotts Valley, CA	http://www.Seagate.com	Seagate's hard drives are used in a variety of computers, from servers, desktops, and laptops, to other consumer devices, such as digital video recorders, video game consoles, and in portable media players, and automotive navigation systems.	Seagate makes hard drives for consumer DVRs.
Seven Media Group	Melbourne, Australia	http://www .sevencorporate.com.au	Seven Media Group offers a complete range of services for designing, implementing, and maintaining business computer systems.	An Australian media company with whom TiVo has partnered.

Company	Location	URL	Description	Notes
Sky+	Glasgow, UK	http://www.sky.com/portal/site/skycom/skyproducts/skytv/skyplus	Personal video recorder with the added advantage of a remote recording functionality enabling recording through mobile devices.	Deploys DVRs for its 9+ million U.K. BSkyB customers.
Sling Media	San Mateo, CA	http://www.sling.com	Provider of hardware and software that enable remote access to television programming over the Internet to a PC; access also includes DVR content.	Provider of hardware and software that enables remote access to television programming over the Internet to a PC; access also includes DVR content.
Sony	Minato-Ku, Tokyo, Japan	http://www.sony.net	Multinational manufacturer of electronics, video, communications, video game consoles, and information technology products for the consumer and professional markets.	Designs and manufactures home entertainment servers with large hard drives for storing video, music, and photo content.
Speco Technologies (1)	Amityville, NY	http://www.specotechnologies.com	Offers the highest quality residential and commercial sound, security, CCTV closed circuit video and electronic accessories.	Speco Technologies designs and manufactures DVRs used for video surveillance equipment.
Sprint	Overland Park, Kansas	http://www.Sprint.com	Telephone service provider.	Allows customers to use mobile phones to remotely record television shows through its venture with cable providers such as Comcast and Time Warner Cable.
Star Hub	Singapore	http://www.starhub.com.sg	Star Hub is the second largest mobile operator and the sole cable television operator in Singapore.	Deploys DVRs to its video customers.

(Continued)

Company	Headquarters	Web site	Company's Description of Key Business	DVR Connection
Teldat Security (1)	Madrid, Spain	http://www.teldat.es	The key business is data voice and image transmission, designing, developing, manufacturing, and commercializing data network interconnection and access devices.	Teldat's subsidiary Telesec designs and manufactures DVRs used for video surveillance/ security equipment.
TeleEye	Hong Kong, China	http://www.teleEye.com	TeleEye is a Hong Kong-based audio–visual, information technology company with its key focus on delivering network CCTV and DVR applications.	TeleEye's key focus is on delivering network CCTV and DVR applications.
Thomson	New York, NY	http://www.thomson.net	Thomson is the world's leading provider of solutions for the creation, management, delivery, and access of video for the communication, media, and entertainment industries.	Thomson supplies cable and satellite operators with set-top boxes that include DVR capabilities.
Time Warner/ Time Warner Cable	New York, NY	http://www.timewarner .com	Time Warner is the world's first fully integrated media and communications company.	Cable and entertainment company, the former of which provides DVRs to its subscribers.
TiVo	Alviso, CA	http://www.tivo.com	Pioneered the DVR and brought DVR to mass market based on a subscription service.	Pioneered the DVR and brought DVR to mass market based on a subscription service.
Topfield	South Korea	http://www.topfield.ca	A producer of digital free-to-air systems, embedded receivers, DVRs, positioners, and common interface systems by continuous change in technology and innovation.	Designer and manufacturer of DVRs.

Company	Location	URL	Description	Notes
Toshiba	Tokyo, Japan	http://www.toshiba.com	Key business is in infrastructure, consumer products, and electronic devices and components.	Designs and manufactures DVRs for use with cable and satellite platforms.
Tri-ed[1]	Mississauga, ON	http://www.tri-ed.com	North America's largest independent distributor of security, low voltage, and home automation products.	Designs and manufactures DVRs for use with video surveillance equipment.
UltimateTV	MountainView, CA	http://www.ultimatetv.com	*UltimateTV®* service from Microsoft provides digital recording devices with an internal hard drive, which is used to store the shows whenever the user needs.	*UltimateTV®* service from Microsoft provides digital recording devices with an internal hard drive, which is used to store the shows whenever the user needs.
Verizon	New York, NY	http://www.verizon.com	A leading American broadband and telecommunications company. Core businesses include mobile phones, broadband Internet.	Supplies DVRs to subscribers of its FiOS service.
Vivid DVR (Security)	Fremont, CA	http://www.vividlogic.com	VividLogic software reduces system complexity by preintegration with popular HD decoders, provides interoperability by plug testing, compliance testing, and CableLabs testing and accelerates time-to-market by offering a complete solution.	Vivid Logic creates DVR software.
Yahoo (Yahoo Go for TV)	Sunnyvale, CA	http://sites.mobile.yahoo.com	Initiative taken by Yahoo to view photos, video clips, and record TV shows on the television.	Initiative taken by Yahoo to record TV shows on the television.

[1] Connotes a company presently focussed on the security side of the global DVR business.

Appendix C

Nielsen's Audience Insight: U.S. DVR Penetration and Usage

Introduction

Nielsen first introduced DVRs in its National People Meter (NPM) panel in January 2006. Over 2 years later, U.S. DVR penetration and usage continue to grow and evolve. This report provides new insight on the characteristics of DVR households and their time-shifted viewing. It also includes a special analysis of how the viewing behavior of a household changes when it first acquires a DVR and after it has had a DVR over a long period of time.

Some highlights of our findings include the following:

- U.S. DVR penetration is now 25%, according to NPM panel.
- In all, 30% of DVR homes have more than one DVR. Among homes with more than one DVR, more time-shifted viewing but less overall television usage takes place.
- Over 90% of DVR homes have DVR cable set-top boxes or DVR direct broadcast satellite (DBS) set-top boxes. Less than 10% have standalone DVR devices.
- The type of DVR that a household has does not have a great impact on its amount of time-shifting.
- The playback audience is getting older as DVR penetration grows and as more people adapt to the technology.
- Homes that acquire a DVR are likely to start viewing more of other dayparts and watch more cable programming but time-shift more broadcast television.
- With the exception of live sports programs, top-rated programs are typically the most time-shifted.
- For persons aged 18–34 years, commercials during children's programming are most likely to be viewed, compared with other genres.

DVR Penetration and Usage

Penetration and Growth

Since DVRs were first introduced in Nielsen's NPM sample two and half years ago, U.S. DVR penetration has grown significantly to 25% in May 2008. While this growth can be attributed to many factors, one important contributor to this growth is the integration of the DVR into the cable or DBS set-top box. While the DVR was initially introduced years ago to the marketplace as a standalone device, over half of DVR homes in May 2008 had a DVR that was integrated with their cable set-top box. An additional 40% had DVR DBS set-top boxes.

At the same time, the penetration of multi-DVR homes has also risen; in May 2008, 30% of DVR households had more than one DVR.

Chart 1

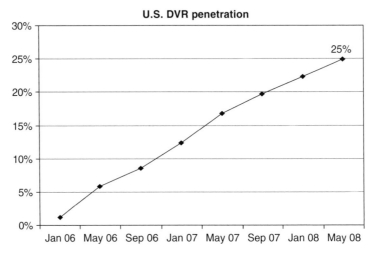

Chart 2

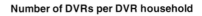

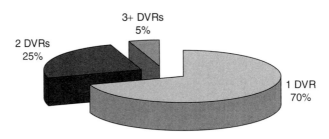

Chart 3

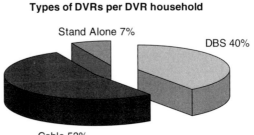

Charts 1–3 are based on NPM scaled installed counts

Usage Levels

Prior research has shown that DVR households view fewer hours of live television. This is a reflection of their changing viewing habits, as these households are able to easily record programming and view it at a later time.

"Primetime Live" ratings among DVR households continue to be lower than "Primetime Live" ratings for total United States. However, as 7-day playback of Primetime programming is included, "Live+7" ratings are close, if not higher, than total "U.S. Live+7" ratings. This trend is consistent in other dayparts.

The number of DVRs present in a household, as well as the type of DVR, can affect usage levels. In May 2008, "Live" and "Live+7" ratings were lower for homes with multiple DVRs. In these cases, it is probable that having multiple DVRs encourages more fast-forwarding of programming and commercials. However, when compared with homes with only one DVR, homes with more than one DVR show a greater lift in usage when including 7 days of playback. Homes with only one DVR exhibited a 6.64 lift in ratings, while homes with two or three or more DVRs had a lift of 8.54 and 9.89, respectively.

When analyzing usage by DVR type, homes with DVR cable set-top boxes have higher usage, but less of a seven-day lift than those that have DVR DBS set-top boxes or standalone DVR units.

Audience Composition

"Live" compositions of various viewers and "Playback" viewers show key differences. In both January 2006 and May 2008, the "persons older than 55 years" demographic contributed the majority of live viewing among the total United States. In DVR households, persons older than 55 years are viewing less live television and the younger aged 25–44 years demographics have the most "Playback." This trend has held true since the beginning of DVR measurement in Nielsen's panels.

Table 1 Prime (Monday–Sunday 8–11 p.m.) PUT[1] Persons Aged 18–49 Years

May 2008	Live AA%	Live+7 AA%	Lift
Total United States	33.28	35.45	2.17
Total DVR	28.33	35.56	7.24
1 DVR	29.40	36.04	6.64
2 DVR	27.09	35.63	8.54
3+ DVRs	25.03	34.92	9.89
DBS Set-top box only[2]	27.07	34.69	7.62
Cable set-top box only	29.16	35.95	6.79
Standalone only	21.44	29.10	7.66

[1] PUT = People Using Television.
[2] Households with multiple types of DVRs within a household were excluded from the type of DVR table above. Sample counts are not large enough to provide reliable data.

Chart 4

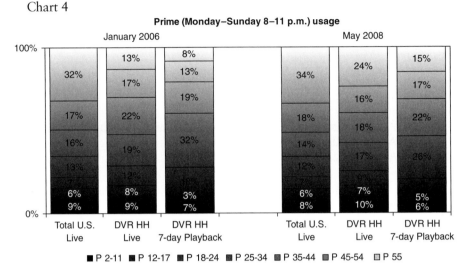

Prime (Monday–Sunday 8–11 p.m.) usage

■ P 2-11 ■ P 12-17 ■ P 18-24 ■ P 25-34 ■ P 35-44 ■ P 45-54 □ P 55

However, the audience compositions for both "Live" and "Playback" viewing in DVR households are changing and, in particular, are getting older. In January 2006, persons older than 55 years contributed to only 8% of "7-day" "Primetime" playback; in May 2008, this contribution has almost doubled to 15%. At the same time, "Primetime" playback contribution from persons aged 18–24 years has decreased. This is an important shift that shows that as DVR penetration increases, people across all demographics, young and old, have become more willing to not only acquire but use this technology.

DVR Playback

An analysis of DVR playback demonstrates that people using DVRs to playback recorded programming is taking away "Live" viewing in those dayparts.

Chart 5 shows the distribution of viewing minutes of when people are using their DVRs to playback recorded content (when the device is in playback mode). Included in this data are time spent using a DVR trick mode (pause, fast-forward, etc.), as well as any playback older than 7 days.

Consistent with previous findings, the "Prime" (Monday–Sunday 8 p.m.–11 p.m.), "Early Fringe" (Monday–Friday 6 p.m.–8 p.m.), "Late Fringe" (Monday–Sunday 11 p.m.–1 a.m.), and "Late Night" (Monday–Sunday 1 a.m–6 a.m) dayparts show the highest DVR usage. In May 2008, 33% of all DVR usage throughout the day took place during the Monday–Sunday 8 p.m–11 p.m. daypart. "Primetime" playback is often high because viewers begin watching programs later in order to fast-forward through content and continue to view these programs into the hours of "Late Fringe." Furthermore, this chart illustrates the current dilemma faced by evening local newscasts; during early fringe, viewers in DVR homes are now watching content that they recorded previously.

Chart 5

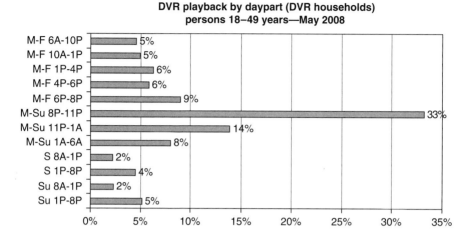

DVR playback by daypart (DVR households)
persons 18–49 years—May 2008

How Acquiring a DVR Changes Viewing Behavior

This section of the report is an analysis of how viewing habits change when a household acquires a DVR. This analysis is based on a comparison of common homes between May 2007 and May 2008. Approximately 180 persons were included in this analysis; these persons were in homes that were in our sample from May 2007 to May 2008, during which time they acquired a DVR.

In many cases, when a home acquires a DVR, its cable status also changes. As depicted in Chart 6, in May 2007, 7% of persons aged 18–49 years in homes that acquired a DVR between May 2007 and May 2008 were in broadcast-only homes. After acquiring a DVR, nearly all of these broadcast-only homes converted to *Cable Plus*.[1] As a result, in May 2008, 99% of persons aged 18–49 years within homes that acquired a DVR were Cable Plus.

This *Cable Plus* growth can be attributed to the year-to-year increase in both wired digital cable and DBS. From May 2007 to May 2008, persons aged 18–49 years in wired digital cable homes increased from 33 to 54% and persons aged 18–49 years in DBS homes increased from 34 to 45%.

This analysis shows that the acquisition of a DVR and upgrading to wired digital cable or DBS often occur at the same time. Therefore, along with acquiring the ability to time-shift programming, homes that acquire DVRs are also gaining additional channel choices.

Prior research has shown that the biggest difference among households that acquire a DVR is that they typically watch less Live television. However, this was not the case for May 2008; in May 2008, homes that acquired a DVR viewed more Live television compared to the previous year. Usually, the addition of a DVR also causes homes to watch dayparts that they did not watch before acquiring a DVR.

---

[1] *Cable Plus* is typically a programming package offering more channels and other features.

Chart 6

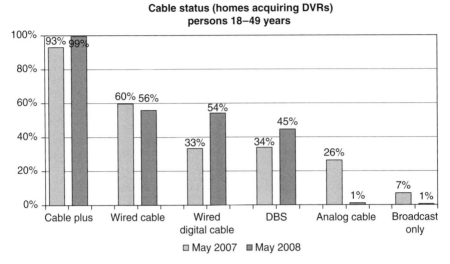

Cable status (homes acquiring DVRs)
persons 18–49 years

☐ May 2007   ■ May 2008

Table 2 compares "Live" usage in May 2007 to "Live" and "Live+7" usage in May 2008 for persons aged 18–49 years. It shows clearly that, among these DVR acquirers, viewing increased year-to-year. Even "Primetime" usage, a highly time-shifted daypart, shows a 9% increase for "Live," while "Live+7" is up 20% year-to-year. As depicted in the table, other dayparts show similar trends.

For homes who had a DVR throughout May 2007 and May 2008, usage in all dayparts show either no change or, in many cases, an increase from the prior year. However, the impact is much less significant than homes who had acquired a DVR over the past year. For instance, while "Prime Live" to "Live+7" usage went up 20% among DVR acquirers, "Live Prime" viewing for this group is virtually unchanged and "Live+7" is up only 2%. The difference between the two groups shows that homes that have had a DVR for a while, in this case at least one year, have already developed time-shifting viewing habits, whereas new acquirers are just accustoming themselves to the new device.

The acquisition of a DVR also has an impact on a household's share of viewing sources. Among persons aged 18–49 years in homes that did not have a DVR in May 2007, but acquired one by May 2008, 40% of their May 2007 "Primetime" viewing went to English broadcast networks. However, in May 2008 after acquiring a DVR, "Live" and "Live +7" primetime share to English Broadcast networks for this same group of homes decreased 26 and 16%, respectively. At the same time, viewing of ad-supported cable networks for "Live" and "Live+7" increased significantly by 25 and 18%, respectively. It is likely that homes that acquire a DVR upgrade their DBS or cable service to include more viewing sources. It is also important to note that along with the acquisition of a DVR, the writers' strike may have also played a role in these viewing trends in May 2008.

Table 2 Persons Aged 18–49 Years PUT[1]% (Homes Acquiring DVRs)

Daypart Live	May 2007	May 2008			
	Live	Live	Live+7	Live 08/ Live 07(%)	Live+7 08/Live 07(%)
Monday–Friday 6 a.m.–10 a.m.	11.35	13.00	13.40	15	18
Monday–Friday 10 a.m–1 p.m.	11.68	12.68	13.36	9	14
Monday–Friday 1 p.m–4 p.m.	12.26	14.52	15.44	18	26
Monday–Friday 4 p.m.–6 p.m.	14.18	17.56	18.64	24	31
Monday–Friday 6 p.m–8 p.m.	19.97	24.31	25.52	22	28
Monday–Sunday 8 p.m.–11 p.m.	32.94	35.86	39.62	9	20
Monday–Friday 11 p.m.–1 a.m.	21.17	24.37	25.44	15	20
Monday–Friday 1 a.m.–6 a.m.	9.96	10.48	10.77	5	8
Sunday 8 a.m.–1 p.m.	12.02	15.58	16.17	30	34
Sunday 1 p.m.–8 p.m.	14.54	16.63	17.65	14	21
Sunday 8 a.m.–1 p.m.	13.14	15.23	15.86	16	21
Sunday 1 p.m.–8 p.m.	18.04	21.50	22.52	19	25

[1] PUT = People Using Television.

Table 3 Persons Aged 18–49 Years PUT[1]% (Homes with DVRs Both Years)

Daypart	May 2007		May 2008		% Difference	
	Live	Live+7	Live	Live+7	Live 08/ Live 07	Live+7 08/ Live+7 07
Monday–Frdiay 6 a.m.–10 a.m.	9.50	10.07	10.30	11.09	8	10
Monday–Friday 10 a.m.–1 p.m.	7.66	8.76	8.62	10.10	13	15
Monday–Friday 1 p.m.–4 p.m.	8.34	10.20	9.37	11.47	12	13
Monday–Friday 4 p.m.–6 p.m.	11.06	13.12	12.24	14.62	11	11
Monday–Friday 6 p.m.–8 p.m.	16.70	18.72	18.40	20.84	10	11
Monday–Sunday 8–11 p.m.	26.29	33.58	26.20	34.40	0	2
Monday–Friday 11 p.m.–1 a.m.	19.31	20.97	19.47	21.68	1	3
Monday–Friday 1 a.m.–6 a.m.	7.18	7.67	8.48	9.10	18	19
Sunday 8 a.m.–1 p.m.	11.85	12.80	12.49	13.70	5	7
Sunday 1 p.m.–8 p.m.	14.38	15.75	15.34	17.04	7	8
Sunday 8 a.m.–1 p.m.	13.55	14.69	14.07	15.32	4	4
Sunday 1 p.m.–8 p.m.	18.21	20.18	18.99	21.00	4	4

[1] PUT = People Using Television.

Table 4 Persons Aged 18–49 Years Prime (Monday–Sunday 8–11 p.m.) Share of Viewing (Homes Acquiring DVRs)

Sources	May 2007	May 2008		% Difference	
	Live	Live	Live+7	Live 08/ Live 07	Live+7 08/ Live 07
English Broadcast	40.1	29.8	33.8	−26	−16
Spanish Broadcast	6.1	3.0	3.0	−50	−52
Ad Supported Cable	38.6	48.2	45.6	25	18
All Other Cable	1.7	3.1	2.8	85	70
Premium Pay	6.0	6.6	6.2	9	4
Independents	1.4	1.1	1.0	−21%	−27
PBS	1.2	0.4	0.4	−70%	−70

Table 5 Persons Aged 18–49 Years Prime (Monday–Sunday 8–11 p.m.) Share of Viewing (Homes with DVRs Both Years)

Daypart	May 2007		May 2008		% Difference	
	Live	Live+7	Live	Live+7	Live 08/ Live 07	Live+7 08/ Live+7 07
English Broadcast	37.2	45.3	34.2	43.6	−8	−4
Spanish Broadcast	1.7	1.4	1.5	1.2	−14	−12
Ad Supported Cable	41.2	35.6	46.5	40.2	13	13
All Other Cable	2.5	2.0	2.2	1.8	−12	−8
Premium Pay	9.3	8.6	7.1	6.0	−24	−31
Independents	0.5	0.5	0.7	0.7	27	24
PBS	0.9	0.8	1.1	0.9	17	15

A similar analysis of homes that had a DVR both years shows a slightly different story. Similar to DVR acquirers, "Live" and "Live+7" for homes that have had a DVR in both years are down slightly year-to-year for the English broadcast networks and Ad Supported Cable is up. However, the magnitude of differences is much more subtle than that of DVR acquirers. It seems that share differences among homes that have owned a DVR in both years are less dramatic because they have already adjusted to viewing habits.

In summary, the acquisition of a DVR dramatically changes a home's viewing behavior in terms of usage levels and viewing sources. However, an analysis of homes that had a DVR for at least 1 year shows that over time, these effects remain present, but to a much lesser degree.

Program Types and Time-Shifting

Program Ratings

This section evaluates whether higher rated programs are time-shifted more than lower rated programs. To answer this question, the amount of programs that are most time-shifted were compared to the standard top 10 program ranking for May 2008 among persons aged 18–49 years across English broadcast, Spanish broadcast, cable and syndication programming.

For the most part, most programs that are time-shifted for English broadcast, Spanish broadcast, and syndication match the top 10 overall program ratings. For cable, on the other hand, only two of the time-shifted programs match. The eight programs that do not match are live sport programming, which are the highest rated programs on cable and are not generally time-shifted. In this case, both the *NBA Playoffs* and *NHL Stanley Cup* finals are aired during May 2008.

Commercial Retention

An analysis was conducted to study the relationship between program genre and commercial retention: are commercials for certain genres more likely to be viewed?

Table 6 depicts the top 10 genre-based "Live+3" commercial (C3) indices for persons aged 18–49 years across English broadcast, Spanish broadcast, ad supported cable and syndication programming for May 2008. The index is the relationship between the commercial ratings within a program and the overall program rating. Therefore, a high index for a genre group signifies that during playback, commercials are less likely to be fast forwarded among these program types.

Table 6 Persons Aged 18–49 Years–May 2008 Live+3 Commercial Index

English Broadcast		Spanish Broadcast	
Child—live	98	Child day—Animation	103
Audience participation	98	Child multiweekly	98
Sports commentary	98	Comedy variety	96
Child multiweekly	97	News	96
Child day—Animation	97	Evening animation	95
Sports anthology	95	Situation comedy	94
Comedy variety	93	General variety	94
News	93	Daytime drama	94
Sports event	92	News documentary	93
Daytime drama	92	Conversations, colloquies	92

(Continued)

Table 6 *(Continued)*

Ad-Supported Cable		Syndication	
Quiz panel	98	Quiz give away	101
Official police	98	Instruction, advice	99
Child multiweekly	98	Situation comedy	98
Private detective	97	General variety	98
Devotional	96	Adventure	98
Western drama	96	General documentary	98
Adventure	95	General drama	98
Sports news	95	News documentary	98
Quiz give away	95	Unclassified	98
Situation comedy	95	Feature film	97

Breakouts and programs less than 5 minutes have been excluded

For English broadcast networks, children's programming and audience participation programming achieve the highest commercial indices among persons aged 18–49 years. Children's programming also indexes high for the Spanish Broadcast networks. For ad supported cable and syndication, game shows exhibit the most commercial retention.

In just the last few years, the DVR has clearly had an impact on U.S. television viewing trends. As DVR penetration grows and usage continues to evolve, Nielsen will provide ongoing insight about the characteristics and behavior of DVR users.

Index